17 95

THE
AGONY
OF
EDUCATION

THE
AGONY
OF
EDUCATION

BLACK STUDENTS
AT
WHITE COLLEGES AND UNIVERSITIES

JOE R. FEAGIN HERNÁN VERA
NIKITAH IMANI

ROUTLEDGE NEW YORK LONDON

Published in 1996 by
Routledge
29 West 35th Street
New York, NY 10001

Published in Great Britain by
Routledge
11 New Fetter Lane
London EC4P 4EE

Library of Congress Cataloging-in-Publication Data

Feagin, Joe R.
    The agony of education : Black students at white colleges and universities / Joe R. Feagin, Hernán Vera, Nikitah Imani.
      p. cm.
    Includes bibliographical references.
    ISBN0-415-91511-2. — ISBN 0-415-91512-0 (pbk.)
    1. Afro-American college students—Social conditions.
2. Discrimination in higher education—United States.   I. Vera, Hernán, 1937– . II. Imani, Nikitah, 1967– . III. Title.
LC2781.7.F43   1996
378.1'98'296073—dc20   95-53032
                                              CIP

CONTENTS

PREFACE

In the fall of 1994, Francis L. Lawrence, the white president of Rutgers University, spoke to a faculty assembly on the admission of African Americans. In a rambling comment he noted that average SAT scores for African Americans were low and asked, "Do we set standards in the future so that we don't admit anybody with the national test? Or do we deal with a disadvantaged population that doesn't have that genetic hereditary background to have a higher average?" When his words became public months later, Lawrence apologized, saying he had misspoken and had intended to say "that standardized tests should not be used to exclude disadvantaged students on the trumped-up grounds that such tests measure inherent ability."

On February 7, 1995, at half-time some 150 mostly black student protesters sat down at mid-court interrupting a Rutgers University basketball game. In the following days numerous students demonstrated on campus and demanded the university president's resignation. President Lawrence was quick to admit his words were false and insensitive. Yet much damage was done. Lawrence's phrase and the subsequent press coverage sent an injurious message to millions of African American students. And unfortunately his kind of comment is common. The African American parents and students at a major state university who shared their experiences with us for this book receive many messages of this sort. Consider the recent public debates on the balanced budget, affirmative action, social welfare, drugs and violent crime, issues that usually become marked by racism in this country. Consider the scholarly works that every decade or so claim to have discovered a genetic inferiority in the average intelligence levels of African Americans and other people of color. It often seems that there is a concerted cultural war against African Americans and other people of color.

The mainstream press generally gave positive reports on President Lawrence, noting that, as the *New York Times* put it, his career showed a "lifetime effort to open campuses to more minority students, faculty and administrators."[1] Indeed, the *Times* article contained very little in the way of criticism of Lawrence. Similarly, *U.S. News & World Report* opened its account with the sentence "Let us pity Francis Lawrence . . . his career is in tatters because of a careless phrase." Lawrence is presented as having an "impeccable record." The Rutgers campus was reported as bristling "with the enforcement tools of diversity," and among other things, with "professors who learn not to raise unapproved ideas about race, gender, and the campus power system built around multiculturalism." Student protesters were characterized as having been trained by "the bishops" of the multiculturalism church.[2] Most other media outlets followed suit in condemning the students. In most reports we did not get the African American students' view of what happened or why it happened. The reporters' accounts were usually more calls to arms against campus multiculturalism than probing news accounts. The fact that Lawrence's comment about black students was "a debilitating disappointment, the kind of blow that strikes your spirit dumb," was not widely chronicled.[3]

One had to read the *Village Voice* to learn that this supposed "church of multiculturalism" had actually imposed a gag order on Rutgers University athletes and reportedly pressured them not to participate in the student protests. In this publication alone did one learn that as the black protesters sat on the basketball court some white fans called out "nigger," and "kill them all." The *Village Voice* reporters commented that white fans were used to being entertained by African Americans but could not tolerate being enlightened by them.[4] The black students at Rutgers heard their president echo some of the racial insults often leveled at them. When the students protested, the media blamed the university's alleged political correctness and multiculturalism. The students were denied respect and humanity once again with the accusation that they were trained followers of a multicultural church on a "radical" college campus.

The students at Rutgers are not alone in their protests over racism. In the spring of 1995, at the University of Texas (Arlington), black students and community leaders protested what they regarded as patterns of racism on campus, including a lack of black professors. In addition, in the 1990s, student protests over racism have occurred at colleges and universities as diverse as Purdue University, Olivet College (Michigan), and Grinnell College (Iowa). The unwillingness of white analysts to face the real causes of student protests is commonplace. A fall 1992 issue of the *Chronicle of Higher Education* devoted a major discussion to protests by students of color on several college campuses. The article probed a number of explanations for the protest, including "rising expectations" among students of color, the impact of the movie *Malcolm X,* the state of the U.S. economy, and the election of a presidential candidate who had "fired students up."[5] The serious problems that students of color have with racial discrimination on their campuses was not mentioned in this account from the major U.S. publication on events in higher education.

Significantly, President Lawrence's comment came in the middle of much national discussion of a 1994 book by Richard Herrnstein and Charles Murray, *The Bell Curve,* which argued for genetically determined differences in intelligence that favor white over black Americans. In the fall of 1994, African American students at Howard University held a press conference to protest *The Bell Curve* and to promote measures to counter the new racist ideology on education and IQ.

Recent books by best-selling analysts like Allan Bloom, Dinesh D'Souza, Richard Bernstein, and Arthur Schlesinger assert that historically white colleges and universities have gone through a radical revolution in recent years. In their view, which is shared by many media commentators, the majority of predominantly white colleges and universities are now strong bastions of entrenched multiculturalism. In these colleges and universities African American students and faculty members are alleged not only to have a disproportionate share of the control over campus discussions and rules, but also to dominate a significant portion of the curricula and many classroom discussions. Even some black neoconservative authors, such as Shelby Steele, have portrayed desegregated white campuses as devoted to real equality between white students and students of color and as "among the freest and fairest in society."[6]

For these much-heralded authors, the new dominance of multiculturalism and students of color is an "academic revolution" that has radically decentered white interests, power, and concerns. Indeed, Richard Bernstein, a self-described liberal, begins his book with an extreme metaphor, likening the influence of multiculturalism today to the workings of the Committee of Public Safety during the French Revolution. The Committee perpetrated many atrocities on the French people. Bernstein argues that the rise of multiculturalism has similarities to this historical French "terror" in its preoccupation with a "narrow orthodoxy" and "the occasional outright atrocity."[7]

This portrait of major colleges and universities is so strong that many academic analysts are at a loss to explain the relatively high black student dropout rate. For any evaluator, the data on black student enrollments and dropout rates are not encouraging. In the mid-1990s black students constitute about 9.3 percent of students in college and universities across the nation. Compared to white students, a substantially lower percentage of African American students complete their degrees at four-year institutions. These statistics cannot be explained adequately by resorting only to such factors as preparedness for college, students' family backgrounds, or personal values and attitudes.

In this book we take issue with the misinformed portraits of what goes on in the corridors, classrooms, offices, and byways of predominantly white colleges and universities in the United States. Even a casual glance at the black student and parent commentaries in this book will reveal that these conventional views are out of touch with campus realities. Indeed, these portraits are so often imaginary and ungrounded that one has to wonder if the mainstream critics of higher education have spent significant time on a predominantly white college or university campus talking with black students and other students of color. We argue that these conventional analyses often represent little more than the fears and ill-founded assumptions of many white Americans about the possibility and reality of racial change in U.S. educational institutions as well as in the larger society.

In our data we find much racial discrimination and many other forms of racism in what at first appears to be an unlikely place, the U.S. system of higher education. In the United States, major colleges and large universities are usually thought to be centers of diversity and global knowledge, centers showing the way for the nation in solving problems of racial intolerance. Yet, as we will see, U.S. colleges and universities are frequently permeated with much subtle, covert, and blatant racism. Racial barriers and difficulties are created not only by white undergraduate and graduate students (who, oddly enough, are portrayed as too liberal by many mainstream observers) but also by white professors, administrators, police officers, and other college staff members.

Because of the negative climate at many predominantly white colleges, very difficult, painful choices are forced on African American students and parents. The choices and concerns of the black parents we interviewed are those of parents deeply troubled about their children's present and future experiences with white-dominated educational institutions. These parents brought to their focus groups real life experiences and frustrations regarding discrimination at a predominantly white college campus. In the interviews we constantly sense that daily life for them and their children is a racial struggle. Their educational choices have been hard, and often agonizing.

Significantly, the parents' struggle is perpetuated in the racial struggles and dilemmas of their children, both before and after they choose a college. At traditionally white colleges in particular, racial "integration" has in actual practice been a major failure. Indeed, "integration" has been designed for the most part as a one-way assimilation process in which black students are forced to adapt to white views, norms, and practices. Predominantly white colleges and universities are still places that are more than demographically white; typically, they are white in their basic cultures and climates. In our chapters we will see that this monochromatic culture continues to pose difficult choices for black parents and for black students deciding on whether to stay in, or to flee from, the white-dominated college environments.

Surprisingly, only a handful of research studies in the 1990s have examined the racial barriers that African American students encounter in predominantly white colleges and universities. Moreover, some of these reports (which we will cite) have not been published commercially, or are not widely available. To our knowledge, our analysis is the first to explore systematically and in depth the racial experiences of African American students in their daily rounds on a predominantly white university campus (called hereafter State University). This book is based substantially on focus group interviews with thirty-six randomly selected black juniors and seniors at State University and with forty-one black parents in nearby metropolitan areas, areas that often send students to the university. These black students and parents were not selected because of their activism in regard to racial matters. They are typical of the students and parents who grapple with the barriers faced by African Americans in higher education in this state and in the nation.

Our analysis preserves the voices of African American students and parents who have directly or through friends and relatives experienced racial demarcations and barriers at State University. While we will keep this university anonymous in our analysis, it is typical in many ways of our large universities. It has thousands of students, many of whom are drawn from the best high schools in the United States. It has hundreds of faculty members, a majority of whom are graduates of prestigious graduate programs. Many are important scholars in their disciplines. State University has good undergraduate and graduate programs and a substantial athletic program. State University is one of the nation's important public universities.

Today, higher education remains a principal dream or goal for most African Americans. Thus, in a recent opinion poll virtually all the black youth aged eleven to seventeen stated that their biggest hope for their future was to go to college.[8] These students represent yet another generation of African Americans who see in higher education the possibility of personal and racial liberation. W.E.B. Du Bois, the great black educator and sociologist, saw education as part of the plan for the racial liberation of African Americans. Education provided the critical path for group survival and a way to contribute to the larger society. In a major speech delivered in 1933 at Fisk University he told the students:

> Let us not beat futile wings in impotent frenzy, but carefully plan and guide our segregated life, organize in industry and politics to protect it and expand it, and above all to give it unhampered spiritual expression in art and literature.[9]

Many decades later, the spiritual expression that Du Bois was calling for continues to be severely hampered by racial discrimination at the predominantly white colleges and universities in the United States.

Acknowledgments

We are indebted to a number of people who commented on portions of this manuscript or otherwise helped in our research, including Harry Shaw, Elaine Lyons-Lepke, Clairece Booher Feagin, Michelle Dunlap, Melvin Sikes, Debra Van Ausdale, Rhonda Levine, Janell Byrd, Kim Battle, Walter Allen, John Schweitzer, Hsiao-Chuan Hsia, Felix Berardo, Bill Sedlacek, Robert Parker, and Eugene Labovitz. In addition, numerous students in our graduate seminars at the University of Florida have participated in discussions that sharpened our interpretations. We would like to thank the moderator of the focus groups for her excellent efforts, and certain government officials in the state where State University is located for support and for giving us permission to use the group data. Above all, we are grateful to the students and parents who gave of their time for the focus group interviews. In addition, we would like to thank the numerous other black and white Americans who have provided critical ears for the arguments in this book; discussions with them have clarified and sharpened many points. We especially appreciate the strong support from our editors Jayne Fargnoli and Anne Sanow at Routledge. Nikitah Imani would like to thank Aaronette Carter, Cherice Roldan, the McKnight doctoral fellows family, and his parents, Eulas and Eloise Strong, for their strong personal support and understanding. Joe Feagin and Hernán Vera would like to thank their life companions, Clairece B. Feagin and Maria I. Vera, for their strong personal support and understanding over many years.

BLACK STUDENTS AT PREDOMINANTLY WHITE COLLEGES AND UNIVERSITIES
The Rhetoric and the Reality

The Modern University: Under Attack from "Barbarians"?

In the United States public and private universities have long been viewed as particularly open and tolerant places. Universities are seen as intellectual settings that house and disseminate the best knowledge society has to offer. Essential to the ideal of the university is that it be a place where diverse students and teachers seek knowledge without hindrance and intolerance. The university is usually viewed as guiding serious inquiry, verifying discoveries, and exposing errors through, to quote John Henry Newman, "the collision of mind with mind, and knowledge with knowledge."[1] In this vision, as Newman put it, a university is "a seat of wisdom, a light of the world . . . and Alma Mater of the rising generation."[2] Critical to this ideal is the view that excellence should be the only criterion for the admission of students and teachers to its ranks, as well as the criterion for the quest for knowledge.

In recent years this ideal of the liberal university has been featured in mainstream critiques of racial events and multicultural trends on our university campuses. The values of excellence and tolerance are frequently viewed as under attack from misguided administrators, radical professors, multiculturalists, and students and professors of color. According to widely publicized analysts like Allan Bloom, Dinesh D'Souza, Arthur Schlesinger, and Richard Bernstein, traditionally white colleges and universities have experienced a "revolution" that sets aside concern for excellence in favor of the allegedly corrupting goals of certain racial groups, particularly African Americans. Indeed, the problem with the modern university, many critics suggest, is that it has become *too* tolerant of the views and interests of African Americans and other people of color.[3]

Allan Bloom, for example, has portrayed modern universities as peopled by white students who "just do not have prejudices anymore."[4] White students and faculty members are today "egalitarian meritocrats who believe each individual should be allowed to develop his special—and unequal—talents without reference to race...."[5] Bloom goes so far as to argue that "when students talk about one another, one almost never hears them saying things that divide others into groups or kinds."[6] In this view white students and faculty members are still the primary carriers of the ideals of tolerance for diversity and of academic excellence. In *Illiberal Education,* Dinesh D'Souza's portrayal of white students who arrive on college campuses is that they are "tolerant" and want to "build friendships and associations with people who they know have been wronged through history."[7] Other conservative authors, such as Shelby Steele, have echoed this view of desegregated white campuses as devoted to fairness and equality between white students and students of color and as "among the freest and fairest in society."[8] U.S. college and universities are idealized as true melting pots.

For these analysts of higher education, however, the predominantly white colleges and universities are under siege. At the heart of this threat are black students, who from this perspective are seen as challenging the hoary ideals of excellence and tolerance. Bloom has argued that there is "a large black presence in major universities, frequently equivalent to the black proportion in the general population" and that this black presence has become "indigestible" because of black student desires for self-segregation and political power. Bloom blames black students for being unwilling to melt into the melting pot, "as have *all* other groups."[9] Black students, with their allegedly exaggerated assessments of universities as racist and their pressure for political change, are viewed as a threat to the ideal of the university. Shelby Steele contends that most black students have "an unconscious need to exaggerate the level of racism on campus—to make it a matter of the system, not just a handful of students."[10]

One of the best advertised of the analysts of college and university life, Dinesh D'Souza, agrees with this portrait of U.S. universities as captured by students of color and their professorial allies, with both groups being substantially under the control of multicultural dogmas. He asserts that "minority activists dominate race relations" on traditionally white college and university campuses.[11] In his view these campuses also teach students to be cultural relativists and to be hostile to the traditional American values on which they were raised. The core curriculum has been "diluted or displaced" to make room for new course requirements celebrating non-Western cultures. The "current revolution of minority victims" (who are described as "barbarians") is destroying higher education.[12]

Other best-selling authors, including white liberals, have accepted and amplified this image of colleges and universities as losing their historic commitments to the ancient ideals of academic excellence and tolerance. According to Richard Bernstein, offices of multicultural education and mandatory training in multicultural courses are "becoming nearly universal" in colleges and universities.[13] He further suggests that there is "a predominating antiracist ethos on campuses" and that college and university administrations are "eager to assuage the anger of minority students."[14] Bernstein concludes that discussions of diversity, race, and ethnicity have "become mandatory in the way that attending religious services was once mandatory at American universities." These discussions have become an official part of university life "organized by a growing multiculturalist bureaucracy."[15] Echoing the ideas of Bloom and Steele, Bernstein contends that there is no real need for this multiculturalism at colleges and universities because "racism is no longer the social norm in American life."[16]

Another white liberal, Arthur Schlesinger, Jr., has also bought into this rhetoric. He views the multiculturalism perspective as becoming dominant at various levels of education, not just at the colleges and universities. A major concern here is with the fragmentation he feels is ushered in by the multiculturalists, who are alleged to have made "an astonishing repudiation" of the idea of "a unifying American identity." Moreover, "the United States had a brilliant solution for the inherent fragility of a multiethnic society: the creation of a brand-new national identity, carried forward by individuals, who, in forsaking old loyalties and joining to make new lives, melted away ethnic differences. . . . The multiethnic dogma abandons historic purposes, replacing assimilation by fragmentation, integration by separatism. It belittles *unum* and glorifies *pluribus*."[17] Here the ideal of a unified perspective in U.S. education is seen as the only antidote to the fragmentation brought by people of color. Schlesinger rails against what he calls "the assault on the Western tradition," one example of which is the "invasion of American schools by the Afrocentric curriculum."[18] Schlesinger's diatribe against multiculturalism in education and other societal arenas reveals his bias in the terms he uses liberally, such as "tribalism" and "separatism," to characterize what he views as the dominant multicultural perspective.

At the heart of this analysis of U.S. educational institutions is the view that racial barriers and impediments are not important problems at predominantly white colleges and universities. These authors, like many media analysts, political commentators, and politicians, deny the reality of discrimination and other aspects of racism not only in education but also in society at large. As a result, the problems faced by students of color in education are often said to be located in the students themselves, their families, or their communities. For example, the educational analyst, George Keller, has attributed the lack of black advancement in education to causes primarily within the black community. Faulting community leadership, he argues that "petulant and accusatory black spokespersons will need to climb off their soapboxes and walk through the unpleasant brambles of their young people's new preferences and look at their young honestly. . . . Critics will need to stop the fashionable practice of lambasting the colleges as if they were the central problem."[19]

Many conventional analysts have joined the chorus suggesting that racism is no longer a serious problem that needs government action, except perhaps in the confused minds of many African Americans. For example, Martin Seligman, a prominent psychologist, has echoed the common white accusation that black Americans are generally wrongheaded in focusing on racism in U.S. institutions. Black explanations of their problems that often accent white racism or the "system" are, he argues, "superficially appealing," but they are not nearly as good as personalized explanations like "bad housing," "drugs," or "poor education." In his view,

> The reflex of thinking "racism" when thwarted or when justice is not done produces more hopelessness, giving up, and depression than do these alternatives. "Racism," the "system," and "white people" are just as destructive explanations as "I'm stupid" or "I'm lazy" ever were.[20]

Like many conventional white analysts of U.S. society today, Seligman goes on to suggest that this blaming-racism view should also be avoided by government policymakers: It is time to question the view that "racism is to blame for all the barriers between African Americans and success in our society."[21]

A Strikingly Different View of Campus Racism

In a national interview study that included a number of African American college students, one black honor student at a public university reviewed her pre-college trip to a leading Ivy League school:

> I applied to a lot of different schools besides here, and I got accepted to a major Ivy League university. And I went up there, checked it out. . . . I deserved to be there, simply because of my merit. And I felt bad; I felt out of place. One reason I didn't go to there, besides the money (I couldn't afford it), one reason I didn't go was because it reeked of whiteness. And that is no joke. And I am not exaggerating. I was only there for two days, and after one day I wanted to leave. And I mean, really, it just reeked, everywhere I went, reeked of old white men, just lily whiteness, oozing from the corners! [laughs] I wanted to leave. And I knew that socially I would just be miserable. And I talked to other black students; I talked to all of them because there aren't a lot. And so I said, "do you like it here?" And they were like, "no, we're miserable."[22]

If white students and faculty members are as receptive to black students as is claimed by the conventional commentators on education cited above, why is it that this black student feels "bad" and "out of place"? Why is it that the other black students at this Ivy League school feel "miserable?"

Or take the case of Michigan's Olivet College. During the spring of 1992 trouble began brewing when some white students openly objected to black male students dating white females. Then there was a major incident. A white female student reported that she was sitting in the dorm with a white male friend when four students, three of whom were black, came to her door to discuss various matters. One black student had come to ask about a paper the female student was typing for him. After some discussion, the black students departed. Later, the female student telephoned friends to report receiving a threatening phone call, which she felt had come from the black students. As a result, a dozen or so white fraternity men came to the dorm, where they confronted two of the black students. The white students directed racial epithets at the black students, who responded in kind; more students gathered, and an interracial fight ensued.[23]

Over the next few days black students became worried that they might be attacked on the campus. White students and anonymous callers directed more threats at the black students, and someone distributed Ku Klux Klan literature on the campus.[24] Many white and black students who were friends ceased speaking to each other.[25]

Significantly, two thirds of the black students left the campus within a few days of the initial incident. Soon after the interracial fight, moreover, black students organized a "black caucus," which would come to play an important role in pressing the Olivet administration to take action to promote racial justice on campus.[26]

One black student present at the fight noted reported hearing comments like "We're sick of these niggers. We're going to get them."[27] Later the black student commented: "Many students you thought were your friends, roommates, teammates, guys who'd give you answers during tests were . . . calling you all types of names—coon, spearchucker, nigger. . . . [Were] everyone's true colors shown that night? And were the first three years a facade, a fake, and finally everybody showed how they really felt?"[28]

One black student leader commented: "Right now we're in the midst of a civil war on this campus, and you can't turn your back on it. You have to face it. . . . I feel as though I have to make a stand here."[29] One of the black students who remained on campus following the incidents commented on feeling unwanted and isolated: "People I never would have expected have called me names. None of us feel we can trust white people anymore."[30] A student who returned home told a reporter that they "recruit us here, but they offer nothing to keep us here. I think the blacks you see here are the last you will see here in a long while. I wouldn't advise them to come here. They can see there is racial violence, and they are not going to want to come here."[31]

Could these black students be talking about the same type of college setting that the critics of higher education are discussing? Was this college, which was founded by a white abolitionist in the 1800s, a place where the multiculturalism philosophy was so pervasive that whites were no longer dominant in determining the campus climate or curriculum?

At a number of colleges and universities, African American students and other students of color have recently organized to protest various types of racism on campus. For example, early in 1995 at Iowa's Grinnell College more than sixty students of color, most of them African American, organized a protest over racist incidents on campus, including the use of racial slurs by disc jockeys on the campus radio and by white spectators at a basketball game. The students reportedly wore tape over their mouths on campus, with the message, according to a student leader, of "Through our silence, you will hear our rage."[32]

Is this a college where racial barriers are no longer of any significance, as many of the critics of higher education allege? Is this a place where black students and faculty members dominate the campus climate?

Racial Intolerance on College Campuses

Recent studies of students at predominantly white institutions of higher education have found that black students have higher attrition rates and lower rates of going to graduate school. On the average, they do not perform as well academically or adjust as well psychosocially as white students.[33] In the mainstream literature there is a debate as to why black students do not do as well as whites. As we have seen, many contemporary critics of higher education blame the black students, their families, or community leaders for the students' college troubles.

This view of higher education is myopic because it fails to examine the persisting role of white racism in creating serious barriers and dilemmas for black students and other students of color, the point emphasized by the students quoted above. One analyst of higher education, Walter R. Allen, has underscored the finding that U.S. schools and colleges have been settings for black "contest and struggle, as African Americans fought for full citizenship and participation in the society. Historically, educational institutions and educators have been among the most active and effective instruments for the oppression of black people."[34]

As we will demonstrate in later chapters, on predominantly white college campuses racial barriers and impediments are still commonplace. This racism is situated in particular places and at particular times as it is practiced by numerous white students, faculty, staff members, police officers, and administrators. Today as in the past, racial discrimination involves erecting physical, legal, and social barriers to make certain places, situations, and positions inaccessible to, or difficult for, members of racial outgroups. In the process of developing strategies to cope with racial barriers, black and other targets of discrimination are injured physically, psychologically, and socially and forced to waste much energy and time.

For the white-on-black racism we accent in this book, racial discrimination can be viewed as the *socially organized set of practices that deny African Americans the dignity, opportunities, spaces, time, positions, and rewards this nation offers to white Americans.* What we call *racism* encompasses subtle and overt discriminatory practices, their institutional contexts, and the attitudes and ideologies that shape or rationalize them. Discriminatory practices—for example, the legal exclusion of black students from many colleges until the 1950s or the informal discrimination directed against these students at majority-white colleges today—are generated by a range of white motivations, including prejudice, fear, and hope of personal gain.

Universities are embedded in local, state, national, and international communities, and what happens in these larger arenas can have important effects on campus life. National surveys in the 1990s have documented the antiblack attitudes of a majority of white Americans. For instance, in one national survey white respondents were given a list of eight blatant stereotypes of black Americans, including that they are "more prone to violence than people of other races," "prefer to accept welfare rather than work," are "less ambitious than people of other races," and possess "less native intelligence than people of other races." Fully three-quarters of the whites agreed with one or more of these antiblack stereotypes; just over half agreed with two or more. This survey also found that younger whites (those eighteen to twenty-nine years of age) had a little *higher* level of racial prejudice than the general white population.[35] Other surveys have also found substantial white acceptance of antiblack stereotypes.[36] In addition, a majority of whites do not view discrimination as the major barrier to opportunities for African Americans. In a 1994 survey, when asked the question, "On the average blacks have worse jobs, income, and housing than white people. Do you think these differences are mainly due to discrimination?" more than six in ten whites said no. When asked if the differences were mainly due to the fact that most blacks "just don't have the motivation or will power to pull themselves up out of poverty" the majority of whites said yes.[37] In another 1994 survey a substantial majority of whites agreed with the view that today black Americans have equal opportunities for skilled jobs and for a quality education in the United States.[38]

In the United States racial prejudices and stereotypes are often linked to white superiority ideologies, including those developed or fostered by white political and business leaders, intellectuals, and scientists. The ideological foundations of discriminatory practices have been elaborated, at different times and places, in Western religion, philosophy, anthropology, literature, legal scholarship, and psychology. As each ideological effort has been discredited, a new attempt has been made to support the view that African Americans are inferior to whites in regard to intellectual, psychological, or cultural characteristics. Within this white rationale the world appears as place of "superior whites" and "inferior blacks." A major example of this is the best-selling book *The Bell Curve* by the late Richard Herrnstein, a longtime professor at Harvard, and Charles Murray, a conservative intellectual. Reflecting a pseudoscientific tradition going back to the early nineteenth century, these notorious white authors have alleged that differences in "intelligence test" scores are not determined just by environment, learning, and socialization but reflect genetic differences in mental abilities between black and white groups, differences they argue can be reliably measured by brief paper-and-pencil and object manipulation tests. Although these reactionary views have been successfully critiqued by many social and physical scientists, they are accepted by many white Americans.[39] Most striking, moreover, is the fact that a book like *The Bell Curve* has appeared at least once every decade since World War II.

Discriminatory Practices in Education: The Historical Background

As we noted above, most white Americans do not see racial discrimination as a pervasive and serious problem for African Americans in the United States. What discrimination remains is mainly seen as created by isolated racial bigots, including extremists such as Ku Klux Klan members and skinheads. Moreover, judging from opinion surveys and other opinion indicators, the general white view of college campuses appears to be much like that of the critics of multiculturalism cited previously. Racial barriers are no longer seen as the norm on traditionally white college campuses.

As we will see in the next chapters, however, our data strongly contradict this well-publicized view. Claims that serious racial hurdles and animosities are no longer common in higher education are disproved by much evidence from the past and the present. The historical background is important to an understanding of more recent evidence. Indeed, U.S. educational institutions have long institutionalized an array of discriminatory practices, and not just in the South. Many educational facilities in the North were legally segregated in the nineteenth century. In the late 1860s, for example, thirteen states outside the South, including New York, Illinois, Indiana, and Ohio, mandated or allowed school segregation for local communities.[40] As late as 1940, moreover, Arizona required segregation in public schools; and Kansas, Wyoming, Indiana, and New Mexico permitted local communities to practice public school segregation. Southern areas of the states of New Jersey, Pennsylvania, Ohio, and Illinois used local regulations and pressure to maintain segregated schools.[41] Moreover, in most Northern areas, nearly complete housing segregation made for segregated public schools even where they were not implemented by law or custom. Indeed, housing segregation that was enforced by restrictive covenants was not ruled unconstitutional until 1948.

After slavery was abolished in the South in 1865, the states there gradually adopted the Northern plan of legal segregation of African Americans in schools and other areas of society.[42] With the substantial development of public educational facilities in the early twentieth century in the South came a very strong commitment to keeping black and white children segregated. By 1900 all southern states, and some northern areas, had legally segregated schools as a means of creating and maintaining a racial caste system. Most other northern areas maintained segregated schools by school regulations or local custom.

The history of the admission of African Americans to traditionally white colleges and universities does not reflect the traditional ideal of the university as a place of tolerance and meritocracy. From 1826, when the first black American graduated from Bowdoin College, to 1890, only thirty black Americans graduated from historically white colleges and universities in the United States. By 1910 the number was still fewer than 700, with the largest number graduating at Oberlin. In response to a survey by W.E.B. Du Bois in 1910, Fordham, a Catholic university in New York, responded: "Fordham has had no applicants for admission from the black race. What we should do were the applicants to come, I just cannot say."[43] Indeed, a number of universities in the North excluded black students prior to 1940. After 1940 no Northern state university outside the border states officially excluded black students, although some placed discriminatory restrictions on black students on campus. Even at that time, however, some private universities in the North significantly limited black students to token numbers or excluded them entirely. For example, the first small group of black students was admitted to Princeton University only in the mid-1940s, and the first black student to receive an A.B. degree did so in 1947.[44] Most border state universities did not abolish their racially exclusive policies until the 1950s. Significantly, the entry of African American students into most traditionally white universities on a significant scale, in the North and the South, did not begin until the 1960s.[45]

Even today, the full desegregation of higher education remains more of a goal than a reality in some areas of the nation. Recently, a study by the Southern Education Foundation found that in the mid-1990s most southern universities remained racially concentrated. Most historically white universities in the South were more than eighty percent white, and more than sixty percent of black first-year students attended historically black colleges and universities. In eight of the twelve states studied, less than ten percent of black first-year students were enrolled in their state's historically white flagship universities.[46] Moreover, in the mid-1990s the proportion of black students at the majority of major four-year colleges and universities in the North was well below the black proportion in the general population. Black students tend to be best represented in the community and technical colleges and, of course, in the historically black colleges.

Discrimination against black faculty members is also part of the nation's racial history. During the entire nineteenth century very few African Americans taught at U.S. universities.[47] As late as 1940, not a single one of the 330 black doctorates in the United States taught at a white university. Even in 1960, there were no more than two hundred black faculty members in traditionally white colleges and universities around the country.[48] Most traditionally white Northern and Southern universities had very few black faculty members until the 1970s. Even today, most of the nation's predominantly white colleges and universities have only token numbers of African American faculty members.[49]

It is important to note that even the segregated black schools, whether elementary schools or colleges and universities, were not under the full control of black educators. Writing in the 1930s, Carter Woodson noted that the segregated schools created by whites for African Americans were places where black students were taught to be inferior:

> The thought of the inferiority of the Negro is drilled into him in almost every class he enters and in almost every book he studies. . . . Much of what [universities] have taught as economics, history, literature, religion, and philosophy is propaganda . . . that involved a waste of time and misdirected the Negroes thus trained. . . . When a Negro had finished his education in our schools, then, he has been equipped to begin the life of an Americanized or Europeanized white man. . . . The education of the Negroes then, the most important thing in the uplift of Negroes, is almost entirely in the hands of those who have enslaved them. . . . The present system under the control of the whites trains the Negro to be white and at the same time convinces him of the impropriety or the impossibility of his becoming white.[50]

Black schools and colleges were created and run in a white-oriented framework that downplayed the contributions of African and African American cultures, a framework that, as we will see in later chapters, is still to be found in ostensibly desegregated higher education in the United States.

By the early 1900s open resistance to legal segregation in a number of areas was the major agenda of newly organized civil rights organizations. From this period to the present, numerous desegregation lawsuits have demonstrated the fallacy of the old "separate but equal" doctrine, as, for example, in data showing long-persisting disparities in the funding of black and white schools in many school districts. Beginning in the 1930s, the National Association for the Advancement of Colored People (NAACP) began a large-scale attack on legal segregation in education. The NAACP and other civil rights lawyers won a series of cases that over the next several decades expanded the legal rights of black defendants, protected the voting rights of black citizens, reduced job discrimination, voided restrictive housing covenants, and desegregated public schools.

Between the 1930s and the early 1950s a series of federal court decisions outlawed explicit racial exclusion at historically segregated white universities, including the University of Missouri, University of Oklahoma, University of Maryland, and University of Texas Law Schools, and the University of Oklahoma graduate school. These cases built the foundation for *Brown* v. *Topeka Board of Education*, which marked a major thrust against blatant discrimination in public education. This ruling, handed down in May 1954, declared that blatant racial exclusion in education violated the U.S. Constitution. "Today, education is perhaps the most important function of state and local governments," wrote Chief Justice Earl Warren in the *Brown* decision. He continued:

> Compulsory school attendance laws and the great expenditures for education both demonstrate our recognition of the importance of education to our democratic society.... In these days, it is doubtful that any child may reasonably be expected to succeed in life if he is denied the opportunity of an education. Such an opportunity, where the state has undertaken to provide it, is a right which must be made available on equal terms.[51]

However, the high court did not order immediate relief for black children. It waited a year to hand down an implementation order that stipulated school desegregation "with all deliberate speed," the first of many actions that guaranteed that racial change in schools would come at a snail's pace.

This break with racial exclusion was not intended to mutually integrate black and white young people in public schools and colleges, but at most was designed to assimilate black young people in a unidirectional manner to the dominant white perspectives, goals, and culture. The reciprocal adaptation of white youth and teachers to black perspectives or views was never a consideration for whites in authority. In fact, during the process of desegregation, many black schools were closed, and black teachers and administrators were fired. Black children bore the brunt of the burden when they were ordered to endure long commutes by white judges unwilling to bus white children to black schools. Generally, there was no mutual, democratic negotiation about how to desegregate or about what was to be taught or how it was to be taught. Bringing black students into historically white schools usually meant an aggressive emphasis on fitting them to white social and cultural molds. The Eurocentricity of education for black students did not change with the abolition of racial exclusion in public schools and colleges. As a result, desegregated schools and colleges have taught, and still teach, black young people to be "Europeanized whites" culturally, but without the privileges of that status. At least as serious is the fact that most white children in desegregated schools and colleges learn little about African and African American cultures or about the harsh realities of U.S. racial relations history.

Today, as we document in subsequent chapters, racial discrimination is well entrenched in higher education in the United States. This institutionalized discrimination both reflects and molds the attitudes and ideologies many whites hold in regard to racial matters. Racially restrictive practices in U.S. educational institutions have occurred over a large geographical area and for centuries. Clearly, isolated bigotry is not sufficient to explain the past or present racial picture in education. The coordinated repetition of discriminatory practices suggests that their roots are not just in individual psyches; individual perpetrators are compelled, in part, by social forces and perspectives that they feel to be irresistible. Many harmful racial actions taken by whites are supported by their families, social networks, and organizational contexts. For a long period, blatantly antiblack discrimination at most colleges and universities was prescribed by law or local customs. In many areas no African American students were allowed; in most others they were discouraged from attending or restricted once on campus.

Although outright exclusion is now illegal, much discrimination persists in a variety of forms, ranging from blatant actions to subtle but still destructive practices, and is carried out by a range of white perpetrators. Discrimination targeting black students on contemporary college campuses is still carried out by a large number of whites guided by the informal norms of white-dominated social networks and organizations. The examples of discrimination on campus today include racist joking, the recurring use of racist epithets, racist skits and floats by white fraternities, the neglect or rejection of black students' goals and interests, the mistreatment of black students by white professors, and racial harassment by white police officers.[52] Most damaging is the taking for granted by most white administrators, faculty, staff, and students that the campus is a "white" place in which blacks are admitted, at best, as guests.

Dimensions of White-Black Interaction: Recognition, Space, and Time

In our analysis we make particular use of three concepts that have enabled us to probe deeply into the patterns of racism in higher education. We pause briefly here to introduce these concepts, but fuller explanations will be provided later. The three concepts are human recognition, social space, and social time.

The question of human recognition is at the heart of U.S. racial relations. As we have seen in the black honor student's account above, black experiences at predominantly white college campuses bring to mind Ralph Ellison's famous book *Invisible Man*, in which a black protagonist comments:

> I am an invisible man. No, I am not a spook like those who haunted Edgar Allan Poe; nor am I one of your Hollywood-movie ectoplasms. I am a man of substance, of flesh and bone, fiber and liquids—and I might even be said to possess a mind. I am invisible, understand, simply because people refuse to see me.[53]

A central theme found in our group interviews is this black invisibility, that is, the experience of white professors, students, staff members, and administrators refusing to see, and to recognize, African American students as full human beings with distinctive talents, virtues, interests, and problems.

In this book we use the concept of *recognition* to capture the importance of this question of human visibility. As Ellison suggests, being forced into invisibility is an insidious denial of all that makes us human and equal. The failure to recognize someone else indicates a serious lack of respect and implies, for the misrecognized, a "loss of face," and a denial of a place in the social world.[54] This concept bridges several disciplines with a distinct, readily accessible meaning. For example, political scholars have used the idea of recognition to think through the issues of cultural identities in constitutional democracies. In this sense, Jurgen Habermas argues that constitutional democracies thrive on conflicts generated by different cultural identities so long as the citizens are united by mutual respect, that is, so long as everyone's right of coexistence is clearly recognized.[55] A similar concept of human recognition is used by psychoanalytic scholars examining the inner self. Jessica Benjamin proposes that "domination and submission result from a breakdown of the necessary tension between self-assertion and mutual recognition that allows self and other to meet as sovereign equals." For the individual there is a delicate balance between self-assertion and recognition of the other. Social psychological research has established the importance of being recognized by others in healthy human development. This interpersonal "recognition is so central to human existence as to often escape notice." In this sense, recognition is the "response from the other which makes meaningful the feelings, intentions and actions of the self."[56] In addition, sociologists have long written about a similar idea—that the feelings, intentions, and actions of a self are rendered meaningful in the "looking glass" provided by other selves.[57]

The data in subsequent chapters will make clear that African American students at predominantly white institutions often do not receive full recognition and respect from many white students, teachers, advisors, police, and other campus personnel. This white failure to recognize is very serious, for it teaches lessons of out-of-place-ness and self-worthlessness to black students. We use the term *misrecognition* here in the sense of a failure to see who or what is actually there. Moreover, from this viewpoint, the type of recognition that others give to an individual creates a "place" in the structure of a particular social institution. Consider the case of two students at a university. One student, through relentless messages from many professors, feels respected and recognized, as intelligent, worth listening to, and filled with potential for academic success. By means of similar interpersonal messages, another student is not fully respected but is misrecognized by numerous professors as troublesome, not worth listening to, and lacking in potential for success. The professorial messages quickly communicate to the students where they stand in relation to significant others in their social world. Given the power differential between professors and students, few students have the psychological and social resources to alter dramatically the social position crafted for them by professors. Moreover, it is not difficult to predict that the former student, who is more likely to be white, will typically have fewer academic difficulties than the latter, who is more likely to be black. The recurring messages of recognition and misrecognition create mental blueprints for both sides of the interaction, and thus become central constituents of the social structure of a predominantly white university.

Personally, structurally, and ideologically, white racism on college campuses and elsewhere in the society denies full human recognition to the racialized "others." This is achieved both through the fictions of whites as superior (the misrecognition of self-attributes) and through antiblack prejudices and stereotypes (the misrecognition of the attributes of the racial other). These racial constructions are part of a mind-set that influences behavior and alters emotions in regard to racial others. The cognitive stereotypes of modern racism—which include myths about black inferiority and incompetence noted previously—are not provable but are fictions honestly believed by a majority of white

Americans. It is not enough to enjoy white privileges, these must be seen as legitimate. These images become more than an individual matter when whites collectively, especially those whites with great power, construct and circulate widely a developed racial ideology.

Two other important dimensions of contemporary racial relations, often ignored in social science analysis, are space and time. The African American parents and students we interviewed consistently marked personal and group experiences by giving their location in time and space. For these African Americans, as for most other Americans, the basic unit of human reality is not the individual human being but rather a cluster of social ties and relations that extend across space and time. The experiential reality of *space* is at the heart of interpersonal ties and is a critical element of U.S. racial relations. The experience of the space around oneself, between oneself and others, and within oneself is deeply meaningful in many cultures.[58] Indeed, in these cultures the idea of human freedom has long incorporated the integral dimension of space, as something that gives freedom both being and meaning.

We use the concept of space for two purposes. First, we call attention to the ways in which the black parents and students described the physical spaces they live in. They repeatedly described these physical spaces as "white," "hostile," "alien," and the like. These spaces were defined principally by social not physical characteristics. Second, we want to call attention to how these physical spaces and their representations are read by whites and blacks for clues as to their social nature. Significantly, those with the greater power and resources ordinarily control the use and meaning of many important spaces in a society. Certain people are included or excluded from important places, in many different institutional arenas. The concept of *racialized* space encompasses a number of cultural biases that help define specific areas as "white" or as "for all," with the consequent feelings of not belonging or belonging. When the black honor student quoted above said that the Ivy League university she visited "reeked of whiteness," she was speaking of the overall character and tone of that campus space. Throughout the chapters of this book, we will see that many spaces on majority-white campuses like that of State University are racially marked and delimited, often in subtle ways. To a significant degree, the strong symbolism attached to white spaces on predominantly white campuses becomes part of the personalities and identities of the individuals associated with those spaces.

Like the case of space, the individual and collective sense of time and memory is socially and racially colonized. We are not primarily concerned with time as a quantifiable entity but rather with time as qualitatively experienced and collectively understood. Through interpersonal communication and cultural definition, the memories of times past are made into collective goods that are shared and contested across human groups. To have substantial power in society is to control the important memories and histories that are recorded in some form, such as in books or the mass media. Reflect for a moment on the centuries of U.S. history during which large numbers of white Americans used coercive intimidation and physical violence to control the bodies, lives, and spatial displacement of African Americans, first as slaves, then as segregated semi-slaves, in both the North and the South. The semi-slavery of legal segregation has been followed by pervasive informal and illegal discrimination in all areas of U.S. society. Yet, as we will document later, most white Americans either do not know this history or accept versions of it that play down the extreme brutality and human destruction that are at its center. It appears that over the last century or so, the majority of white Americans, particularly white officials, historians, and movie makers, have tried to forget or sanitize the nation's collective memory and understanding of the interracial history of the United States.

In contrast to this selective white amnesia about U.S. history, African Americans retain within the oral and written traditions of their families and communities much knowledge of this racial history. They and their ancestors have experienced this history in painful detail. Thus, we will observe throughout the accounts of black parents and students in later chapters the many ways that the knowledge and understanding of personal, familial, and communal racial histories play a role in reactions to present-day racism on a university campus.

Witnesses to Educational Apartheid

The importance of our ideas of racial recognition, space, and time will become clear as we examine the experiences of African American students at State University (SU) and as we assess the experiences of African American parents who have children of, or approaching, college age. As we noted in the preface, SU is fairly typical of predominantly white universities in the United States, with thousands of well-educated students and hundreds of distinguished faculty members. Yet, as we will see, like many U.S. colleges and universities, State University has a continuing problem of racial barriers and hurdles for African American students.

A thorough, in-depth examination of the context and meaning of African American students' experiences at predominantly white universities requires something more than quantitative data gathered in surveys or in classroom testing. It requires careful listening to what

African American students and their parents have to say about their experiences, feelings, thoughts, and actions, and it requires looking at the university from the African American perspective. To accomplish this objective, we used focus groups, a type of group interview in which several people come together to discuss questions posed by the researchers. The open-ended format of the focus group encourages participants to cover issues not anticipated by the researchers, to move back and forth between issues of importance, and to build on each other's ideas by associating personal experiences and opinions with what has been described by others. Our research project included three focus groups with black juniors and seniors at State University and four focus groups with black parents who have children in college or are considering colleges for their children. Members of each focus group were randomly selected; all were African American, as was each group's moderator.

Randomly selected focus groups can be a powerful tool for social scientists interested in obtaining nuanced and meaningful accounts of lived events. This methodology can provide more in-depth information on actual experiences and a better-rounded understanding of important issues than are possible using standard survey techniques. The focus group format allows participants to discuss their experiences and those of relevant others at some length within a group setting.[59] One participant's comment often triggers comments from others, and each individual's views are subject to a reality check by the rest of the group. As we promised them, we have kept the respondents' identities anonymous in our research analysis. Details on this and related methodological issues can be found in the endnotes to this chapter.[60]

The three student focus groups included thirty-six black juniors and seniors at SU. We chose juniors and seniors to take advantage of their longer period of experience at the university. The students represented a variety of college majors, and their average age was about twenty-one years. Sixty-one percent of the students in the three groups were male.[61] Participants in the four parent focus groups represented a range of working-class and middle-class black Americans from urban areas that send black students to SU.[62] Thirty-nine percent of the parents were men. Most of the participants had blue-collar or white-collar jobs outside the home. Some of the parents had only a high school education; a majority had a year or more of college. Most were between thirty and sixty years of age. All the parents saw higher education as important for them and their children.[63]

After a general description of the focus group's purpose by the moderator, the group discussion focused mostly on the university's reputation, its social and racial climate, the participants' experiences on campus, and the participants' views on a range of other subjects, including university recruitment efforts and scholarship programs.

Conclusion: Difficult Choices

A distinguished university appears, at first, to be an unlikely place in which to study racial discrimination, the barriers it erects, and the injuries it inflicts. We have underscored the ideal of the university as a fortress of enlightenment, excellence, and tolerance. In spite of this powerful ideal, universities in the United States have frequently been centers of racial exclusion, animosity, and discrimination. Historically and in the present, the recruitment and treatment of faculty members and students have seldom been guided solely by the unbiased standards of excellence claimed by the ideal. Historically, African Americans were denied entrance to, or discouraged from attending, most U.S. colleges and universities, often by the force of law. Even in recent decades, many colleges and universities continue to be characterized by racial animosity and discrimination. Under these conditions, the colleges and universities are centers, not of wisdom, but of white Eurocentric wisdom. They are lights, not of the world, but of a Eurocentric world. The fact that racist ideologies have been able to corrupt the ideals and knowledge of many white students and teachers for generations makes predominantly white U.S. universities appropriate sites in which to study racism in our time.

The experiences of the black parents and students with whom we talked are often different from those presented by well-advertised analysts of higher education like Bloom, D'Souza, Bernstein, and Schlesinger. Drawing on their own experiences, these parents and students often see predominantly white campuses as white-dominated and dangerous, psychologically or physically, for African American students.

In many ways the black parents in our groups are like nonblack parents in the United States. Most share similar hopes for the education and success of their children. They are willing to seek out information on colleges, to sacrifice, and to do whatever is needed to help their children succeed. While black and white parents share a common hope for the success of their children, black parents and their children frequently face hard educational dilemmas that white parents do not face. Black parents often must help their children to choose between a black college and a white college. (White parents and their children rarely even consider a black college.) If black parents chose predominantly white colleges, then they must help their children to navigate the colleges' shoals and tempests of racial hostility and maltreatment.

Another major contrast between black and white parents is that black parents and their children often confront a poor racial climate at public educational institutions that the parents help to finance with their taxes. Indeed, black communities as a whole reap a disproportionately small share of the higher-education rewards they help create with their taxes. The racial maltreatment of black young people at predominantly white public colleges and universities can thus be thought of as involving a serious misappropriation of public funds.

The concerns the black parents expressed and the judgments they made in our groups are those of parents deeply troubled about their children's present and future experiences with certain white individuals and institutions. These parents brought to the groups real-life concerns, experiences, and frustrations regarding racial patterns and racial discrimination at State University, as well as in other educational institutions and in the larger society. In listening to their articulate voices, we will regularly get a sense that life for them means an ongoing racial struggle. Their educational choices have been hard, and often agonizing.

Black parents' difficult choices and racial struggles become part of the lives of their children, both before and after they choose a college, particularly if they choose a predominantly white institution. At most such places, racial "integration" in actual practice often means the one-way assimilation of black students into white space and culture. Traditionally white colleges and universities are white-normed spaces that are more than demographically white; they are white in their basic cultural components. African American students entering such campuses often find that they are expected to accept positions as racial subordinates and to accept one-way cultural assimilation as a legitimate goal. Many whites seem to expect African American students to view their educational experiences in the mostly white university as a great privilege. Yet most of our student and parent accounts contain stark and disturbing testimonials of the difficulties posed by supposedly integrated social spaces. In this book we examine how white in culture and character predominantly white colleges and universities remain and how they continue to pose difficult educational choices for black students deciding on whether to stay or flee racially oppressive environments.

2

EDUCATIONAL CHOICES AND A UNIVERSITY'S REPUTATION

The Importance of Collective Memory

Like space and territory, the individual and collective sense of time and memory can be socially and racially colonized. What passes for a society's history is usually the dominant group's version of that history. White Americans, particularly white officials, historians, media commentators, and moviemakers, have long tried to control and sanitize the collective memories and understandings of the interracial history of the United States. A whitewashed version of this racial past has often been popularized in the mass media, especially in major movies such as *The Birth of A Nation* (1911), *The Littlest Rebel* (1935), *The Little Colonel* (1935), and *Gone With The Wind* (1939). These and other movies, together with most white-authored novels and nonfiction books until the 1960s, portrayed a gallant American South run by genteel white aristocrats who had earned the loyalty of faithful black slaves. The black struggle for freedom was of no interest. Not until 1989 was the heroism of even one of the many black units in the Union army chronicled, in the movie *Glory* (1989). To this day, Hollywood's white moviemakers have shown very little interest in most other aspects of the lives of African Americans during slavery or legal segregation. Significantly, the white prohibition during slavery on teaching African Americans to read relegated the understanding of the slave past from the black slave perspective mostly to oral traditions.[1]

During slavery and ever since, not only white filmmakers but also white historians and publishing companies have largely controlled the record of the racial history of the United States. For example, in a recent review of a dozen leading high school textbooks, sociologist James Loewen found that most tiptoed around the harsh realities of America's racist past. He found no discussion of white racism as a persisting causal factor lying behind the racial barriers faced by African Americans. Most strikingly, not one of the major high school textbooks makes significant use of African American sources; not one "lets African Americans speak for themselves about the conditions they faced."[2]

One consequence of the white control of the understanding of U.S. racial history is that the African American oral tradition has had to place a heavy emphasis on familial and community memories of African American history. The black students and parents that we interviewed repeatedly emphasized the time dimension of their experience by drawing on a strong and often perceptive sense of the racial past and present, recalling memories and understandings that are not only individual but also familial and communal.

African Americans place a heavy emphasis on education because of its role in family and community. Education is about a liberated future that must be better than the oppressive past. Pressing hard for higher education for children today is linked to the strong educational aspirations of African Americans in the distant and recent past. The prospect of a successful future for one's children and grandchildren helps to justify and give distinctive meaning to the collective suffering and struggles of the past and the present. In many ways, black parents do not differ from other parents who work hard to put their children through college. However, for black parents the education of their children gives meaning to their struggle against racism as well as to other aspects of their individual and familial histories.

The biography of each student who comes to college is rooted in individual and familial histories. Chances for success and for intellectual growth depend in part on skills, predispositions, and discipline developed in the home and community. The parents in the focus groups provided illustrations of how they regarded their children coming to college as part of a collective history. One father noted the pressure he felt during his school years:

> If I don't perform I [lose] my scholarship; if I don't perform, I'm not going to be able to get a job; if I don't perform, I'm not going

to be able to perpetuate the family's goals. In other words, I have to do better than my father. My father had to do better than his father, so forth down the line.[3]

This familial pressure is common to many American families, but it takes on an added dimension for those who are members of an oppressed group that has faced major racial barriers to education. The ways in which such cross-generational pressures shape black parents' conceptions of their own and their children's futures will become apparent as we examine accounts of the racial reputation and climate at a predominantly white university. As we will observe, a university's reputation is generally a condensation of individual and group memories of experience with that university.

Significantly, the concept of a collective past and future allows one to understand many African American responses to encounters with antiblack discrimination. In addition to the immediate pain and stress that comes from hostile encounters with whites, such experiences have over time a significant *cumulative* impact on individuals, their families, and surrounding communities. The lives of most African Americans are regularly disrupted by racial mistreatment suffered personally or endured by friends and family members. The cumulative impact of these instances of discrimination is often very distressful and damaging. Typically, a black victim of discrimination communicates the incident to family and friends, and the pain of the incidents is passed along to a larger social group. Moreover, the negative effects of present discriminatory incidents are enhanced because they are laden with individual and group memories of centuries of racial oppression, which include accounts of lynchings and other antiblack brutality and violence.[4]

The black parents and students in our focus groups did not view most acts of discrimination as unusual disruptions in their everyday lives, but rather as recurring and integral parts of the experience of being black in a white-dominated society. In this sense, the past is a constant part of the present; African Americans speak about events and evaluate them based on both their own and their historical group experience. Some analysts have argued that a traditional African perspective, elements of which are present in African American thought, includes two concepts of time—sacred cyclical time and ordinary linear time. Sacred time has no "past" because it is not part of a linear conception; ancestors and their experiences live in the present. This sacred cyclical time joins the past, present, and future at any point in time and space, making the present especially significant.[5]

Other cultures and groups share aspects of this perspective on time, but it can be particularly important for those groups that have suffered oppression. One critical dimension of time is the sense people have of the character and pace of social change. This understanding of change is important because an appraisal of the future—Are things changing for the better or worse? What type of world will our children face?—affects to a substantial extent how we view the past, experience the present, and see the future. This sense of the possibility for social transformation is particularly momentous for groups, such as African Americans, that have a long history of oppression.

We noted in Chapter 1 that certain heralded analysts of higher education have argued that predominantly white colleges and universities are undergoing a dramatic revolution that is radically decentering white interests in favor of the concerns and interests of racial minorities.[6] According to this interpretation the racial reputations of most predominantly white colleges and universities are now quite liberal and signal correctly that minorities dominate much of campus life, much of the curriculum, and much of the discussion in college classrooms.

However, the images of the majority-white colleges and universities held by the black parents and students we interviewed are often dramatically different from these critics of higher education. These black parents and students view majority-white campuses as generally inhospitable for black students. In this regard they are much like other parents and leaders in communities of color across the nation. For example, the University of Texas (Austin) has long had a reputation for academic excellence and liberalism both nationally and in its own region. Yet, a recent survey of black and Latino leaders at the university and in local communities found that the university had a reputation for being racist and unwelcoming to students of color. According to one report, the black and Latino leaders objected to the university's failure "to remove statues of Confederate leaders" and its failure "to recruit and retain black and Hispanic students."[7] Here we see a clear example of the importance of collective memory in shaping the reputation of a university campus. The symbolism of campus statues of Confederate officials is very negative in communities of color in Texas and many other states, although most whites do not seem to understand the strong linkage of this type of symbolism to a predominantly white university's negative reputation for people of color or to its problems in retaining students of color on campus.

In this chapter we investigate the question of a university's racial reputation and explore the educational dilemmas that the continuing racial barriers at a predominantly white university force on parents and students of color. The temporal dimensions of a university's reputation and its campus climate—including collective memories and their present and future effects—are a central concern in this chapter.

Parental Hopes and Aspirations:
"You're Going to Get an Education, Period"

African American parents and students told us about their daily lives and basic choices—what their past was like, what was happening to them in the present, and how they saw their futures. For these parents, the children's college education was the natural continuation of their individual and familial hopes and ambitions, and their children's success in college is understood as justifying many sacrifices. The parents in one focus group began with a discussion of educational plans for their children. One successful entrepreneur described the pressure to fulfill the family goals he had felt in his youth. He contrasted this pressure with his desire for his son to get an education for its intrinsic value:

> I want him to go get an education for one reason only—to broaden his mind, period. See, he's not going to go to school or college like I did with the pressure of—if I don't perform I [lose] my scholarship. . . . If I don't perform, I'm not going to be able to perpetuate the family's goals. . . . In other words, you're going to go to school. You're going to get an education, period. And then, we'll see how things work out after that.

This father's education was a multigenerational family project that transcended the individual. He wants to spare his son the heavy familial pressures that he experienced. Still, his parental concerns and demands on his son suggest a continuing familial dimension to the educational decisions.

A little later in the discussion the mother of a teenager who was considering a community college took up the last speaker's topic. She noted a contrasting family history and how her experience has affected what she wants for her children:

> I want them to do things better because I didn't, and you know I really didn't have nobody to talk to me, like, "What you want to do?" Push me, you know. So I kind of talk to them: "If that's what you want to do, go for it," as long as they want something that's right, not messing with drugs or nothing.

In this focus group the participants build on each other's ideas. Like the father above, this mother wants a better life for her children, a life without the pitfalls she has had to live through. While her experience is different from the previous parent, like him she shapes her behavior to help her children. The hopes and plans for a child's education are rooted in the parent's and student's familial past and extend into the family's future.

Selecting a College:
"It's Important for All Children ... to Be Nurtured,
as Far as Education Is Concerned"

All the parents we interviewed, whether they had graduate degrees or had never been to college, consider the selection of a college for their children a serious matter. In addition to taking account of their children's particular needs, they make college decisions in light of issues of racial identity and African American culture. The problem of racism in predominantly white institutions often came up naturally as the parents talked about general college matters.

In response to a general question about what colleges the parents were considering for their children, one father noted his displeasure with his son's going to a business college. He indicated that his son needed to learn to spell and write better, skills apparently not provided by the college. He suggested, thus, that his wife would be to blame for his son's getting a low-end job since she "pushed him" into that business college. There was parental conflict over the son's needs and the college he should have attended. Although this man's response did not address the question directly, his emotional statement had an impact on the group that set the tone for the following statements. As the conversation moved around the table, other parents took up the theme that colleges should be chosen according to the children's needs and abilities.

The next person to speak, the mother of two children nearing college age, cast her comment in the temporal terms we have described. For her there is a personal and collective past, and a future that in this case looks hopeful:

> I think I would like my children to go to [names a local university], a black institution. And that's because of the topic that we're discussing—racism in higher educational [settings]—there is or has been a lot of racism within this state's institutions. . . . I didn't attend that school [State University], but I know lots of people who did, and the black people who attended . . . all experienced racist attitudes among the students and among the teaching staff there. I think things may change. . . . They now have a black administrator.

The past experience of racism at predominantly white universities is an important element in black parents' decisions concerning their children's college choices. The future—in this case the hope that things may change because of the presence of a black administrator—may also guide some parental decisions.

Next, an educator and mother of two children presented a past experience at a predominantly white university, which she contrasted with that of a previous speaker:

> I didn't experience the racism that you're talking about. And I guess because when I was in school, I was very naive. I mean, I had gone to a predominantly black state university in a nearby state prior to going to a local white university like State University. And I went there for two years. . . . But when my father died, I decided to come home to go to school, and I think going to the local university really helped me as far as a broad perspective, as far as getting . . . my career, or my job, or my profession as a teacher, but as far as my children are concerned, . . . a lot of it depends on your child. . . . Well, this child needs to be close to home, this one can, you know, go off on his or her own. So I really haven't considered it but I know they will go to college. I do know that.

This parent, while not denying the problem of campus racism the previous parents brought up, notes a different personal experience. Looking to the future, she refocuses the discussion by making children's abilities and inclinations a key to a decision about a predominantly white or a black college. In each of the parent groups one or more parents introduced contradictory experiences or disclaimers about not facing discrimination, and each group examined the matter of racial barriers openly and critically.

As the group continued, the collective effort to examine the difficult issues thoroughly became apparent. To illustrate the idea that children's abilities and interests are the key element in a college decision, another mother addressed the issue of identity:

> Well, I have two sons who are . . . very different. One is extremely bright and could go anywhere, and the other one struggles, so we really worked hard to find a college for them. Now, . . . I didn't consider a college in this state; my husband did. My son received a scholarship to an Ivy League college, but he refused to take it. [He] had gone to predominantly white schools in the lower grades and high school, and he decided for himself that he wanted to go to a school that was predominantly black—that he . . . would be more comfortable [there] even though he was quite competent academically, but he wanted to immerse himself in this culture. And so for that reason, he decided that he wanted to go to a predominantly black university.

The interest in this question was intense and several parents raised their hands seeking to participate in the discussion. The previous speaker continued:

> The second one . . . who's not as bright, . . . didn't want to go [to
> the black college], so he chose State University . . . and he strug-
> gled with it academically . . . and they're now both in grad school.

In the beginning of this line of discussion, we should recall, the issue
of choosing a college was posed in the conflict between a husband and
a wife who pushed their son into a business school. In subsequent
comments that initial issue was framed broadly to encompass the matter of children's talents and interests, including an interest in African
American culture that can usually be nurtured best at a predominantly
black college.

In her comments the last speaker indicated that the choice
between a predominantly black or a predominantly white college
involves more than academic matters. Predominantly black colleges
have much to offer, including a more hospitable social and cultural
environment. Some research shows that, on the average, African
American students at predominantly black colleges make greater relative academic gains than those on white campuses because there is a
more supportive academic environment and because there is a better
match between the academic and social needs of the students and
existing campus programs. On mainly black campuses students make
better psychosocial adjustments and have a stronger awareness of
African American history and culture.[8] The group discussions make
it clear that African American parents do not make the often agonizing choice about colleges for their children abstractly. The abilities,
needs, and inclinations of the children are factored into the decision,
as are the academic, social, and cultural environments of the college
campuses that are considered.

Then another educator in this group introduced another time-related
factor relevant to college choices, that of late-blooming children:

> . . . sometimes people tend to say that a child is a certain way
> when they see them growing up as children. However, when
> they become older, they blossom. Sometimes, experiences make
> them not do as well in school as maybe parents would like for
> them to do, but if they have the ability, and if they have guidance
> that parents have already given them, and nurturing, more than
> likely they'll do well. They just need average ability in order to
> go to college, so I feel that a child should never be discouraged
> from going to college. Just like she said, her son, who she felt was
> not as strong academically as the other child, made it, and that's
> the key—making it, making it into a college. But now, my chil-
> dren . . . will go to college. My husband graduated from a black
> institution. . . . My children are living in an environment where
> they are truly a minority. . . . It's important for all children . . . to
> be nurtured, as far as education is concerned. And I find some-

times that there is not a sensitivity to African American children
... by teachers that are non–African American. . . . I just believe
that African American schools nurture our children more.

A father of two children doing well in school then asked the last
speaker a question to settle the issue of white and black colleges:

Based on . . . you being a graduate of [a predominantly white uni-
versity] and your husband being a graduate of a black college . . .
have you thought about a comparison as to the level of educational
environment made available by both schools? How would you
compare that—one-on-one equal or one more than the other?

Thinking deeply about the matter, she replied to him and thus com-
pleted her previous thought about the critical role of classroom teachers:

To me, the key is the person that's standing in front of that classroom presenting the information. That is the key. It's not private,
public, this reputation, that reputation. Sometimes reputation is
an important factor, but the person that is giving out that information, that is teaching, is the key to the learning.

At this point the line of discussion reached closure. More than
which college or university has a superior academic reputation, the
critical issues for these mothers and fathers included the interests of
children and the sensitivity of teachers. These parents confronted the
issues of academic quality, racist reputations and attitudes, campus
culture, a child's skills and desires, and the sensitivity of teachers as
elements in the decision to choose a college. Very important here are
what we have called the temporal aspects of these college choices.
The personal, familial, and community events these parents note are
not inert quantities that can be ignored. Past events and experiences
are powerfully active factors that must be considered in order to act in
the future. The discriminatory or unsupportive climates of predominantly white institutions versus the supportive climates at black institutions are among the important college realities that are faced by
black parents and their children.

State University's Reputation:
"You Go to School for a Lot of Experiences, Not Just the Academics"

We have just followed an important discussion where difficult decisions about colleges involve, among other factors, a consideration of a
college's racial reputation. Parental and student judgments regarding
the degree to which a predominantly white university will facilitate
personal and cultural development are based in large part on reported

experiences of other African Americans who have attended or attempted to attend that university, as well as on events involving the university that are reported in the media.

The parent focus groups generally opened with a dialogue about questions regarding higher education which were not initially focused on racial matters. Soon, the parents or moderator turned the discussion to State University. One of the questions explored in the focus groups was the reputation this predominantly white university had in local black communities. Both in their focus group comments and in responses to an exit questionnaire, the black parents were often explicit about SU's reputation. On the exit questionnaire we asked each participant, "What would you say is State University's reputation today as an institution of higher education for blacks within the black communities you know in this state?" The overwhelming majority (eighty-three percent) replied that SU's reputation was somewhat or mostly negative. Only ten percent said that the school's reputation was somewhat positive, and not one parent chose the option of "mostly positive." The rest were uncertain. In reply to the question, "In regard to serving the black community and black students in this state, has the reputation of State University changed in a positive or negative direction over the last five years?" thirty percent felt the reputation had become somewhat or a lot more negative, and twenty-four percent said, "No change." Only seventeen percent thought SU's reputation had become somewhat more positive, and no one thought it had become much more positive. The rest were uncertain.[9]

In the focus groups the parents engaged the question of SU's reputation and some attempted to achieve a balance in their opinions. Their views of negative aspects of State University were frequently mixed with their views of the good they saw there, as in the following statement:

> Very often, blacks will feel that [at] State University . . . they can get a good academic background. However, for blacks, they feel that there's a lot more negative kinds of feelings, emotions, considerations going on there. In fact, even with their black programs here that they have—the student programs—there's not enough knowledge of the cultural differences, not enough allowances for expressing the cultural differences. So the students—while they may be academically sound, you're talking about a total person, and especially in the undergrad level—are not able to develop into a full-fledged whole person who feels good about himself or herself.

African Americans quickly pick up on certain white aspects of the campus. The lack of knowledge of cultural differences and the lack of "allowances for expressing the cultural differences" are traits of State University as a distinctive place. Thinking in terms of a positive-to-negative scale, another parent added this comment on SU's reputation:

> I would say that definitely not on the positive, but in between neutral and negative . . . because when you hear blacks talk of State University, "Oh certainly it does have a good academic program," but just like [a previous speaker] said, you need [to be] a whole person. . . . You go to school for a lot of experiences, not just the academics, and I hear that black students have negative experiences there. They're called various names. They're treated a certain way, and that cannot be positive as far as I'm concerned.

These parental evaluations of a major U.S. university's image illustrate the problems for African Americans considering predominantly white universities in the United States. Like other black parents across the nation, these parents weigh the value of such a university's academic programs for students' careers against the racial costs of schools that fail to provide support for the development of the "whole black person."

Both the moderator and the parents made a serious effort to include positive points about predominantly white universities in their discussions, although their attempts to do this were sometimes punctuated with laughter, thereby indicating this was a difficult task. Asked by the group moderator if anyone there had heard anything positive in support of State University, one parent responded:

> In support of? [Group laughter] Yeah, you do hear things. A few years ago the media came out with this . . . Do you know Mr. Jones [a black professional]? . . . I believe he's employed out at State University because of the perception that had gone up.

This is a modest example, one that notes the efforts of SU to add racial diversity to the campus; it suggests that black communities pay attention to small gains. Previous research has found a tendency on the part of many African Americans to try hard to find something positive to say about whites even in situations of serious racial barriers and hostility.[10] The desire to acknowledge a situation's positive aspects seems to involve more than a concern with avoiding the appearance of being one-sided. Some social analysts have suggested that among many people of African descent there is a view that the "good" often emerges out of the substance of the "bad." Such a perspective accents change and sees human interactions and situations as in the process of being transformed from one state to the other.[11] For the university to represent a legitimate educational option for many African Americans, it must have some positive dimensions, as well as at least the possibility for future change in the positive direction.

In the focus groups the black parents sometimes viewed SU's sports programs as a positive aspect of the school's reputation. Commenting on the university's image in the black community, one father noted:

> They have a positive image in as far as people that I'm in touch with . . . in my neighborhood. . . . I gather the kids around and try to show them something positive as I take them along with me. And . . . their older members of their family, cousins and brothers, . . . some of them are in different schools. Some aspire to go to State University. . . . Lots of guys [say], "Hey, I can get there and get some exposure playing football and possibly prepare myself into professional sports."

However, other parents' assessments of the sports programs at SU had a less positive tone, as in the case of this mother who only knew SU by its reputation:

> We were just discussing the issue of the sports thing there. It's just not happening. They won't accept you there, and they just won't accept you if you're not involved with athletics there.

Another mother also noted that SU's reputation was one of seeking black students for their sports abilities:

> It's just really like for sports, if you're good in sports.

A father noted how he saw the university as keeping itself separate from local black communities:

> Now, where all the black people live, that's something else. That is totally separate from State University. The only reason why [the university] ventures out, in my opinion, back in the 70s . . . to make any contact with the black people, they needed athletes. That was the only reason. [Another parent added] They needed federal monies, you see.

Although many African Americans, especially young people, see sports as an avenue of upward mobility, these black parents were aware of the racial contradictions in college athletic programs. College athletics provide a means for some talented black students to finance their college educations, but from the perspective of white university officials and alumni these athletes are often little more than grist for the athletic mill. There is evidence that black athletes are important in the generation of revenue for white colleges and universities, as well as in the building of a regional or national reputation. Recent figures indicate that about thirty-seven percent of NCAA Division 1 football players and fifty-six percent of Division 1 men's basketball players are African American. However, well over half of these black football and basketball players score in the lowest quartile on the SAT, and sixty-one percent have high school GPAs in the lowest quartile.[12] Once admitted to predominantly white colleges, these students are worked very hard by the coaches in their primary occupation, which is college athletics. During the season for their sport they typically spend more time practicing and playing than on academic matters. In one survey, three quarters of black athletes at predominantly white institutions reported it was hard for them to make the grades they were capable of achieving. More than four in ten had been on academic probation. Seven in ten gave their coaches a "fair" or worse rating in regard to encouraging good coursework and listening to their academic problems. It appears that many black athletes are not recruited to enhance their educations and career prospects outside the area of athletics.[13]

Black parents know that the role of black athletes at mainly white colleges is primarily to enhance the reputation and revenues of the school. Still, some parents and students gamble on the athletic route in the remote hope of recruitment by a professional athletic team. We will return to this important issue in the next chapter.

Racism and the University's Reputation: "A Bad Reputation"

In the previous section we saw the attempts of the parents to balance their positive and negative comments, and they noted the importance of the university's academic programs and athletics in shaping its reputation. On the whole, however, the positive comments about State University were drowned out in a chorus of negative sentiment about racial barriers on the campus. When asked if State University had a reputation in black communities, one group's spontaneous comments went this way:

> *Group:* Yes.
> *One father:* I say yes.
> *Moderator:* And what is that reputation?
> *Group:* Racist.
> *First father again:* I hear that.
> *Moderator:* Now you have to talk up. You're the lowest speaker.
> *One mother:* Racist.
> *Another mother:* Racist.
> *First father again:* Because my daughter just the other day was ask-

ing about that. And a friend of ours, their son is going to come out of there, and they're the ones that said, "No you don't want to go there because it is racist." My wife went there for one semester going at night, and I can see how it is there.

The comments in another focus group about the university's reputation in local black communities were similar:

> *One mother:* A bad reputation.
> *One father:* Yes! A bad one. . . .
> *Another mother:* Negative. Negative. . . .
> *Another father:* I'm neutral only because my knowledge of it is limited.
> *Another mother:* My sister went to State University, and she said it's very prejudiced; there's a lot of racists there. And I'm going by word of mouth.

Parents in the other groups replied in the same vein to a question about whether the reputation was positive or negative:

> *One mother:* For me it would go towards neutral to negative. [Neutral to negative? Okay, what makes you say that?] Well, it's a majority white school. I think that the black kids there, . . . this is just my perception, they get kind of lost there if they're not an athlete, and the focus there is on the athletic team.
> *One father:* I've heard from other students, some white, some black, and from what I get, they are still prejudiced at State University.
> *Another father:* Getting back to the school: Nobody ever said anything good about it. I never heard anybody say anything good about the school at all.

Unquestionably, SU has a reputation in the state's black communities of being socially inhospitable to blacks. The black parents' willingness to use the strong word "racist" in assessing SU's reputation, together with the resolution and emotion shown in many of their comments, suggests that such an appraisal is common in black communities and not considered excessive. In each focus group the negative views expressed by individual parents were generally validated by the group as a whole. Contrary to much white commentary on black "paranoia" about racism, most African Americans usually do not choose such strong words until the experiential evidence is substantial.

The parents' sources of information about SU's racial reputations are diverse, as one speaker made clear:

> I've only heard that, you know, basically what I'm hearing now, that there were some problems, racial problems, out there. [Who

did you hear it from?] . . . I've talked to several people . . . because I was thinking about going to State University. . . . After I started to talk to some people about myself and going to State University, then it started coming up that they were racial. . . . And then just looking at the news, you know incidents that have happened out at State University, the racial incidents that are going on out there.

Personal contacts and the mass media both play a role in the black construction of a predominantly white university's reputation and image.

Drawing on what he had heard and on his own experience, one father described the SU campus and its reputation in chilling terms:

The first time I rode through it looked like Ku Klux Klan country. . . . State University . . . just looked cold when I rode there, and I didn't like it, and I had already heard negative things before I went there. [What did you hear?] They were racist. And just driving through, I was only through a half hour, and I felt like I was in the heart of Alabama.

The image of this white campus as "Klan country" is a strong historical association for a black man to make. The Klan was created after the Civil War as a white organization designed to create a condition of semi-slavery for ostensibly free black Americans. Certain unnamed aspects of the campus triggered in his mind personal or familial memories of racial oppression. The Klan, still a white supremacy organization in many states, is part of a seamless web of white racism that reaches from past to present.

Indicating yet another source of information on SU's reputation, one mother presented some evidence suggesting that SU was not viewed positively in the local black communities:

I interview students, graduating high school seniors, who are going to college in the fall. I interview about fifty a year, and out of each group of fifty students, I don't think I have five students who are interested in State University. [Now, is that all of your students or African American students?] All minority students, and very few are interested in [State University].

Sources of information about SU's reputation include peer networks, as another parent explained in his assessment of how a racial reputation spreads:

Among the [black] undergraduate college group and so forth it [SU] has a very negative reputation. And I think the reason for that is students from schools in the area effectively party together and so forth, and they hear the sad stories and so many non-success stories from so many students at State University. . . . Now when my son was going to college he was very lucky. He was offered a four-year, expense-paid scholarship to State University, and I really begged him to take it, but he turned it down flat. I think it was specifically for this reason, what the peers were saying.

Peer groups among young African Americans are important receptacles of collective memory; they accumulate positive and negative accounts of students' experiences with a variety of colleges and universities. The poor reputation of white universities acts as a powerful deterrent so some black high school students' consideration of SU as a desirable locale to obtain an education.

Reflecting on how a black state university welcomed black students, one mother noted the different attitude the black community perceived at State University:

This is to tell you how they [SU] reached out to their population. [The black] people who lived right in that [SU's] community, the students that I met that summer—well you know how you spend the summer on campus—from SU's area, they didn't go to SU; they went to a black state university. So, if they [SU] were interested in bringing these black people in, and if they were being good servers to the community, I would think that . . . [black people] would say, "You know what? That school right there will really service us well. We should go there." But no! They go all the way over to the black university.

The decision of black students living nearby to attend other educational institutions signals that SU has a reputation of little interest in serving nearby black communities. Some students report that black students, in their experience, are not actively recruited by State University. This absence of aggressive recruitment evidently contributes to black parents' and students' lack of interest in State University.

Parents' View of SU's Service to Black Communities: "It Can Burn Down"

The collective memory of African American families and communities accumulates accounts of negative experiences with SU, which can affect present-day views and decisions. On the exit questionnaire we asked the parents if they agreed or disagreed with this statement: "In the past, historically, State University has done a poor job of serving the black community and black students." Three-quarters said they agreed with this negative assessment of SU's past performance, while only fourteen percent disagreed. The rest were uncertain or gave no answer.

In the group discussions some parents noted that SU's historical background of referring or discouraging black applicants played a role in their current thinking, as was the case in this dialogue:

> *One father:* Looking back, I was raised here, and I've been in this county most of my life, and I can remember people applying to go to State University, and they would be referred to, because of their race, you know, "Wouldn't you be more comfortable at the predominantly black universities?" They would invariably try to refer you to a black school.
> . . .
> *One mother:* That's true. . . . They would do that. If you go to them, they would refer or they would recommend or suggest that you could go to another college.
> *Moderator:* I wonder is that [referrals to black colleges] to keep down racial tension, maybe?
> *Another father:* No, that's to keep blacks out of universities! [Group laughter]

Later in this focus group's discussion the last speaker added this strongly worded comment:

> If you picked up State University and dropped it off the face of the earth, I would not miss it. [Anything driving that feeling?] Well, I thought about it, and I thought, "What drove me to think about it like that?" And I've got to go back to, I'm from this state. And from kindergarten to sixth grade I was a segregated black student. From seventh grade, boom, integration. They dropped you into a predominantly white school. . . . Well I did go to college—to a white college. I was in an English class, and I turned in a paper in the English class, and it came back in three days marked "E—this does not sound like your work." So these are the types of things that made up my mind quick that I'm going to scamper right to a black college where I don't have to worry about that aspect. That qualifies that statement. None of the peers that I grew up with went to State University. They went to the predominantly black universities. Like I said, "It can burn down."

This father's anger is palpable. Significantly, no other parent took issue with his harsh comment. The history of racial separation in the United States lays the foundation for and now blends into current parental decisions, which may sometimes be oriented away from unwelcoming, predominantly white colleges and universities and toward more hospitable, predominantly black colleges and universities.

Students' Views of State University's Reputation: "Whites Really Rule the Campus"

As we have seen in the parents' comments, the parent and student decisions about college settings are affected by a college's reputation. Before most black students in the focus groups came to SU, they had heard about the university's reputation. As with the parents, we asked all the students on the exit questionnaire a question about SU's reputation: "What would you say is State University's reputation today, as an institution of higher education for blacks, within the black communities you know in this state?" The pattern of student responses was generally similar to that of the parents. A large majority (seventy percent) felt that SU's reputation in local communities was mostly or somewhat negative. Twenty-two percent said that SU's reputation was somewhat positive, and only three percent (one student) replied, "mostly positive." The rest were uncertain. Taken together with the strong parental views, these results are unmistakable—they show that SU's racial reputation is substantially negative in the state's black communities.

In the focus groups the black students discussed what they had heard about SU's reputation before they came and about their reasons for choosing SU. Their comments were similar to the parents. They included some positive assessments of the location, sports programs, academic reputation, and reasonable cost of this university. In their college choices the students indicated a desire for an academically first-rate university that would prepare them well for good careers in business or the professions. Not surprisingly, most of these young scholars relied on family and friends in sorting out SU's and other colleges' reputations, as this student indicated:

> Well, my mother liked the idea. My two choices for college were both predominantly white anyway, and this was the better of the two. Because it was between this and another predominantly white university, which was having a lot of racial problems right before I came to college. So she was O.K. with it.

Also noting the importance of the academic reputation, one male student described his college choice:

> I have a cousin who recently graduated from here. She had nothing but good things to say about this university. She graduated with honors, and she's in law school right now. She kind of swayed me in this university's direction.

Another student also noted that he had heard good things about the academic program:

> I didn't hear anything about any racism or nothing like that. All I heard, all I knew was that they had a good business school, and that's basically why I decided to come.

Interestingly, another positive factor about SU's reputation cited by several students in the group interviews was the fact that this predominantly white campus does have some African American students. As one male student noted, "I didn't know the percentage when I decided to go here. I just knew they had blacks."

This issue of the visibility or invisibility of black students on campus is important in shaping SU's image as a hospitable place, for parents and students. The relatively small number of black students there has caused the residents of the state's black communities to see SU as a *white* university. Several of the black students reported that they were discouraged from selecting this university by friends or relatives who felt they would be relegated to the margins in a mostly white setting. Replying to the moderator's question about whether people said things to discourage students from coming to SU, one young woman replied:

> Yeah. Because it's a predominantly white school—and that I should go to a predominantly black school, which I did not want to do. Because I knew the whole world was not black, and with me coming from an all black town.

Bringing up the large size of the university, one student in another focus group reported that she faced tough questioning from some of her black friends:

> "Why are you going to that white school? All those white people up there." And then . . . a lot of my friends were talking about the fact of how this university was so big, "Oh, you are just going to be a number. You're just going to be a number. You should go to a smaller school."

Here the common student complaint of "just being a number" takes on racial connotations. Being lost in a crowd is a common experience for all college students at large universities, but being lost in a sea of white faces elevates the common problem to another level of difficulty for black students.

As we have noted previously, such experiences are not unique to black students considering State University. Advice from relatives and other black adults that warns students away from mostly white universities is commonplace in many black communities across the nation. For example, a junior at the University of North Carolina (Chapel Hill) was recently quoted in *Essence* magazine: "Before I decided to go to North Carolina, a lot of people encouraged me to consider universities that were a little less racially intense. UNC had a history and a reputation for being a racist campus."[14] Collective memories shape black student decisions about education in many communities.

Reflecting a realistic tone about post-graduation opportunities, another student at State University noted the university's image among his friends:

> I heard something like that too, . . . not from my parents but from friends. They say that since it was an all-white school I might have some problems. But to me I just looked at it [as a] situation where if we're talking about going to an all-black college—but the world is not all black. So if you have to deal with these people eventually, you might as well deal with them now.

In reply to the focus group moderator's question about what he had heard about SU's reputation before he came, one student discussed the views of his parents about the white-oriented staff at State University:

> I heard that since it's predominantly white that the whites really rule the campus. And my parents tried to tell me not to come. . . . Like programs that would go on—most of the stuff was geared toward the white. . . . The staff would tend to you more, care about you more, if you went to a black college.

In Chapter 1 we assessed how racial barriers take a variety of forms, blatant or subtle, overt or hidden. One student explained that she had heard about the character of certain barriers on campus:

> The racial atmosphere was OK, but a lot of the racism was like underlying. It wasn't very blatant . . . but that you always have to be on your guard.

Unquestionably, agonizing educational choices are created for black parents and students by the racial reputation of predominantly white universities like SU. The choice of such a college may sometimes be made against the advice of relatives and friends, who may warn the students of subtle and blatant discrimination on a campus where whiteness is omnipresent in student body composition, staff services, and a variety of campus facilities and affairs. Still, these students have decided to come to State University anyway. Some explain, often with an air of resignation, that they might as well get used to dealing with mostly white, socially inhospitable environments while they are young.

We have previously noted the importance of space and place in the way that racial relations are arranged or managed. As we have just seen, a number of the student commentaries indicate the importance of that spatial environment. The interaction in one focus group made the significance of place even clearer. After the moderator asked what factors students considered in choosing a university, one senior commented sharply on the issues pressed on her by family and friends:

> I had so many, like people my parents' age and people older than that, going, "Oh girl, don't go there," you know, and people just telling me that it was the worst place for me to go. "Go to another state university." . . . [Names another] was the one they kept telling me to go since it's predominantly black. But they just said under no circumstances was I to go to State University. I mean I had friends who are a bunch of years older than me going here, and they still said "Don't go there."

This comment is similar to those previously examined, but this student accents both the spatial and temporal aspects of her important decision. The vocabulary of spatial relations is striking: "Don't go *there*," and "it was the worst *place* for me to go." Replying to the moderator's follow-up question about why she had received such advice, the same student alluded to SU's past history in regard to African American students. She suggested that the university had few black students until the late 1960s, then added:

> And the environment just wasn't conducive I guess to black students, so it's just the kind of thing that we knew we weren't wanted here. I guess that was what they meant.

Again, the collective memory of black families and communities in regard to racial discrimination is underscored.

In what at first appears to be a move in a different direction, the next student in the group interview focused on her own parents' fears about substance abuse on campus:

> The thing that my family did . . . and I was coming from out-of-state. So that was like, "That school has drugs. You don't need to go there." So I mean that was just a major thing because that was so much in the news and everything. And every place else was drug-free according to them except State University.

The family's sense of danger is focused on the "place" that is State University. Then the next student speaker in this particular group drew on her past experiences to discuss the reputation of State University:

> I didn't know anything about this school.... I used to pass through this campus all the time. I used to always see these white girls. I'd tell myself, "I wouldn't go to that school...There's no black people here." I live right in the neighborhood. It's like I didn't know one black person that came here.

Racial Climate and Racial Reputation: "You Were ... Just an Unseen Person"

Not surprisingly, the parents' perceptions of SU's racial climate are ingredients in their views of SU's reputation. On the exit questionnaire the parents were queried as to how they felt about this statement: "Today State University is a college campus where black students are generally welcomed and nurtured." Most (seventy-one percent) disagreed with this statement, while only fourteen percent agreed. The rest were uncertain. The parents were also asked, "How often have you heard about racial discrimination or racial problems at State University in the last ten years?" Fifty-four percent replied "fairly often" or "very often," while thirty-two percent replied "not very often." One person said "not at all," and the rest were not sure. In spite of SU's efforts over the last decade to improve its image among African Americans in the state, most of the black parents still have a negative view of the situation of black students on campus.

In the group discussions of SU's racial climate, some of the parents drew on their own or their children's experiences there; others based their views of the campus on discussions with friends and relatives or accounts in the local media. The favorable assessments of SU indicated that acquaintances or relatives had made it through with no serious problems. A few of the parents spoke in this fashion:

> *One mother:* I know of three people who attended [SU].... The three people had no complaints.
> *One father:* A real close friend of mine, ... attended State University. He had no problems at State University. [As] a matter of fact, he raved about [the] school. [That's] my only experience.

Even positive accounts sometimes have an undercurrent that suggests something is amiss. There is no clear suggestion in any of the parental accounts that the experience of black SU students was highly rewarding beyond the attainment of a good education and a college degree. For many white students, in contrast, the university experience doubtless marks a special time in their lives which creates fond memories, a time which enhanced in positive ways their self-esteem and personal and collective identities.

Drawing on the experiences of his wife and his wife's friend, one father suggested that there were positive and negative aspects to SU's racial climate:

> I have negative and positive points about State University. My wife's girlfriend went to State University and . . . we went over there constantly to visit her; she stayed on campus. We never got any negative response from her about the school. . . . My wife [is] . . . a high school teacher, and they approached her about taking a job, or her internship at State University's computer program. But, being the so-called aggressive black woman she is, she said, "I'm not taking the position where I would be a clerk typist or whatever." I mean, she has her master's degree.

Several participants noted that some relatives and acquaintances had positive experiences at SU or at least had not made negative complaints. A few referred to specific events. One black student was offered a university job; another was welcomed back by a mixed group of friends. Two parents specifically mentioned that black athletes had a more positive environment. Again there is the hint in such comments that black students who are athletes may be seen by many whites as in their appropriate "place" at a predominantly white university.

Significantly, some participants had relatives who did not talk much or at all about their personal experiences as students at SU. Providing some family details, one parent mentioned the eloquent silence of a sister-in-law about her student days at SU:

> My sister-in-law graduated from State University, and I had a lot of respect for her because I thought highly of that institution as far as academically being able to graduate. Now, she never ever had anything to say about the college. You know, I graduated from a black public university. And, yeah, we had this, and I had great friends, and we were doing this, and the campus was doing this. And we were political signers. We were signing people up to vote this, that, and the other. [Yet] she never had anything good [to say about State University], I mean, there was nothing. She worked. She went to school. She came home. . . . College is one of the best times of your life! You never ever should cheat yourself out of that. She never had, as far as I'm concerned, she never had that. . . . Because I know somebody who graduated, who was an excellent teacher, who benefited from that education, who was strong enough, academically and socially, and must [have] had a wonderful self-esteem . . . to get through a situation where

you were sort of like, you know, just an unseen [person]—you weren't seen.

This speaker reveals another potential consequence of an African American's choice of a predominantly white educational institution. She interprets her sister-in-law's lack of any commentary, either positive or negative, about her experiences at SU as a sign of social isolation. She concludes that it took great personal strength for her sister-in-law to succeed as an "unseen" person on the campus. Comments touching on the lack of recognition were numerous in the parent and student focus groups. Such experiences bring to mind yet again Ralph Ellison's comment in his *Invisible Man* about the white inability to truly "see" African Americans as individuals: "I am invisible, understand, simply because people refuse to see me."[15]

Significantly, *not one* participant in the parent groups indicated they had *often* heard from friends, relatives, or other black residents of the state that SU's campus was strongly supportive of its black students. The best many could say was that their acquaintances or relatives had gotten though the university with "no serious problems."

Advice to Potential College Students: "I Wouldn't Recommend Anybody to Go to That School"

The ultimate test of one's views of a university campus is the type of recommendation one would make to a young person selecting a university. In this way, individual, family, and collective knowledge of a university's reputation moves from the present to future generations. The reputation of a university is linked in central ways to its position in local communities, black or nonblack. On the exit questionnaire we asked parents, "If you were asked by a black high school student to recommend a college in this state, would you recommend State University very favorably, somewhat favorably, somewhat unfavorably, or very unfavorably with respect to the racial climate there?" Two-thirds said that they would give a somewhat or very unfavorable recommendation to a high school student, while a quarter said that they would give a somewhat favorable recommendation. Only one person would give a very favorable recommendation, and a few others were uncertain.

Several parents gave a very negative reply to an open-ended question about recommending SU. For example, one parent answered this way: "I wouldn't recommend anybody to go to that school, with low self-esteem." And another parent underscored his point this way:

To most of them I would say, just because of experience and because it's tough enough, there are enough challenges, and you don't want to add that one on unless there's some overriding reason. [Moderator: I get a sense you're discouraging them.] For most black students, yes, I would discourage them from going to State University. Whereas two years ago I would have offered some encouragement. Basically the only competitive edge it has is cost.

Drawing on their *experience*, a common process in the interview groups, some black parents judged the personal and psychological stress generated by racial hurdles at SU to be so great as to outweigh the benefits for potential students.

However, the majority view seemed to be that their advice on colleges would be tailored to the needs and strengths of a particular student, a point this expressive parent underscored:

I think that an individual brings an experience to their own education. Everyone's isn't always the same. [Another parent: Even if it makes them uncomfortable?] No. Different people react differently to a situation. And there are many people who are successful—African Americans who have had successful experiences. So I wouldn't limit anyone by saying, "Don't go because of the racial attitude." I might say, "You'll run into racism at the university just as you'll run into racism [Another parent: Any place else.]" . . . It's how you handle it and how you feel about yourself. My only problem is how I feel about young people in the seventeen-to-nineteen age group. It's such an evolutionary period that so much harm can be done. It would depend on the person.

A number of the parents amplified this point by arguing that only those students who are "tough" should take on the racial climate at universities like State University. In these probing commentaries the parents bring up issues that we saw them discuss in regard to their own children; we see the accent on individual and collective experience with racism as the inevitable backdrop of much black decision making about higher education.

One mother answered the question about encouraging a high school student in this manner:

I think if I was going to encourage someone to go there—because, for instance, they want to go to the school of [names a SU program] because it's one of the best in the country . . . it would have to be someone who is very highly motivated. And

... there has to be some kind of support system there for them. And I think it would be incumbent upon the parents and the other students to, [in the] freshman year, try to get together and at least form some kind of unit to help these kids get through there because, like he said, otherwise they're just lost.

Suggesting that SU is for the highly motivated, this speaker recommended the defensive strategy of banding together. In contrast to certain critics of higher education like D'Souza and Bloom, many black parents see black students' sticking together in traditionally white places as necessary for their personal and academic survival, not as some type of organized antiwhite activity. These peer group settings give many first-year college students a place to be themselves, and to find supportive friends, without the intrusion of racial barriers.

Accenting the requirement of mental toughness, one focus group participant added this penetrating social commentary:

> The people that I've spoken with over the past couple of years . . . who attended [State University] . . . have had negative things to say. But they all graduated, and they are all successful in their respective careers. So, I guess . . . it strikes a balance. I think there are some things they went through that were challenging, and I guess, if you're mentally strong enough, you can rise above and get what you want out of the program. But a lot of the stories I remember and the one that I related—just little things that I felt were kind of demeaning to us as black people—just should not have [happened]. It's sad that . . . a person has to learn in that type of atmosphere, that you have to go through that kind of thing.

The approach of the majority of the parents to advising students about how to deal with predominantly white universities like SU was not usually one of avoidance and retreat. For many of the parents the choice of a predominantly white college must be made with eyes open and a certain realism about the omnipresence of racist attitudes, as this parent emphasized:

> I think they have a lot to offer. I think there's a good academic program there. I think once you get a degree, . . . you can go far. It's something that is respected nationwide, and I would not steer a young person away from the university simply because it's racism everywhere. . . . You can tell the child to go down [to] the basement, and I'll open up a college down there, and that's going to be perfect. But I just wouldn't, I would not steer this child away from State University solely on racial climate there, because . . . it may be moving worse than somewhere else, but it's still tension; it's everywhere.

A certain resignation about racial impediments and animosity in everyday life in the United States creeps into many of the answers of both the parents and the students. The predominantly white university is not an island of tolerance in an ocean of intolerance, as it has often been pictured. From the black perspective it is another major arena of everyday intolerance and racism.

Phrasing his answer eloquently, one father noted that advice giving and decision making about majority-white colleges and universities was like being part of military campaign:

> I don't think that I could ever be so shallow as to say to a student or a guy or a girl who wants to go to college or State University, "Don't go there because [of the] prejudice or there's a history of racism." . . . So, if a student, . . . —let's say that this is an intelligent child—is looking at the academics that they could achieve at this university, and they're looking at what I could get at this university [that] will help me do what I want in life. Okay, then, I would say, "Well, this university's a good school for this thing, that, and the other. However, I think you should be well advised to know that you will probably, I'm not saying you will, but you may probably experience this sort of problem, so I'm just telling you so." [What sort of problem?] Racial prejudice. . . . A white student is treated like a number; a black student is treated . . . less than a number. See, because the white student goes to school, he says, "Well, I'm going to get an education first, and the college has this atmosphere." A black student going to a white town is war.

The parental remarks on the recommendation they might or might not make to a high school student considering State University illustrate the complex situations and difficult choices that confront black parents and children in dealing with higher education in the United States. Many felt that SU's academic programs warranted a young black person's consideration, yet they suggested that the black student who chooses SU will likely require much familial, peer, and other social support to survive personally and academically. These African American parents generally seem to believe that only strong and highly motivated black students should choose a predominantly white college or university.

Conclusion

Across the nation African American parents and students face distinctive, difficult, and often agonizing dilemmas in making choices about higher education. Central to these dilemmas are the racial reputations of traditionally white college and university campuses. The military language—such as "struggle" and "war"—sometimes used in the focus groups indicates the painful labor and effort that a racist environment imposes on African American students seeking greater academic opportunities. African American students in majority-white university settings must be able to put up with racial slurs, to avoid becoming "lost," to protect themselves from personal "harm," and to endure or confront the often negative racial climate. Such conditions do not describe a truly positive educational experience for any person.

Within the geographical area that it serves, a predominantly white university's reputation is a condensation of individual and collective memories. From the data we have seen on predominantly white universities this reputation can be very different for black and white families. Judging from academic quality reports and alumni publications, most major public universities have reputations accenting excellent academic programs and supportive social environments in the white communities which send students to these universities. However, while in black communities these universities' academic programs are typically regarded as very good, their racial climates are often another matter. Many African American parents feel that a typical black student will pay a heavy personal price for participation in the desirable academic environments at these traditionally white colleges and universities.

In general, African American parents and students want the same things from a college education as white parents and students do. They seek solid college credentials and a broadening of the mind within a personally and socially supportive campus atmosphere. Yet the choice of a college for African Americans involves serious dilemmas and major struggles not generally faced by white Americans. The racial barriers of the past and the hope that the racial situation will change in the future color the temporal aspects of these educational choices and dilemmas. African American parents' expectations for their children are grounded in their own experiences as well as those of other family members and the larger African American community. References to past racial segregation and violence-prone supremacist groups like the Ku Klux Klan are notable because they point to how violent white hostility has been in the past and the present. African American parents cannot afford to ignore this nation's racialized past, whether it be the racism of yesterday or of decades past, if they are going to make intelligent decisions about their children's futures.

CONFRONTING WHITE STUDENTS
The Whiteness of University Spaces

The Character of Racialized Settings

In describing their experiences with a major university, the African American parents and students often used spatial and temporal metaphors. Their social relations extend in many directions in both space and time. As we noted in Chapter 1, the experiential reality of space is at the heart of social interaction. Experiencing the space around oneself, between oneself and others, and within oneself is meaningful in many cultures.[1]

For the most part, social scientists in Europe and North America have regarded space as a passive container of events, as the environmental vacuum where human lives take place. Yet, space plays a very active role in social life. Social relations are physically structured in material space, and human beings often view space expressively and symbolically.[2] In most societies those with the greater power and resources ordinarily control the use and meaning of important spaces in a society. For example, large amounts of land and other real estate are disproportionately consumed by the higher classes as evidence of their power and monetary position.[3] Indeed, the control of space has often been discussed in terms of a territorial imperative, for individuals and nations.[4]

Humans seek to conquer territory and maintain dominion over territory that can be used to demarcate in-groups and out-groups. The ethnic war in the former Yugoslavia provides one example. The struggles with police officers and the destruction of many city blocks in recent uprisings by African Americans and other people of color in Los Angeles, Miami, and other U.S. cities illustrate the significance of these places as racialized territories. Over the course of U.S. history, whites, from the white slaveholders and segregationists of yesteryear to many white homeowners, real estate companies, banks, insurers, and law enforcement officers today, have clearly demarcated their territories, usually taking the lack of melanin in the skin as a principal marker for the dominant culture and in-group status. This centrality of territorial demarcation along skin-color lines for Europeans, and their descendants elsewhere, has been underscored by a number of social analysts who have examined the long history of European emergence and development.[5]

Particular places not only contain recurring movements of people and ideas but also are set within larger social contexts which provide additional meanings. The concept of racialized space encompasses the cultural biases that help define specific areas and territories as white or as black, with the consequent feelings of belonging and control. Consider the following interaction in a State University parking lot, a space with a clear campus function, but one not usually thought of as significant in racial terms. One black student made this comment in a focus group interview:

> I was walking to class. . . . It was about twelve noon and I had my backpack. I'm a black student, right. And there was this white girl in the car, and she pulled in the parking space, right. And she's about to get out. And I'm walking up. I'm not even paying attention to her, and the next thing I hear is "click, click." And she's looking at me like I'm going to rape her.

Although he was clearly recognizable as a university student, this young man was subjected to degrading gestures of suspicion by a white student. The white student's actions and look, and the black student's taking offense, can be understood fully if one probes the elaborate biases, fears, and presuppositions that steer racial relations in the United States. The parking lot was not simply a passive container of events but played an active part in what the actors perceived about each other and in the behavior they displayed towards each other. The black man was assumed to be in the wrong place. Many whites at universities like this assume, consciously or half-consciously, they are in *white* places.

This assumption is evident in much recent writing about African American students on mostly white college and university campuses. For example, in *The Closing of the American Mind,* Allan Bloom, a white University of Chicago professor, reveals a preoccupation with the black presence in the spaces of predominantly white universities with which he is familiar. Although the book was published in 1987, in it Bloom is still greatly concerned about black student militancy at Cornell two decades earlier in the 1960s. Commenting on the present, Bloom contends that there is a "large black presence in major universities, frequently equivalent to their proportion in the general population."[6] This statement is demonstrably false, for the percentage of black students at predominantly white colleges and universities is rarely equal to the black percentage in the general population. As we will see, this underrepresentation is part of the problem that black students face in coping with predominantly white places like State University. With such exaggerations Bloom and similar white critics reveal the importance of the black student presence for the white mind.

Bloom argues that black students have "proved indigestible" because they "keep to themselves." He goes so far as to assert that at the moment when everyone "has become a 'person,' blacks have become blacks."[7] The use of the bodily function, digestion, as a metaphor to characterize black incorporation into certain universities reveals that in Bloom's view desegregated education involves one-way acculturation of the black out-group to the dominant culture. The physical and social spaces of predominantly white colleges and universities generally embody the presumption of one-way assimilation for students of color. As we will see throughout this book, black students regularly encounter white students, professors, and administrators who treat them as if they were socially and educationally "indigestible."

Bloom construes the spatial separation of black students as a major campus problem, but not one that is "the fault of the white students, who are rather straightforward in such matters and frequently embarrassingly eager to prove their liberal credentials."[8] Bloom is not unique in this view, for other critics of the so-called "multicultural revolution" make similar assertions about the alleged "segregation" of black students at major universities. Indeed, many white students on these campuses look at the grouping of students of color negatively, as "segregation." For example, a study at the University of California (Berkeley) found that whites were the most likely among the students to articulate a strong concern that the campus was too balkanized and segregated, with separate political and social groups for different groups of university students.[9]

Other critics of the modern university share Bloom's critique of African American students and place a positive patina on the actions of white Americans. For example, George Keller has examined a number of books, reports, and journal issues devoted to problems of black access and achievement in higher education. After reviewing what he terms the "massive effort to encourage equality of opportunity in higher education" and the surprising lack of black advancement in the last decade, Keller suggests that the reasons for the latter problem must lie primarily "within the black community."[10] While Keller recognizes that there are traces of racism in the college cultures, he downplays the importance of racism as a major factor in explaining black student attrition. Instead, he emphasizes individual and family factors, including the allegedly problematical black attitude toward education and the lack of black leaders who recognize that racism is not the central problem. Keller suggests further that

> Petulant and accusatory black spokespersons will need to climb off their soapboxes and walk through the unpleasant brambles of their young people's new preferences and look at their young honestly. ... They will need to encourage, lift up, and argue with those youths who do not see the urgency of education in a scientific, international, and information-choked world ... where knowledge is the principal sword and shield against decline, poverty, and inferiority. Critics will need to stop the fashionable practice of lambasting the colleges as if they were the central problem.[11]

Similarly, Dinesh D'Souza avers that white colleges are not the problem. He views whites as sincerely seeking to rectify past wrongs by welcoming black students into historically white college spaces.[12] Such writers seem to view whites as the victims on contemporary college campuses and to see black students and professors as primarily responsible not only for the black attrition rate but also for the social balkanization of racial groups on campus.

Significantly, in these white-centered analyses the authors reveal no understanding of the action and courage involved in large numbers of black students' coming to, and graduating from, predominantly white campuses. In this chapter we turn to an in-depth examination of the experiences of these courageous black students with whites at one of the nation's major universities. We will see that the African American students suffer at the hands of white students and pay a heavy price for their choice of a white college. The costs include not only personal degradation and mental anguish but also academic costs. These problems are not unique to State University. Recently, for example, researchers at another predominantly white university found that most of the African American students questioned knew of incidents of racial mistreatment on campus. Fifty-nine percent had personally been verbally insulted. Apparently, much of this mistreatment came from other students. The researchers came to the conclusion that "the climate for African American students in this sample, was sufficiently problematic to interfere with academic success."[13]

The Symbolism of College Spaces:
"Black Students Aren't Even Represented in the Yearbook"

In a variety of ways, the strong symbolism attached to spaces on college campuses becomes part of the personalities and identities of individuals associated with those spaces. A particular college or university commonly takes on a high level of significance in individuals' lives not only while they are there but also after they graduate. Many college graduates look upon their alma mater with great nostalgia. A diverse assortment of rings, yearbooks, and other paraphernalia emblazoned with college insignia fosters and facilitates the public display of individuals' association with their college. Alumni associations, class meetings, cruises, and various consumer gimmicks designed to build a school's reputation and endowment fund promote the continuation of the graduates' identification with the school.

Parents participate in the display of school allegiance and in the consumerism associated with it, as the following example from a female student illustrates:

> It just made me think about my freshman year. My mom sent away the order for the yearbook. And I wondered why, since I was a freshman. . . . But it was the first thing she wanted me to have before my college experience. So I got my yearbook, and I was going home, so I was reading on the train. And I'm going through it, and I'm not seeing very many black people. And the one—they had a picture of, I think, blacks in pre-med. That was the only black scholastic organization that they had. They had two pages for the homecoming step show; that was about it. They did their traditional dorm life, students moving in, all this for white students, like I guess the black students didn't move in. They, like, landed on the roof and snuck in, into the dorms. I'm so—I'm getting a little—I'm just wondering why there were no pictures. And then to top it off they had two or three pages of the white students hanging out . . . standing in line outside a local cafe, and I was like, "This isn't even a part of the campus. But yet it's a part of the yearbook." You know, glorifying their life and their recreational activities, and where black students aren't even represented in the yearbook. That really made me mad.

Here something as innocuous as a yearbook delivers eloquent messages about the collective racial identity of a modern university. Like many others of its type this college annual glorified white life and recreational activities. The college yearbook is a textual and pictorial record of classes of students, their activities, and the campus spaces they have occupied. Yearbook photos are among the campus representations that make different groups of students visible to others on and off campus. This personal and group visibility, or invisibility, is a critical aspect of our idea of racialized space. To be recognized as valued members of the campus community is important to all groups of students, but especially to those who are underrepresented on a large campus like State University. The omission of African American students from the yearbook suggests a general lack of recognition of the black presence and achievements on campus and hints at the low status the whites who prepared the yearbook apparently granted to black students. This kind of neglect encourages black students to congregate in their own groups and plan their own activities and publications, a reaction that may bring white condemnation of this black "segregation."

Most campus activities at majority-white universities reflect white student traditions. In a study of black students at predominantly black and predominantly white colleges Walter Allen found that just under two-thirds of black students on white campuses, but only one-third on black campuses, felt that the campus activities there did not relate to their interests.[14] A 1990s survey of a large national sample of college students by Sylvia Hurtado and her associates found that just over half the African American students felt excluded from certain activities on their campuses because of skin color; the comparable figure for whites was six percent.[15]

Many campus activities become localized, white-dominated rituals in which to display college symbols, promote school solidarity, and spur student, alumni, and public celebration of a college's geographical and educational identities. In one group interview with the black parents, a father reviewed the most important spatial event for alumni, Homecoming ceremonies:

> Homecoming is supposedly what it says: Coming home; coming back to where you're from. I know of no black students who go to State University's homecoming. I know at one point they had separate homecomings, so to speak. There were functions that were set up specifically for the black students, specifically for the white students, because they knew they were not going to mix.

Homecoming events usually include sports activities that have become important rituals involving a display of college spirit and symbols. Yet, at many predominantly white colleges and universities these ceremonial events have long been white-oriented. For example, in 1994 black students at the University of Georgia organized a protest of homecoming activities because an all-white screening board selected an all-white slate of ten finalists for homecoming queen, ignoring seven students of color who were candidates. In recent years two black homecoming queens at the University of North Carolina endured racial harassment and vandalism directed at their cars from whites opposed to their participation in traditionally white ceremonies.[16] Not surprisingly, African American students and alumni often feel uncomfortable at traditional homecoming rituals.

Even the meaning of school traditions and events can be different for black and white students. For example, one of the authors attended Georgetown University as an undergraduate. He and his fellow black students there took great pride in the basketball team as the major black institution on a mostly white campus. At the Georgetown basketball games, the black students sat beside the white students, with all the students yelling "Go Hoyas" (the name of the team) at games. However, in this activity the black students did not feel solidarity with the white students. For most black students, "Go Hoyas" urged on the players as *black* players. It was thus a cry of African American unity in a sea of white faces. For most white students, in contrast, "Go Hoyas" was likely linked to a lofty sports tradition going back many decades. The students were side by side physically, but not joined in their commitments or understandings of the events taking place.

The entrenched whiteness of place that is State University was eloquently underscored in the frustrated commentary of one very articulate student in the focus groups:

> This university does cater to white students. You know, the commercial strip near the university is for white people. You know, bars everywhere—all white boys in it, no black people. The frat row's white, no black Greeks, nothing, so they're coming from where they're coming from. . . . [She added later] Sometimes I'm like, "God, if I was white I'd have the best time." . . . They get to have parties at frat houses. They don't have to pay for it. You know, they just have the best time. Everything is geared toward them. Their [campus] paper is geared toward them. Everybody agrees.

For the most part the black students that we interviewed more or less felt unwelcome. They were asked on an exit questionnaire to assess this statement: "Today State University is a college campus where black students are generally welcomed and nurtured." Eighty-nine percent of the students *disagreed* with the statement. Because of the negative racial messages and racial barriers, black students at SU and similar universities frequently identify the schools as places in which they are not wanted, by white students as well as by other whites on campus. The campuses become sites of daily struggle to survive rather than arenas where educational experiences are savored and where their personal development is central and nurtured.

The physical space of a traditionally white college campus has many meanings. We noted in Chapter 2 how the racial reputation of the University of Texas was affected by some of its Confederate statues. Recent debates on other Southern campuses have centered on similar statues or the use of Confederate battle flags in campus parades and ceremonies. These white symbols are oppressive in certain respects for African Americans. Moreover, African American history is generally burdened with violence and oppression perpetrated by many white people, some of whom have become national heroes (for example, Thomas Jefferson and George Washington, who were major slaveholders) whose names are affixed to statues, streets, libraries, and buildings on predominantly white campuses, both in the North and the South.

The Aggressive Defense of White Territory: "Is That a Nigger with a White Girl?"

Ideally, the college experience should represent a special place and time in student lives that enhance in positive ways personal and collective identities. For students who sense that they are not wanted, however, the college campus becomes an unfriendly place and is likely to have a negative impact on both self-esteem and personal identity.

On or near predominantly white college campuses a significant number of white students, as well as other whites, regularly communicate hostile messages to black students, while many other whites stand by and take no action to stop such activity. In the focus groups there were several examples of aggressive white reactions to black intrusions into "white space." A university campus typically has geographical boundaries that blend into a surrounding array of student-oriented stores, restaurants, and night clubs, with students moving between the campus and the surrounding environment. One student gave the following account of an experience walking near the SU campus:

> I was walking down the street with my girlfriend—I guess it was over the summer—and out of the blue comes this guy driving in a van. He had one of those, you know, loudspeakers on the van, and he's like, "Is that a nigger with a white girl?" You do not understand how hard it was for my girlfriend to keep me from running and pulling him from the window of that truck because I knew he had to stop at the stop sign, you know, and I saw him there.

African American students walking on or near predominantly white universities have a heightened visibility for whites, both for students and for non-students. Here an ostensibly neutral space, a public street, was transformed into a place of significant pain and anger for a black student. The white hostility seems to reflect not only the view that the black student is "out of place" but also the deepest of all white-racist preoccupations, a concern about racial miscegenation.

Thinking about her time at SU, a female student spoke of an incident that happened while she was walking near campus:

> I don't remember everything that happened, but I know once I was down on [a campus-area street], and somebody drove by. Yeah, it was ignorant, I mean because it was kind of night, and maybe I shouldn't have been down there by myself to begin with, but I think I was walking back home. And somebody yelled "nigger" out of the car. And I was like, "Oh, what am I supposed to do?"

Commenting on SU students, one father in our focus groups noted that the male athletes he knew had an easier time than the female students with racial slurs:

> The ones that I know who have attended it did not feel welcome.... The guys felt welcome; the girls didn't.... [After another parent interrupts, he continues] See, the guys that I knew that were athletes, they were readily accepted among the general population. Where they went they did not come into any, I guess you'd say, "racial" situations. The women who I knew went there, from what they told me, they were constantly bombarded with racial slurs, so to speak, as they walk from their dorms to the campus.

Walking on or near campus is an everyday activity that should not be racially threatening. Yet it periodically becomes a stressful act for black students. They are vulnerable to a range of racist acts, including many which can be carried out impersonally and with impunity.

Pain-creating racist epithets, like "nigger," "coon," and "boy," are used by whites as a way of defining certain areas as white spaces. The epithet is frequently meant as an insult and as a warning to a black person: "You should not be in that place" or "Watch your step." One student described this type of ritualized behavior on a shuttle bus:

> I work for the shuttle bus at State University, and I usually drive on Friday nights. And on Friday night all these white people go down to their club. You know what I'm talking about? And one night, it was about one o'clock, these frat boys were on the bus.

And there's no smoking on the bus, right? And they were smoking. And I stopped the bus, and I told them to "put out your cigarettes," right? So they put them out, and then I kept on, and then I was at a dorm, right? They got off up there. And then when they got off they said, "Coony" or something.

The fact that this epithet was delivered at night probably intensified the target's pain because of the racial dangers that nighttime spaces can bring for black men. The common experience of African Americans is that there is usually a potential for violence when epithets such as these are hurled in public places.

Fear of direct physical attack is not unreasonable. One father in our focus groups noted briefly that he had heard about a racial attack at State University: "I did have one kid tell me that [he was] attacked by other students . . . a black student by some white students." And in a student focus group one young woman gave an account of whites moving from a racial epithet to a physical attack:

A friend of mine . . . walked me to the bus stop. He was going back to his dorm . . . say three o'clock in the morning or whatever. These kids come by, these three white guys come. And they call him a "boy." He's about five feet ten inches, thin built. He kind of freaks out, you know. He's like "I ain't nobody's boy." You know, freaks out. And all of a sudden they're kicking his ass. And they beat him down. The next time I'd seen him, he had stitches under his eyes, eyes out to here, and whatever. We had to go to [the] little student court. The [three white students'] old friends, black student athletes, stood up and tried to say their white friends were not racist. It really freaked me out. The case— I mean people saw these . . . three white guys beat one guy down —and the judgment was he could've run. Because he had a cane and he hit them with his cane, and . . . [they] said he could've run. He's just as [much at] fault as the white kids. O.K. [It] freaked me out. I was freaked out from that point on. State University is just so racist.

Some sociologists have suggested that "home territories" are those in which the occupants have a broad freedom to act, which is coupled with a sense of control over the area.[17] The white students' sense of what is home territory appears to underlie this attack. As in the previous incidents, the white words and gestures are ritualized and have well-known, shared meanings going back centuries in U.S. racial relations history. Here the student court (likely run by white students) concluded that because the black target of racial hostility had attempted to defend himself he was as culpable as the whites. In this way the student justice system plays an active role in creating a hostile climate for black students. Discrimination in white-dominated student justice systems is a complaint as well of black students at other colleges and universities.[18] In the above incident the victim did not suffer alone; at least one other black student shared his suffering. The latter's reaction illustrates again the importance of blacks' collective memories of white hostility.

How widespread are the black students' problems with white students? Their answers to the exit questionnaire indicated that a substantial number of whites on SU's campus were involved in actual instances of discrimination. In reply to the question, "Since you have been on this campus, how often have you had experiences with whites that you thought were racially discriminatory or hostile?" Sixty-nine percent said occasionally, and another fourteen percent said fairly often. Only seventeen percent replied that they never had such experiences. Asked, "How often have you been mistreated by white students at this campus because of your race?" about half said once or twice, while thirty-one percent replied several times or many times. Only nineteen percent said that they had not been mistreated by white students on racial grounds. Clearly, the overwhelming majority have faced some racial discrimination on campus, including mistreatment at the hands of white students. Moreover, one should recognize that these estimates of discrimination are probably on the low side. Past studies have shown that one way for African Americans to cope with everyday racism is not to "see" as much of it as possible, just to be able to survive in traditionally white spaces.[19]

Most white observers of U.S. racial relations, including many in the mass media, are removed from the daily realities of life for African Americans. Whether out of ignorance or intentionally, they usually associate blatant racism, including the hurling of racist epithets and extreme antiblack views, only with intolerant extremists such as segregationists or Ku Klux Klan members.[20] Moreover, some white analysts such as Allan Bloom, Richard Bernstein, and Arthur Schlesinger have claimed that one indicator of major progress in U.S. racial relations is the alleged elimination of blatantly racist discourse in U.S. society.[21] Nevertheless, the hurling of racist epithets and more violent attacks by whites, including white students, on or near a major college campus are by no means extinct.

Several surveys of black students have found that the problems the SU students discuss are common on other campuses. For instance, a 1980 survey of more than two hundred black University of Michigan undergraduates found that most had faced verbal and other racial harassment since their arrival. The most common forms of mistreatment were total avoidance by white students and subtle actions or statements with racial overtones. The black students reported encountering prejudiced statements about African Americans or other minorities, "nigger" epithets, racist "KKK" graffiti on walls, and racially motivated rudeness in social situations.[22] More recent surveys have found similar or worse patterns. A 1988 survey of more than two thousand black students at twenty predominantly white college colleges in Southern and border states found that "black students are still experiencing verbal attacks, written epithets, physical confrontations, and other more subtle, and in some ways more insidious, acts that discourage their participation in and graduation from college."[23]

In addition, a 1989 survey of black students at a mid-Atlantic university found most had heard negative comments about African Americans by others on campus, with about half noting they heard such comments often. Most reported being victims of racial harassment, and over half feared for their safety on campus. One-third had changed their activities in some way to avoid racial harassment. Two-thirds reported they were aware of other black students suffering racial mistreatment, and the students themselves reported a range of racial abuse. More than half reported they themselves had been verbally insulted. Ten percent of the students had been threatened; twelve percent had property destroyed; nine percent had been chased; two percent had been spat on; and three percent had been punched. The major sources of this racial harassment were other students, university staff, and faculty members.[24] A 1993 study at the predominantly white University of San Diego found that not only had eighty percent of the black students heard derogatory racial comments or jokes in the last year, but seventy-five percent of the white students reported hearing similar comments or joking. In addition, nearly half the black students had seen racist graffiti, and thirty-six percent knew someone who was physically assaulted because of their skin color.[25] In addition, a 1993 survey of African American students at a historically white Southern university, half of whom had been at the university for fewer than four semesters, found that forty-four percent had encountered racial discrimination at the hands of other students, and another eight percent were uncertain whether they had faced discrimination.[26] And a report on the experiences of black graduate students at Michigan State found that the overwhelming majority had witnessed or experienced acts of racial condescension from other students, and half reported incidents of racial hostility from other students.[27]

According to the National Institute Against Prejudice and Violence, there were published reports of at least 250 racial incidents involving physical violence or serious psychological assault on college campuses between 1986 and 1990.[28] Between 1993 and 1996 racist graffiti were reportedly scrawled on dorm doors, on bulletin boards, and in other public places at a number of colleges and universities across the nation, including Harvard University, Yale Law School, Swarthmore College, the University of Colorado (Denver), the University of Wisconsin (River Falls), Antioch University, the University of West Virginia, Central Missouri State University, the Southern College of Technology, Miami University (Ohio), and Heidelberg College. Racist flyers were reportedly posted or handed out at Indiana University, the University of Northern Colorado, and the University of California Law School. Racist effigies were found at the University of Minnesota, and racist cartoons were reportedly published in several campus papers, including one at Princeton. Incidents involving antiblack threats (with "nigger" epithets) were reported at Salisbury State University, the University of Pennsylvania, and Michigan State University.[29]

In assessing campus hate crimes, *New York Times* reporter Richard Bernstein has argued that the data are "rather heartening" because this racist violence is "sporadic at most" and "always deeply disapproved by vast majorities at just about every university."[30] He further suggests that "only" a small minority of the 3000 U.S. college campuses reported racist incidents and that many of those incidents seemed minor. Remarkably, Bernstein argues that "nigger" graffiti is *not* a form of violence against African Americans, that those African Americans who only "see" the racist graffiti are not really victims.[31] The insularity and naivete of much white thought about the state of racial relations on mostly white campuses are clearly suggested in Bernstein's comments.

Other Markers of White Space: "We'll Walk in, and It Seems Like People Just Slowly Disappear"

Not all actions by whites that mark off white spaces involve open hostility in the form of verbal attacks or real or threatened violence. Some antiblack actions are more subtle but still mark off white territory. Even relatively passive behavior can have a destructive impact if it plays a role in reinforcing the racial character of college places. Reflecting on their accumulating experiences, the juniors and seniors in our focus groups cited numerous examples of whites signalling the campus was "home territory" for whites. Recall this comment of a male student who described a white student pulling into a parking space:

> And she's about to get out. And, you know, I'm walking up. I'm not even paying attention to her, and the next thing I hear is "click, click." And she's looking at me like I'm going to rape her.

For many whites, blacks, or black men, are by definition intruders in white territory. A black male presence is frequently seen as a dangerous and threatening anomaly. That the white student's action here was probably unreflective and automatic makes the act even more grievous.

Some black parents in the focus groups had visited the campus of State University, not just to check it out as a place to send their children, but also for conferences and other purposes. One father reported a hostile rejection he had personally experienced, apparently at the hands of white students:

> One day me and four of my friends were coming by the college. And we saw a lot of commotion going on. So we were saying, "Well, let's stop and see the game that was going on." It was a lacrosse game, and they told us, "You all are not invited here. You've got to go. Your kind of people don't know anything about this. You all might as well just turn around and leave." We just laughed at them and ... left. It was just a crazy experience, but, you know, there are still a lot of racial hostilities at State University.

These African Americans were treated as unwelcome intruders in what was apparently viewed as a white sports activity and arena. Implicit in the exclusionary actions here is an assumption that sports like lacrosse are not a black person's game.

Reflecting on direct contacts with State University, one mother noted that she had experienced unfriendly reactions from whites there:

> For myself, I would go over there and make copies of notes and letters and all kinds of stuff that I'm doing. And the majority are white students. And they're very rude and ignorant, and they don't know it. I'm just going to say they don't know it. They'll look at you. They'll walk over, talk to you, trying to do something. It's like they're better, like, "Why are you here?" And they kind of give you that look because they're in their group of friends, and I'm like, "You just don't know who I am." But they don't say anything. They might laugh behind your back. They just do real ignorant things, and I think ... they feel that you don't know what they're doing to you or at you.

The black experience is again one of being treated as an intruder. Negative or hateful glances and actions imply an unspoken question, "Why are you here?" The unfriendly atmosphere is palpable in the way whites even look at blacks. This type of cold glance or "hate stare" on the part of white bystanders is reported by African Americans in many institutional and street settings.

Similar white reactions were cited by some of the students in the focus groups, as in this account of whites moving away:

> I sometimes come up here on the weekend, and I'll let a [black] friend use my account. We'll walk in, and it's like we're the only group of people of nonwhite origin inside the computer lab. And we've had weird situations where we'll walk in, and it seems like people just slowly disappear. And we do sometimes go in there and we'll be a little goofing off and silly, but for the most part it just feels like there's this casual migration away. And it feels like there's something like, "These black people are here. Well I think I'll just scoot because you know how they are." And I've seen people of other ethnicities doing their thing, goofing off, laughing a lot, but there doesn't seem to be any fear of them. But one thing that might be it is [that] my friend is kind of imposing. He's tall and heavy. I mean, he and I walk in, and we're not wearing a three piece suit or whatever, and we may talk intellectually.

The gradual "migration away" may have been rooted in the stereotypical notion that black men, especially large black men, are a threat, but we cannot be sure. It may have reflected white discomfort with a black presence that was more or less unreflective or automatic. In any case, it caused unnecessary pain. The student's sense of humor here does not hide his distress, and his choice of words indicates that the black students were aware they were somehow violating a strongly felt sense of place among some of the whites.

African American students frequently perceive they are not valued as part of the student body. Many white students, faculty members, and administrators seem to be chronically unable to acknowledge, or to recognize properly, the presence of black students. In a detailed example illustrating another problem with some white students, one of the African American students described a certain rudeness, again in the computer lab context:

> The subtle thing is waiting in line for things. Like when you go to the computer lab, if you've got something to do, people get crazy about getting on the computer.... If you're standing, and you sign on a list, so you're waiting to get on that list. And [white] people will look at me and try to walk in front of me to see if there are any computers. And the other day this girl, I mean I almost slapped her.... The person got up, and she ran over and said, "Are you finished with that?" I said, "Excuse me. I've been waiting here a half an hour. I don't think so." And she's like, "Oh I'm sorry, I'm sorry." And she saw me standing there. She saw me. I made eye contact with her, too, like, "Hello. I'm waiting, too.

You'll have to wait." And she just looked at me like, "Yeah, whatever." . . . I was there before she was. [Moderator: Do you think
it's racial?] I think the computer thing was racial. . . . But when it
comes to courtesy, they're not going to give it to me. And I don't
know if it's racial, or just because maybe they don't know me, or
they don't like what I was wearing. But I just don't count.

In settings where they seek services, black students may be avoided,
overlooked, or become socially invisible. A number of recent research
studies have shown how the white belief that blacks should yield to
the white presence, whether on campus, in employment settings, or
in restaurants, stores, and other public accommodations, is commonplace and has deep roots in white history and culture. What this student experienced is not unusual. Blacks have often reported similar
waiting-in-line incidents in many other societal settings. Here again
we glimpse the human misrecognition that Ellison's black commenta-
tor in his novel *Invisible Man* noted: "I am an invisible man. . . . I am a
man of substance, of flesh and bone, fiber and liquids—and I might
even be said to possess a mind. I am invisible, understand, simply
because people refuse to see me."[32]

Another student, a young woman, gave an account of an even
more subtle way that whites define a situation in racial terms:

Nothing really big, but just the little things. A lot of my teachers
and students handle me with kid gloves. I'm like, "Is anyone sitting here, sir?" "No, they're not." So he's brushing the seat off,
pulling the thing down for me. I'm like, "I'm not gonna go off if
someone is sitting here. I'm not gonna hit you." They just think
we're gonna jump on them, or we need to be handled with kid
gloves all the time. I'm like, "Give me the truth the way it is, and
I'll deal with it and give it back to you." But that's what I don't
like. I can tell when they're being patronizing. And that happens
a lot, so I just deal with it. I just tell them whatever, because I
know if I don't, if I'm not careful, I might do something bad. So I
just deal with it. I just say what I have to say quietly.

SU's black students are in an environment filled with racial meanings,
meanings that are conveyed by many whites through an amazing variety of actions and reactions. Racial interpretations creep into the most
innocent of human interactions. This type of classroom situation is
not, as analysts like Bloom and D'Souza have suggested, a matter of
white students being too eager to show their liberal credentials and a
so-called "political correctness." Instead, it is a matter of racialized
spaces that signal to African Americans that they do not really belong.

Sometimes white Americans are hostile to black Americans because of overt bigotry; at other times whites act inappropriately out of ignorance or a lack of experience with African Americans. This black woman saw a white student's reaction to her ordinary question as the excessive kid-gloves behavior she has periodically encountered. This last point is very important. It is past experience that guides the black interpretation, and not a shoot-from-the-hip paranoia—the latter view a common misinterpretation by white observers observing this kind of black reaction to a discriminatory event. Black students' individual and collective experience with whites is the foundation on which they base evaluations of recurring white actions and motives. The patronizing behavior toward the black student leaves little doubt as to who is regarded as the anomaly or intruder. The offensiveness of such commonplace actions may be hard even for sympathetic white observers to see. Defining an attitude or action as patronizing involves an understanding of the duplicity involved. While kid-gloves treatment can have the appearance of cordiality, here it is coded in an insincere tone that is picked up by the student's antennae, a tone that signals a condescending diminution of the black person. Ironically, although blacks are often accused of being overly sensitive, it is white hypersensitivity to blacks, rather than the reverse, that is at the heart of most racial difficulties in white "home territories."

Certain incidents recounted by black students and parents suggest that some whites conceal their real feelings about people of color. Much white prejudice is not verbally expressed, at least not within earshot of people of color. Since the 1960s many white Americans have moved from openly expressed prejudices to grudging acknowledgment of, or actual politeness toward, African Americans. Still, many white Americans reveal their negative stereotypes and prejudices privately to friends and relatives, attitudes that play out publicly in the grudging or condescending actions that take the form of subtle discrimination. In a striking commentary, one black student explained how his light skin color enabled him to hear how groups of white and Asian students really felt about African Americans.

> I can hear them going, "Those black people, this." ... You sit there, and they think I'm Hispanic.... You'd be amazed what people are saying when they don't think there are black people in the room. They're like, "Oh, I can't stand that black guy." And they'll be saying, "Nigger this, nigger that." But when the black people are around it's like, "Hey Bob. What's up, bro?" And they play this nice little role. It's like there's no way. I'm kind of weird in the sense that I can sit in between, and I can see all this hap-

pening. . . . I've run into it a lot, and it's like I hear complaints
about what other black people do on campus.

What many whites say in public may not be what they feel or what
they say in private. Moreover, it appears that the lighter a black person's skin is, the "safer" he is in white spaces. This is true, however,
only if the student plays along. If he were to complain openly about
the racist comments, he would likely be recognized as "not white"
and be ostracized. Melanin is again a marker of group status and of
real or alleged cultural differences.

White Stereotypes and Images:
"You Can Play Basketball, Right?"

Negative or unflattering white images of African Americans are clear
in the examples we have so far considered. These interracial incidents
are not only about white actions but also about the understandings and
stereotypes whites use to justify and interpret discriminatory practices.
The educational settings at most predominantly white universities
were defined, explicitly and implicitly, as white territories well before
any significant number of black students arrived. These definitions
include many images of what black students should be able to do:

> This one is kind of dumb, but anyway I'll say it. I was in one of
> my history classes when I was a freshman, and these white guys
> were talking about hockey, and I said something about it, and
> they said, "Oh, what do you know about hockey? You're black."
> And I said, "Well, just because we don't dominate that sport too
> doesn't mean I don't know nothing about hockey."

Here is a stereotype of what sports blacks are not good at, an example
similar to the lacrosse incident above. A second example illustrates the
opposite white image, the view that black youth can play certain
sports well:

> I was in a conditioning class, and we were about to play basket-
> ball, and the white girl wanted me on her team. She's like, "We
> got [says black student's name] on our team." [Then she says]
> "You can play basketball, right?" You know what I'm saying. . . .
> I could have not known how to dribble a ball, but just because of
> the fact that I was black she wanted me on her team.

A white gesture that might be seen as complimentary if it were solely
based on achievement criteria is here taken as offensive because of the
racial stereotype implied in the white action.

The assumption that African Americans can play certain sports is not unlike other assumptions that white students and professors sometimes make on mostly white campuses. While these assumptions are not as offensive as others the students reported, they nonetheless have a powerful effect in defining the mental model that black students receive about racial relations on campus. Through these white reactions, eloquent messages are given about who the players are in the social field of campus life.

In another student's example we observe a white interpretation of "black interests":

> All [the] white people that I know who are departmental majors are like, "So, have you had one of his classes yet?" It was like expected: "Oh, so you have to take the black man's class." It was just—it was weird.

These classmates, though likely well-meaning, assumed African American students were obligated by the fact of their racial identity to take courses from a certain black professor. The failure of many whites to recognize the great diversity of interests and inclinations among black students may seem an innocent misunderstanding, yet it nonetheless conveys an eloquent message about white assumptions about social positions on campus.

Well-documented in the student and parental accounts is our point that white racism is a system involving much more than overt and blatant discrimination. Today, racism also encompasses subtle and covert white responses, as well as nonresponses, that make African Americans feel uncomfortable, out of place, or unwanted.

The Injuries of Racism:
"It Stifles You"

The accounts of racial hurdles offer much insight into the personal and collective damage that accrues to black students from mistreatment. We have seen the pain brought by hostile epithets and violent attacks, and the pain that comes from being treated as invisible. Reflecting on the suffering caused by a hostile college atmosphere, one mother provided these penetrating insights:

> Prejudice is something that you can't say, "It hurts my finger," or "It hurts in here. Put the bandage here." You know it hurts. You don't know why. Maybe you say, "Well, maybe I shouldn't think that. I should be above this." But you know it hurts. And it has an

effect on you, but you can't say, "Well, it's right here. It hurts," or, "It's here. It's right here." But it hurts. It stifles you. . . . It's little things that intimidate you that keep you from being your best.

In the group commentaries, it is clear that to survive in a predominantly white environment, African American students must learn to "read" whites carefully, including white students who may constitute the opposition in particular settings. Frustration and anger are evident in the black student comments, as is the frequency with which black students must endure racial mistreatment without the freedom to give an adequate countering response. Some of the students reported that they confronted barbed comments from whites directly, while others preferred not to challenge the source. When asked if he had been racially mistreated, one student explained how he coped with mean-spirited comments:

It might have happened, but I just blow stuff off. I just go about my business and do what I need to do so I can get out. . . . [When you're blowing stuff off, what makes you do that?] Because if I do anything, then I'll be the bad person. As long as they don't touch me, it's all right. . . . [Have you had to walk away?] Maybe, [from comments] by students I guess. [Like what?] Smart comments they make.

The psychological pain of not being able to respond more actively is clear. Ignoring the racist activity as much as possible is a black survival technique. Still, this strategy of nonresponse should not be confused with acceptance of or capitulation to hostile white acts.

Pain and suffering at the hands of white students is not the only cost of racism on campus. There are academic and personal development costs as well. We discussed previously the study of another predominantly white college campus that looked at the experiences of similar groups of white and black students, with a majority of the latter reporting experiences with discrimination on campus. The study also found that the racist campus climate was serious enough to interfere with the academic success of the students.[33] Moreover, another survey of black students at eleven predominantly white universities found they were so concerned about academic survival that they were unable to devote as much attention as they needed to their own social, personal, and cultural development.[34] The consequences of racist barriers on campus are very serious, not only for black individuals' academic success but also for the success and development of black communities—and, ultimately, of the nation as a whole.

White Denial:
"There's No Racism on This College Campus"

The denial that there is widespread white racism in U.S. society by a majority of white Americans is a problem for all African Americans, including African American students on mostly white campuses. Previously, we have cited certain academic commentators, such as professors Bloom and Schlesinger, who deny or downplay the reality of serious racial discrimination in higher education and other societal arenas. They are not alone, for this is the view of many white business and political leaders and white commentators in the mass media. We have already noted the commentary of Richard Bernstein, and there are many others. For example, Thomas and Mary Edsall, writing in the *Atlantic* and in their book *Chain Reaction*, have argued that there has been an "extraordinary integration of the races" and that among whites there has been a "public repudiation of racism" and a "stigmatization of overly racist expression" since the 1960s.[35]

Some students in the focus groups noted that the denial of the reality of white racism was shared by some white students on campus:

> It was a creative writing class, and we had to write stories, whatever, and we had to sit in circles. And we had to tell our stories and read them. And mine was on racism, of course, because I'm always bringing that up. And it was just like a tragic mulatto story, and this girl couldn't stand being mixed.... So she kills herself, right. So this [white] guy goes, "You guys [have to] make the stories ... fit reality. You can't make like a fantasy-fiction whatever." And he says, "Why did you do that? Why did you write a story like that?" [I said] "Because the girl also went to this university." And he goes, "There's no racism on this college campus." Freaked everybody out. And I was the only black. But there was a Puerto Rican, and there was a Chinese person in the room, and they just freaked. And I had never heard either one of them speak before. This guy said: "Where the hell do you live?" You know, "Where do you live? Do you live in this state?" And the teacher ... goes, "Hold up, honey, I don't know what utopia you're living in." This is a white teacher; she said, "But honey you can just, inside of this room, outside of that door, on this campus ... there is a lot of racism." ... She's like, "Open your eyes, open your eyes there's a lot of discrimination and racism on this campus." And that freaked me out.

Then the student added pointedly, "I think white students have the best time at this university. Because I mean, what do they have to go through, what's their biggest problem you know? No beer."

In this poignant incident the intense reaction of the students of color suggests a recurrent experience of maltreatment at this university. Many whites fail to perceive the existence of racism, in part because white privilege is taken for granted and in part because most whites have not experienced being in a subordinate position or have not been educated about the character and impact of racism. Jacqueline Fleming, who has done important research on barriers faced by black students, has suggested that most white students are taught by their elders to ignore the issue of racism. As a result, "the average student does not feel responsible for the racial climate or civil rights."[36] Many whites, both students and nonstudents, participate in subtle and blatant racist actions, or watch while others do, but still deny the reality of widespread discrimination. Moreover, by not educating white students to the reality of everyday racism, the predominantly white faculties at most universities participate as accessories in its maintenance and perpetuation.

Another aspect of contemporary racial relations is the unwillingness of many white Americans, including many students, to listen to a diversity of black voices on matters of racial relations. For example, a few students reported on white reactions to campus visits by controversial Nation of Islam ministers as an indication of a certain white intolerance for diversity in campus points of view.[37] One male student described the effects of certain black-oriented cultural events on the campus climate:

> It's bad, it's bad, when every [time] you try to bring somebody that can actually benefit the black community. It's always bad. Because if you bring Mr. Farrakhan in, "Oh, he's a hatemonger," "He's," you know, "anti-Jew." They never heard anything he had to say except for what the media portrays of him. And ... everybody [will] come, all the Jews, and whoever else. I'm just saying Jews, because that's what happens. They'll come out in force and try to protest them. You bring Kwame Ture; they try to get there before we do so they can fill up all the seats. You bring Abdul Ali Muhammed here, you know; they never heard what he had to say. But yet ... he's a hatemonger, too, because he's under Farrakhan. And they'll try to protest that, but they never hear what people have to say. Anything that, you know, can serve the black community positively, it seems like, somebody is always going to protest it because they don't understand what really goes on with these people, with this activity. So just because they're ignorant of the fact they just ... go by whatever they heard the news say, or whatever they heard, not even second hand. They hear it fifth hand. ... They just have to protest it. That's when the racial climate is definitely bad, as far as my perspective is.

At the heart of this probing commentary is the statement that "they never hear what people have to say." How can white students and staff members on such campuses learn about the history and contemporary situation of African Americans unless they are willing to listen to a range of black community leaders, including those with whom they may disagree?

Reflecting on the texture of the campus climate, another black student noted how heavy the tension was when a Nation of Islam minister spoke on the SU campus:

> I think the racial tension at the university is real thick. It's real indirect, but it's really there from day one. I mean my mother called me. When I first got to this university, Farrakhan came to campus. Freaked every white person on campus out. . . . [Black] people freaked, talking about, "Come home, come home. You don't want to be down there." I said, "Get out of there. You can't run away from racism." And it was really wild that day after Farrakhan came.

These black students brought up the lectures by Nation of Islam ministers as examples of the "thick racial tension" on campus. Clearly, the last student's relatives were alarmed by the potential danger from angry whites. The comment that one "cannot run away" from racism again conveys a sense of being trapped in a racialized space. This is an element of the injuries that racism inflicts, for "from day one" African Americans realize their lives will be marked by racial problems and tensions. At the heart of the incidents seems to be a white notion of what is a "legitimate" black point of view. White attempts to restrict black expression can cause black students to feel like second-class citizens, while also denying whites a chance to learn more about the diversity of perspectives among African Americans.

Group Cohesion for Survival: "I Kind of Saw More and More Black People, and I Said, 'Okay. This Is Going to Work.'"

In the North and in the South, the system of Jim Crow segregation was a legally enforced system that set aside certain places and arenas for the exclusive use of whites. Today, many white and some neo-conservative black observers have attacked the tendency of black college students to "self-segregate." This in-group behavior is frequently lamented and compared with earlier patterns of legal segregation. Black demands for separate dorms and support facilities have been much-discussed issues at major universities such as Brown, Colgate, the University of Virginia, and the University of North Carolina. Many white students there have regularly complained that black groups are a sign of antiwhite hostility and "reverse discrimination."[38] As we have noted previously, numerous white educators and analysts are also upset with this supposedly new trend of student separation. For example, Allan Bloom ignores separate white groups and condemns black student "segregation" on white campuses. He goes so far as to argue that white students are generally open, want to be friendly, and pretend "not to notice the segregated tables in dining halls where no white student would comfortably sit down."[39] It is significant that most white critics of campus racial relations or of multiculturalism have not collected empirical evidence on the actual experiences of black students on these campuses. If they did so, they would discover a problem that has its roots in institutionalized racism. The creation of distinct social support groups by the black students is *not* in any sense the counterpart of the old Jim Crow segregation.

Long ago, whites invented racial segregation based on their views of and practices toward African Americans, and whites have maintained racial segregation through legal and informal means for many decades. Even today, some white practices of exclusion are common on college campuses. As we noted previously, many black students on a variety of campuses report being excluded from some campus activities because of skin color, yet few whites voice similar complaints. In addition, the aforementioned survey by Hurtado and her associates found that half the black students reported studying often with those of other racial-ethnic groups, and fifty-five percent reported dining with students from other groups. In contrast, the white figures were much lower, at fifteen percent and twenty-one percent respectively. White students were much more likely to be isolated from students of color than the reverse. In addition, participation in black student groups did not reduce blacks' interaction with students in other groups. In one news story, Hurtado was quoted as concluding that "These basic patterns of interaction suggest that the current concern about whether minority students are promoting and practicing self-segregation is misplaced. In fact, students of color are crossing ethnic/racial lines the most, while white students seem to be segregating themselves."[40]

On white-centered college campuses, most black student groups are defensive and protective, a response to what whites have done to exclude African Americans from white privileges and places. They are typically an attempt at self-determination and cultural maintenance in a sea of whiteness. The ultimate foundation of racial separation on these campuses is the preference of most whites for their own kind and their own culture. A mass media report of a white student's attitudes and actions, noted by one of the African American parents, suggests the segregative attitude of some students:

> There was an article in the paper some time ago when the same kind of feeling was coming about with State University, and they interviewed two freshmen—one freshman that was white and one freshman that was black. The white freshman was really upset that she had a black roommate. She was upset because she did not understand the black culture, and she thought that [the black student] would be beneath her, but when she found out that [the black student] had Laura Ashley sheets just like her Laura Ashley sheets, she knew that this person could not have been from a certain kind of [poor] background.

White stereotypes and prejudices often blend racial and class considerations, views that can contribute substantially to segregated housing patterns and related problems on a college campus. Here again, there is an initial assumption that blacks are cultural outsiders. Similarly, a report on the racial climate at the University of California (Berkeley) found that black students there often "experience subtle and indirect references to their lack of legitimate 'cultural citizenship.'"[41]

Several of the parents in the focus groups noted the lack of social greetings for black students coming back to campus. One father spoke of bringing his daughter to the dorm:

> My daughter attended State University, and when I went there with her a couple of times—when she came [for] a weekend, we took her back.... You could feel it [prejudice]. I mean, I went in the building with her.... It's like a thing that you can feel. I mean, black people have [antennae]. No, nothing happened. It's just an atmosphere. The prejudice is the thing that nobody has to say nothing to you, to a black person. We know when it's in operation.

In another context he added:

> I had a friend that attended [SU].... When I went there with her a couple of times, it was the atmosphere that you could sense. And she attended one year. And she, in fact, she came home for Christmas holidays, and she didn't bother to go back and get her refrigerator and—she just didn't want to go back anymore. So that in itself said something, you know. [Do you have a clue to what may have driven that decision?] She used to constantly say that she was treated different, you know, and she didn't like the atmosphere, so she didn't go back.

Given this unwelcoming atmosphere in the dormitories and other campus spaces, the desire of one black student to find others of her color is not surprising:

> I lived in a white campus area.... And there's maybe two or three black people. And I remember there, [the] first day I came here. I was standing on the steps with my stuff ready to check in.... I looked around, and all I saw was white people. I mean I saw not one [black person] but my mother and father. And I sat there on the steps, and I had tears in my eyes. I was like, "What did I do? What did I do?" So after I got myself together, I stayed in my room for a couple days. I had to get myself together. And then I went over to the ... black dorm where all their black girls stayed. And I was like, "Hey, how come I didn't get put in there?" They had to put me in the, you know, they put the "little colored" in the white dorm, I guess. I don't know, but it was really scary. That's when I said, "What did I do?" But then when I went to the other side of campus, I kind of saw more and more black people, and I said, "Okay. This is going to work."

She then continued with a comment on the point some other students in the group had made about the need to learn how to be around and deal with white people: "It makes a lot of sense. But on the other hand it's kind of scary if you're going to be by yourself doing that." Clearly, some black students do not desire to take on the role of isolated pioneer in an all-white residential area. The anxiety and fear generated by being a black person in a mostly white university are mitigated by the presence and support of other black students. Another student in one of the focus groups even expressed the opinion that black students at State University stuck together more than black students at other colleges he knew about. In the context of the difficult situations the black students have described, this sticking together allows them to coexist with whites, to defend themselves, and to survive in the white-defined spaces without feeling completely powerless.

Significantly, research reports on other major campuses have noted that many black students seek out other black students for defensive, social-support, and self-determination reasons. For example, a report on the racial climate at the University of California (Berkeley) campus found much anger over racism among black students, anger that had moved them to seek out the nurturing company of other African Americans.[42] One student there noted that "black students feel alienated on the campus. And if you're not, um, plugged into a support group then chances are, um, you're not going to find the support you need."[43] Similarly, students of color at Princeton reportedly avoid white student hostility there by separating themselves from whites, an action which has led to white criticism of these students as "being overly sensitive, defensive, hostile, angry, and isolationist."[44] In addition, finding supportive black organizations in a local black community can be important for individual survival. A recent survey of black students at mostly white universities found they were so concerned about intellectual survival that they were unable to devote as much attention to their personal, social, and cultural development as they should. Significantly, they reported that external black community involvement was essential for their personal and social development.[45] In addition, numerous research studies done by William Sedlacek at the University of Maryland have shown that black students who become part of a smaller community on campus, usually a group of black students, get higher grades and stay in school longer than those who remain more isolated.[46]

Still, the separation of black and white students on campus creates a dilemma for all concerned with the ideal of educational and societal integration. One student captured the anguish of this unresolved problem:

> Another thing is like when we go in the dining hall and everything. Like if you talk—I feel funny, and I don't know why—but when you talk to white people in the dining hall and everything, black people will look at you funny, and white people look at you funny, too. But we all go to school together, . . . and I don't know if I'm just conscious of that, or how does anybody else feel?

Whites as Acquaintances and Friends: "I Never Put It in My Head I Can Trust Them"

Can black and white students break through the wall of racism and segregation created over the centuries? The evidence on this matter is generally not encouraging. Examining the correlates of student success in a sample of black undergraduates at six predominantly white universities, Walter Allen found that, as African American students gained experience with whites in school settings, their views of black-white relations did not become more favorable. Moreover, greater exposure to white middle-class students and culture did not increase their integration into majority-group networks.[47]

Still, significant friendships and mutual understandings do develop between black and white students on college campuses. There were indications in our interviews that even in a hostile racial climate individual blacks and whites can make progress in breaking down racial walls. For instance, one student remarked on his interracial friendships:

> Where I lived at it was black, white, Oriental, this, that, and the other. . . . We all got along. Every time I went out I had no problems. A lot of my friends were all white, all black, all of them this, that, and the other. And I mean I know that a lot of things [discrimination] have been happening, probably happened to a lot of [black] people. . . . I'm sure it has [happened], but it just hasn't gotten to me, so I've never really had a racial problem since I've been in State University. I know it's there, but I don't know [it personally], in the four years. [Moderator: How do you know it's there?] I mean I know it's there from talking to other people.

Encounters with racial barriers are not experienced to the same degree or in the same way by all students. This student's friends have been white and black, and he remembers no serious racial problems over his four years, although he knows they exist for others on campus.

Interestingly, some of the black juniors and seniors distinguished between friendly and hostile whites, as in the following account from a female student:

> When I lived on campus, I had a white roommate. She was from New York. Cool girl, though. And the fact is I don't necessarily love white people. I don't necessarily hate them. I mean, I just, I'm impartial, you know. True, there are some really cool ones out there that you can get along with, and then again there are some that'll call you "nigger" behind your back, you know. . . . So I learned a lot about white people just from living with her. Just as I made sure that she learned a lot—and I mean a lot— about black people.

A positive experience with a roommate here involved mutual learning about the racial other.

In a racially polarized society it is not surprising that many black students feel perplexed about interracial interactions. Black students may be torn between their friendly feelings toward certain whites and negative feelings because of unpleasant experiences with other whites. They may feel pressure from other black students or older black adults, who have had more negative experiences with whites than they have, to be cautious or distant in their relations with whites. In one of the groups, after a student athlete gave an account of racism on a sports team, another male student concluded with this comment about the campus situation:

> Some people make you choose sides. And I live with three white people. There's four black people at our house and three white guys, and we'll hang out together and both get looks from both sides. It's like you're all or nothing.

Student friendships and other positive interpersonal encounters can, as integrationist theory would predict, reduce black generalizing about whites, as the following account by a female student signalled:

> Since you do go to a school that has a majority of white people, you can't help to become friends with some, you know. So therefore you get confused because when you do meet them you become close to them. And then when you talk to your black friends, and they say things on white people, you get kind of confused because you're like, "That's wrong; you're generalizing."

Among other things these accounts indicate that racial integration is far from being accomplished at this major university. The campus environment appears to be in the first stage of fostering the kind of social interaction that can increase real communication across the racial divide. These accounts do indicate that students of different backgrounds can, and do, get along to their mutual enrichment. The comment against generalizing is important because the student refuses to "do unto others" what is often being done to her.

Several students brought up the complexity involved in evaluating whites individually. The female student just quoted also spoke of the confusion she felt when forming bonds with white students:

> I have some white friends, and they're cool, so it confuses me because you don't know which side to take. And I don't know if taking a side is right because you can say there are wrong white people and there are wrong black people, too. I mean ignorance has no color, you know. So I don't think separating yourselves and [saying], "They this, they that," or "Them this, them that"— I don't think you're going to get anywhere that way. Ever.

Continuing the discussion in this focus group, other participants added their own examples. One senior recalled his mother's negative view of SU and how he had convinced her to allow him to attend the school:

> It's kind of like what my mother said to me when I told her I wanted to choose State University, and she said, "This is bad. This is bad." And I went to a predominantly white school, and I told

her, "You've got to judge the person and not the whole." And that's what made her really decide to let me really come to school.

Then the female student who had commented on some "cool" white friends added a statement on the similar pressures and ambiguities that she had faced:

> My parents constantly telling me, you know, "Well, I don't like you to have a lot of white friends" and stuff like that.... And I get kind of mad about it.... I mean, especially my mom. She thinks that I get blinded by hanging around a lot of white people, and she thinks that I will have this thing in my mind that they will never stab me in the back and all. But that's not true. I mean, I never turn my back, you know, never. You can hang out with them and everything, but you never turn your back to anyone, black or white. You know, that's how I get by. I never put it in my head I can trust them.

Significantly, her parents were troubled by her interaction with whites at State University. However, her statement, "I never put it in my head I can trust them," indicates that her method of coping with the confusion that surrounds interracial friendships involves caution and stress for her as well. This comment underscores the point that black students must learn and hone their coping strategies at predominantly white colleges and universities if they are to survive.

Wrapping up one focus-group discussion, a male student who had already spoken gave an account centered on a white friend:

> My best friend was a white guy, and he's in the Greek system, and that's what I think is a racist thing about campus. And I went to a party the other day, and one of his brothers got mad that I was there. Well, he just said, "I just got rid of some little black [epithet]." And my [white] friend went crazy on him. Just because he said that word.... You're going to judge everybody differently, individually.

According to recent reports from numerous college campuses, white fraternities sometimes play a negative role in racial relations on campus. On some campuses, such as the University of Texas, the University of Arkansas, George Mason University, and Texas A & M University, there have been problems with a few white fraternities building homecoming floats with racist themes, holding racist skits, or staging parties with racist themes. At Purdue University a black student reported being called racist epithets and attacked by three whites after he danced with a white woman at a fraternity party. The situation on campus was serious enough that the Office of Civil Rights of the U.S. Department of Education ordered the university to stop the racial harassment on campus.[48] Clearly, the Greek system is central to the physical and social space on many a college campus. In our groups the fraternity system was sometimes mentioned as an example of institutionalized racism. In the last commentary, a white student's rejection of a black student does not take place without a countering action. It seems to us that increasing this type of white response to racism is critical for improving racial relations on U.S. campuses in the present and in the future.

The last few accounts reveal the possibility and importance of cross-racial friendships. For the majority of students the years spent in college mark a period when they make friends who are important in helping them make it through college and into the job market—and who may remain friends for life. Therefore, the failure of whites as a group to create a campus atmosphere where truly large numbers of cross-racial friendships can flourish is serious for black students' lives and careers. It is also harmful for white students' understandings of the world around them and for the general social health of U.S. society.

Alternative Spaces: "I Want to Transfer to a Black University"

African American students and their parents sometimes compare the situation at predominantly white campuses like State University with that at historically black colleges. For example, one parent compared her son's experience at a mostly black university with that at SU:

> I had a son who started out in a predominantly black university. When we, as parents, took him back to school, mainly to take his junk with him, there are people on campus—"Man," you know, "Hey," and that fellowship and that kind of thing. They were there. All along the way, he met people, and he felt like I'm back, *I'm back*. And it was that kind of feeling. When we took his junk back to State University, [some said] "Hey man," but not that full feeling of you know, I'm back, I'm somebody, I'm worthy. "Oh, I have friends," that kind of thing. And while he accepted that and could make it with that, if you had a person who didn't feel quite so sure of himself, that little "hey"—barely part your lips in acknowledgment—may have . . . felt like, Oh, I hate to be back again.

The lack of hospitality for black students at majority-white universities is apparent to black observers even in places where most whites might have trouble seeing it.

One mother carefully related the responses of a black student from a local poor family:

> There was a kid who works in the medical office I work in; and I thought it was just wonderful that this kid was attending the school. I'd ask him, "How's school going?" The more he talked about it, the more reluctant his comments were. And I would say, "Hang in there," and encourage this kid because he came from a real poor family, and I'm just so ecstatic that this kid is attending. I just encouraged him every time I talked to him. And the last couple of times I saw him and spoke with him, he was like, "I want to transfer to a black university."

Then she added that "his grades were fine, but I just got the sense that he just felt like he was really nobody there."

We noted in Chapter 1 the white educators' notion that the black dropout problem in higher education is primarily a problem of black intelligence, character, community, or family.[49] However, in several of the student accounts we discern that even students with very good grades have serious problems in coping with the unwelcoming climate of white colleges and universities. It is clearly time for educational policy makers to face the fact that negative campus atmosphere is a major reason for the dropout (push-out) problem that disproportionately affects black students at predominantly white campuses across the United States.

Conclusion

Many white observers of racial relations at predominantly white campuses tend to see black problems in familial, personal, or psychological terms. An array of critics and analysts, some of whom we cited in previous chapters, blame black students or their parents for student problems on white campuses. The black students are faulted for academic troubles, for self-segregation, and for "paranoia" about racism when they should be working harder. Many whites on predominantly white campuses seem to share this point of view. For example, a white student at Stanford told one black analyst that "Blacks do nothing but complain and ask for sympathy when everyone really knows they don't do well because they don't try. If they worked harder, they could do as well as everyone else."[50] Even in those campus situations where some white authorities recognize the need for racial change, there is often an accent on personal changes rather than on structural and institutional changes. A recent Diversity Committee report at

Colgate University underscores the different perspectives on change among whites and blacks:

> White students tend to see relationships needing development largely in psychological terms; white students emphasize the need for better 'personal' relationships. Minority students much more often (but not always) see the relationships in need of development also to have important, even primary, 'political' implications.[51]

Clearly, the data in this chapter indicate that both psychological and institutional changes are needed. Viable solutions will entail a consideration of how the campus social structure and campus spaces are racialized. We have examined the ways in which African American students and parents experience mistreatment at the hands of white students in the white home territories of a predominantly white university. In these reports we see the racial meanings that campus spaces have for white and black students. Some of the black experiences involved some whites aggressively expressing their racist attitudes and propensities, while other incidents involved whites engaging in subtle forms of discrimination.

Racialized spaces are part of the daily worlds of African Americans at all predominantly white colleges and universities. From our respondents' accounts we acquire clues as to the character of these spaces: Are they safe places? Are they dangerous? Are black students welcome here? Our data reveal that the black students and parents have been told by white students, in a variety of direct and roundabout ways, that State University is white territory. The students' accounts of the underlying racial hostility, even that hidden beneath superficially friendly gestures, indicate that once whites define campus space racially, the meanings of certain white actions within that space are pervaded with negative racial meanings. Moreover, racial interaction on campus is far more complex than is suggested in the naive views of the white analysts who describe most white students as eager to exhibit "liberal credentials" in interaction with students of color. Most mainstream interpretations of racial relations on college campuses are far from the everyday realities of racism experienced by African American students.

Numerous unpublished reports from other predominantly white college campuses indicate that the experiences of the SU students are not at all unique. For several decades research studies about mainly white campuses have found negative racial climates. For example, in a late 1970s survey of hundreds of black students at eight predominantly white colleges in Ohio, Georgia, Texas, and Mississippi, the students reported "institutional abandonment, isolation, and bias in the classroom—factors that created a hostile interpersonal climate."[52] More recently, a 1988 survey by the Southern Regional Education Board of more than two thousand black students at twenty primarily white colleges in Southern and border states found that most felt a sense of alienation and did not feel they were a real part of their campuses.[53] Similarly, a mid-1990s survey of black graduate students at Michigan State University found that half thought the racial climate on campus was tense. Nearly a third of these graduate students knew of departments on campus with a bad racial climate, and twenty-nine percent reported their own departments discriminated against students of color.[54]

The role of white students in these hostile racial climates is clear in our data and in research studies about other predominantly white campuses. Yet, these white students are not alone in their creation of negative college environments. As we will see in the next few chapters, white faculty members, other white staff members, white administrators, and even whites off-campus play an important role.

CONTENDING WITH WHITE INSTRUCTORS

"You Can Feel When Someone Wants You Somewhere"

White Professors and Educational Change

Many critics of higher education have recently portrayed the faculty members in contemporary colleges and universities as flocking to the cause of multiculturalism. In large numbers, according to this theory, many professors are significantly altering their courses to reflect closely the new language and materials associated with what critics call "political correctness." However, these ideologues ignore the substantial evidence that contradicts their arguments. Research studies since the 1970s indicate that only a modest number of white faculty members have made any significant concessions to the presence of African American students on their campuses or in their classrooms. One study, for example, found that when white faculty members were asked the degree to which black issues or pressures had changed their role as faculty members, most replied "very little." Moreover, a majority of the faculty members said that faculty support for black-oriented programs was more likely to be passive than active.[1]

It is clear from our previous chapters that everyday life on college campuses is structured in terms of historical and collective memories, as well as in terms of racialized places and interaction. We have shown how different forms of racialized space, time, and recognition shape the everyday life experiences of African American students and parents. In this chapter we examine accounts of black students' experiences with their instructors, who bear the responsibility of nurturing and teaching students, the university's purpose. Recall the ideal of the modern university: A singularly open and tolerant place for the transmission of learning. The instructors pass on the collective wisdom and understandings of the past to the new learners in the present. They play the central role in the university as the "Alma Mater of the rising generation."[2] Basic to this ideal is the provision of a place where students and teachers can come together to seek knowledge without serious prejudices, barriers, and impediments.

Today, however, the reality of the predominantly white university often does not reflect this distinctive ideal. Thus, on the exit questionnaire the black students at State University were asked, "How often have you been mistreated by white professors at this campus because of your race?" Half replied that it had happened once or twice, while six percent said several times. Thirty-nine percent said never, and the rest replied that they were not sure.

Surveys on student-faculty interaction at other major university campuses have found a similar situation, although the proportions of students facing problems vary. For instance, a 1990s survey of "ethnic minority" (mostly black, Latino, and Asian) students at the University of Nevada (Las Vegas) found only thirty-seven percent of those with an opinion said that they had almost never felt discriminated against on campus by instructors.[3] A survey of black students at a historically white Southern university, half of whom were first-year or second-year students, found that one-fifth of the students had already encountered racial discrimination at the hands of faculty members —and that another ten percent were uncertain whether they had faced discrimination.[4] Moreover, a 1995 report on the experiences of black graduate students at Michigan State University found that more than seventy percent had witnessed or experienced acts of racial condescension from faculty members, while twenty-eight percent reported witnessing or experiencing incidents of racial hostility involving faculty members.[5]

In our focus groups the black students and parents reported on specific black encounters with white professors and other instructors. As in the previous chapters, we preserve the voices of the students and parents as they present their perspectives on racial issues.

White Professors and Course Content:
"I Got Full Support from My White Humanities Professor"

The experiences of black students with faculty at mostly white campuses are regularly confusing and contradictory. Sometimes, white instructors are supportive and encouraging. They seem committed to fair treatment and a respect for different life experiences and perspectives. In other cases, however, white instructors, like other whites on campus, engage in hostile practices or adopt a viewpoint that is aggressively Euro-American. The fact that many discriminatory acts are unpredictable in timing or character makes their effects even more disruptive and painful to their targets.

In one focus group a student commented on positive support from a faculty member in a humanities department:

> In my humanities class, my first humanities class, one of our projects was you had to write a letter to an influential figurehead on campus, and I wrote a letter to our university's president, basically bitching him out about the minority retention rate. And I got full support from my white humanities professor.

As we noted previously, the black student dropout rate is really a "push-out" rate that affects too many black students. Here the professor appears to be doing nothing out of the ordinary, and, yet, this student considers the incident worth mentioning. The student is manifesting an apprehension about expressing his feelings about a racial problem on campus. The lives of black students in white-dominated places are frequently limited by a reluctance to express openly their feelings about racial matters.

Discussing recurring incidents, one student noted the contrast between the attitude of some white students and that of a white professor who specializes in African American studies:

> I'm in a humanities department, so you tend to get a lot of people ... [who are] more open in terms of racial issues and stuff. In a lot of the classes you can end up discussing racial issues.... As soon as we started talking about books by black people, everybody was like this [she sits closed-lipped, with arms crossed]. They sat there, and they looked [strangely] at me ... because they think that I'm really stupid, like they usually do. And as it is, they like claim to be so open, and how they're understanding and everything. All [open], but then when it comes to racial issues or even like gender and stuff or politics, they'll be, like they're afraid to say what they believe, or either they have no opinion. They're like really ignorant. My teacher is like—he's white—but he, I

guess he's a scholar of black studies, which really surprised them. So it's kind of that you don't just have just the black teachers pushing you to read black materials and learn about black books and stuff.

The experience here is not unique. When racial issues come up in this classroom, some white students are tight-lipped, and a black student becomes the center of attention. In previous chapters we have noted that one critical aspect of modern racism is the white *misrecognition* of African Americans, the failure of whites to see a black person as fully human, as like a white person. As this black student interprets these incidents, some of her white peers misrecognize her as "really stupid." Her position in the classroom is socially constructed and defined negatively by some whites because of her skin color and, apparently, her viewpoint. This injurious white view is highlighted, paradoxically, by the teacher's assigning African American materials to read and discuss. As we see it, the inclusion of texts by black authors in the curriculum should be commonplace, not noteworthy as here, because it broadens the knowledge of black and white students about the contributions of Africans and African Americans to world history and to U.S. society.

Another female student related a similarly positive experience with a white professor who tried to incorporate an African American perspective into a course's subject matter:

> I have this women's studies teacher. Great white lady. She's really good, and we read so much literature done by African American women. She kind of makes up for it [mistreatment by other white teachers]. So either you have one end that doesn't address it, or you have one end that overcompensates, and it's nothing in between.

The last two statements on positive experiences with white instructors took place in a university context in which black intellectual concerns and political interests, according to the students, are only occasionally given serious attention. As female scholars and male scholars of color slowly make their way into academia, the interests, ideas, and literature previously ignored by the white-male professoriat are finally being incorporated into a few course syllabi, discussions, and lectures. This intellectual broadening is very important for the health and survival of African American students in these white-normed places, but it is still the exception rather than the rule in courses on contemporary college campuses.

Stereotyping by White Instructors:
"Their Preference Was Not to Have Blacks"

Several students in the group interviews discussed racial stereotyping by some faculty members. For example, one male athlete described the view of his professor about an absence from class:

> I didn't go to class for like maybe a week or two because we have a tournament and everything. And I talked to the [white] teacher on the telephone. . . . The teacher thought I was right and she gave me a break. [The teacher apparently failed him on a test.] And, then, when I confronted [her], and she was like, "You just didn't go to class because you didn't want to," when she found out who I was. [What's your sport?] Soccer. And when I told her I was an athlete, she automatically thought—"Well, the track team wasn't away this weekend." Then, like afterwards, I had to go to my coach and everything . . . so I could take the test over.

The problem arose when the teacher did not trust the student's veracity in regard to the athletic commitments he had claimed. The student's humiliation is compounded by having to obtain a formal excuse from his coach, who is thus informed the student is not trusted. This is a painful situation to be put in, especially when one is a member of a group whites have long stereotyped as undependable and untrustworthy.

Differential treatment based on racial characterizations of the students can take different forms, as another black student explained:

> This university is just so racist. And then all the things with the teachers came out. Everybody remembers the, was it [an] engineering girl, student who, a teacher told her, "Black women don't make it in this field." In another university program they just said you're going to fail because black people don't do well in this subject.

The old stereotype of black incompetence seems to lie just beneath the surface of certain professorial assumptions about African American students.

One female student related this distinctive encounter with another white professor right after class:

> This is one time in a social science department. I had a professor; I guess she just had it out for me. She didn't like me at all. But anyway one day we were talking about black stereotypes, and you

know how they say like, "They're criminals and always wanting
to rob people." So after class I wanted to talk to her. And a girl-
friend and I were standing waiting for her, so she's coming out of
the class, and she's all like "Oh, what?" And I say, "Can I talk to
you, whatever?" And she's like, "Oh, I thought you wanted to
rob me or something."

Whether the offensive remark was in jest is not clear, but it did signal
an imbedded white stereotype whose use had a negative and lasting
impact on this student. The conventional discussion of black crimi-
nality in the classroom reinforced the student's concern about the
comment. Note too that this black student feels disliked and unvalued
by a person who is supposed to be nurturing and teaching her.

One male student reported another type of stereotyping of non-
European students by a white professor:

I don't want to take a lot of time with this professor. One time
she was taking attendance, and there were these two Asian kids.
One was like Japanese and the other was like Vietnamese, right.
So she . . . said the one kid's name wrong. And she was like, "Oh
well it doesn't matter because like you guys all look alike." She
said that . . . I mean she said that! [No one said anything to her?]
Well, most of the people were white people, so they were just
like, whatever? But we . . . the black people just connected right
there. One of these kids dropped the course. I don't know if
that's why, but I'd have dropped it if she said that to me.

Here we see a kind of crude insensitivity that some white professors
still show toward students of color. This comment was disrespectful
not only to its Asian targets but also to the black students who also felt
victimized by such a barbed remark. This type of faculty insensitivity
is reproduced on college campuses because it can, contrary to the view
of critics like Allan Bloom or Dinesh D'Souza, usually be expressed
with impunity. To challenge a professor in such circumstances requires
more status or power than students, black or nonblack, ordinarily have.

As with other types of human interaction, that between students
and their instructors cannot be expected to be free from difficulties
and misunderstandings. However, the racial definition of the problems
documented in this chapter makes them distinctive. One way these
problems are different from many run-of-the-mill classroom problems is that their impact frequently extends beyond the students to
their circle of friends and into their families. Serious incidents accumulate and become part of the collective memory. We see this in the
accounts of some parents who spoke of classroom problems at State

University. For example, in a lengthy discussion one mother noted that she encouraged her daughter to go to SU:

> She's a graduate. I did encourage her. And she transferred into State University. She'd gone to another school and after a year decided to try them and had an essentially positive experience. . . . I'm not saying that it was a typical experience or it was the standard. But it wasn't as negative as we anticipated. . . . I expected racial incidents, and they happened. I expected discrimination in the classroom, and she had it. [Like what?] Instructors who actually let it be known that their preference was not to have blacks in their classroom or that blacks didn't have the thinking ability to be in those particular classes. And they let them know. And they have no reservations about making a comment about African Americans. Like giving them, [an example of] "An African American woman who is below thirty, and to look for her to be whorish." That's not an unusual comment, and with African Americans sitting in the class.

In addition to the stereotyped image of young black men as criminal, a common white image is of young black women as whores or welfare "queens." This gendered racism undergirds the misrecognition of black women as not fully human and has a very negative effect on young black female students. Reflecting some fatalism about the omnipresence of racism, the same mother added this comment about her daughter later in the discussion:

> I believed her experience prepared her for life in white America, because that's what she's going to have to deal with, these people, and having white roommates was very good for her. Not that she was alienated from those people, the white people, but it was good to see that people looked the same. They all bathe or don't bathe, it has nothing to do with their skin color. They get F's and A's, and they react the same to them. It was a good experience for her.

This particular speaker made positive points about State University's academic climate at several points in the focus group discussion. Yet, she is clear that her child encountered discrimination there, including that of professors who signaled that they did not want black students in their classrooms. In her resigned view, this unpleasant *experience* must be endured because it prepares young people for racial barriers they will encounter when they move beyond the university.

As these accounts suggest, the agonizing struggle to deal with racial barriers is a recurring and stressful aspect of black students' lives.

Psychological studies of black students on predominantly white campuses have found relatively high levels of stress, some of it generated by faculty and other staff members. For instance, one research project interviewed 284 black students at the University of North Carolina (Charlotte) in an attempt to inventory stress factors for students in such areas as personal identity, interpersonal relationships, and career plans. Among the environmental stressors found were insensitive white faculty, low academic expectations, unfair grading, and poor academic advising. The study concluded that assessments of stress levels needed to be culture-specific in order to determine accurately the distinctive needs of students of color.[6]

Insensitivity to African American Culture: "And He Just Dismissed Everything"

In the United States white racism is a system of everyday practices that are motivated, buttressed, and rationalized by white notions of the inferiority of the culture, personality, and morality of African Americans. A critical characteristic of racial stereotyping is that it extends to aspects of the out-group's culture and lifestyle. Some of the student accounts illustrated the cultural insensitivity and stereotyping in faculty comments and actions, as in this example from a female student:

> I had an American Studies teacher like that [one who makes racial remarks]. And he really, really irritates my roommate because she is from the West Indies. And the class is on cultural and mental issues, and he has a tendency to generalize. And he thinks that just because he has been to certain cultures ... I am at the point where I don't really pay much attention to what he has to say anymore, but she becomes really, really irritated because he'll talk about, you know, we had something about a West Indian medium. And she tried to explain to him that some of the things that he thought were abnormal, were very normal for her culture. And he just dismissed everything ... and I have to push her to go to the class because she is really, really irritated with the class. She usually doesn't say anything anymore, and she is very intelligent. I mean she has a lot to contribute to the class. And she only speaks sometimes. . . . And the rest of the time she'll just bite her tongue unless he says something that really irritates her.

Some white teachers alienate students from different cultures by being, or sounding, dismissive of practices that seem to them "abnormal." In this case, the classroom space was transformed into a place for the transmission of cultural parochialism in regard to Afro-Caribbean religious practices. While whites in the classroom were reinforced in their biased or fictional images of certain other cultures, these students of color learned to remain silent even in the presence of what they perceived to be ignorance and intolerance. A student who could have become a major resource for the class was not only forced into silence but had to be pushed to come to the class. Here we observe the subtle racism that is central to the pressures that drive many African American students from traditionally white universities across the nation.

Professorial Inquiries:
"They Put the Whole Black Race on Your Shoulders"

The historical absence of black students in traditionally white universities, as well as their continuing underrepresentation there, contribute to whites' lack of knowledge or awareness of the histories, lives, and racial burdens of African Americans. We have noted how black students often become objects of attention when racial issues arise in class. White professors and students can construct social situations where black students are placed in awkward or painful positions. Social situations of this kind deserve a closer look because of the damaging effects they can have.

In the focus groups several students talked of being forced to be the spokesperson "for the race" in and out of the classroom. One student commented:

> Another thing I wanted to say is like in the classroom when it's like a situation when you're like the only black person in your classroom, and they put the whole black race on your shoulders. [How often does that happen? That you are the only one in your class?] [Several voices] A lot!

A characteristic experience of black students in predominantly white universities is feeling the burden placed on them by whites to act as defenders and explainers of their group. This problem seems to be commonplace in colleges and universities across the United States. For example, a 1990s report on the racial climate at a major University of California campus noted that black students talked starkly about problems of academic adjustment there "in terms of their high visibility in classes."[7]

In one focus group a male student noted that sometimes in the classroom white professors

> can be talking about a whole other subject . . . [and] they use the word "minority" in a sentence. And their eyes just look right to you.

The impact of such professorial gestures can be enhanced by their unthinking spontaneity. Even the expectation of unwanted attention can create pressure and discomfort, as another student explained:

> Especially like this social science department. We're just sitting there in the class. And the teacher . . . you can always tell when they want to get a little discussion, a little smile, [a] look at their notes. "So what about the racial situation and detention we had down at [names a local place]?" And you're sitting there like, "OK this is going to be on me, this is big trouble." You're like the only black person sitting there, and it just happens to be an issue dealing with your race. You feel a lot of pressure, a lot of pressure.

Being the unwanted center of attention is stressful and serves to remind black students of the racial position that they are often assigned in predominantly white classroom settings. The pressure reported by the black students does not come from one isolated act, but from a recurrence of similar situations over several years at SU. The repetition of such acts creates a racialized social structure on campus, which the black students have little power to define or significantly alter. In some cases the questioning by whites can take on a probing and personal character, as in the following account:

> One of my teachers . . . was talking to me about black issues. She was trying to drain me of information or something. Like everyone in class knows about the student-teacher conference. I'm sure she treated them [whites] like they were students. . . . I would go there [to her office] and she would start talking about my family. And she was like, "Well what do you think about their racial atmosphere?" and "When I was growing up as a white woman. . . . " She really pissed me off because she thought I was going to sit there and discuss it with her, so she could better understand how black people were. She was using me as a book or something saying, "Let me try and understand this." That's the thing. . . . I guess [whites] think all black people are dumb from the get-go. And [if] you've got a little bit of sense they're like, "Oh, wow. Maybe I can like probe you." And then when you don't want to talk about it she's like, "I don't understand." I mean if you want to know something you go out and find out yourself, like I had to find out. Then they get mad at you and say, "Oh you're bitter," and all that stuff. . . . And it seems like white people feel the need to get in your business and stuff.

The student leaves little doubt about the discomfort and pain this professor caused her. She is caught in a dilemma: If she responds, she has to control her anger at being placed in such a position. Yet if she remains silent, she may later chastise herself for failing to confront established stereotypes. The student is reacting against being treated as a research object. Some white instructors may probe a student out of well-intentioned ignorance or out of insensitivity, but others may be expressing a deeper racial motivation. Whatever the motivation, many white instructors may become irritated when rebuffed. Both the probing and the displeasure at being rebuffed underscore the reality of racially determined power relations on campus. Moreover, this professorial inquisition signals as much about implicit white conceptions of whiteness, such as the presumed right to get familiar with or to probe African Americans, as it does about white images of African Americans.[8]

On college campuses today students of color seem to face more problems with racially insensitive faculty members, who are unreflective about their racial stereotypes or proclivities, than with openly bigoted professors. In another research study conducted by the senior author a talented student at another predominantly white university described how a white professor made a comment on religion that assumed the student was a Baptist. She was Episcopalian and resented the professor's implication that most African Americans were Baptist. She added:

> Probably the thing that angers me the most about white people is their insensitivity and their total inability to see you as an individual. You're always seen as a black person. And as a black woman, you're seen as a black person before you're seen as a woman. It's just a constant struggle. You're always trying to assert your personality, or your style, your individuality. If you want recognition, you practically have to go overboard to get people to see that you are unique with your own style and your own goals, and your own way of thinking about things.[9]

This is a common complaint at traditionally white universities. For instance, a 1990 Diversity Committee report at Colgate University reported on a meeting with students of color, many of whom noted "widespread faculty insensitivity to their feelings and situations" at that prestigious Northern university.[10] Once again, we encounter the experience of not being seen, of being misrecognized.

As we have noted, the mistreatment of students of color on a college campus is often more than an individual matter. Racial incidents can have an impact on friends and family members. In the parent focus groups, some spoke about relatives and acquaintances who had felt singled out in the classroom, as in the case of this mother:

> I did not attend that school, but I've met a lot of people who have, and I've heard different stories that gave me a negative

impression. Okay. I can think of a friend of mine saying from her experience being in a classroom. And I don't remember what class it was, but the teachers engage the students in discussions about whatever, and you're almost intimidated to put your hand up and contribute to the conversation because you are outnumbered so greatly in a classroom. One experience she had was when she actually got the courage to raise her hand, and I remember the story very vividly. And she put her hand up and the teacher stopped and looked at her and said, "Your name is?" And she didn't know her name, and she finally came up with her name. And she—when the teacher called her name, all the students, [were] looking you know like the E.F. Hutton [advertisement], "This person speaks," like, "Oh this thing can talk." And the intimidation was so great to her, and that was a struggle for her as I recall, her expressing to me other little things. Little things that really aren't significant enough to say the school ... has a negative view of blacks, but enough to make it difficult for a person to just move about, not feeling comfortable in that population. It affects you.

Here we observe again the intimidation that a black student perceives in a sea of white faces on a majority-white college campus and the social isolation this produces. Not surprisingly, black students experience being targeted in this manner as social marginalization.

These narratives relate the pain and tribulations of black students at predominantly white institutions. The black students and parents sometimes do not attribute any negative intention to the white professors and students who caused the pain or discomfort. Some of the white teachers were apparently unaware of the hurt or damage that they inflicted. The fact that white teachers, sometimes in well-meaning or spontaneous ways, are able to inflict such pain on African American students signals a more serious problem than if the white actions represented only hostility and ill will. The institutionalization of racism means that certain hurtful ways of acting have become more or less routinized, as taken-for-granted actions linked to traditional ways of doing a professor's job. Unless the black students' side of the story is heard, and heard clearly, there is little hope for eradicating the racial divide that persists in higher education.

Differential Treatment from White Professors: "Things That Build Up Rage"

In any society the subtle and overt distinctions that are made in everyday interactions define the character of the social position one occupies in interaction with others. Being singled out for differential treatment by a professor can cause much pain, no matter what the motivation may be, and this distress effectively marks the actual position one occupies on campus. For example, one young woman noted what seems at first glance to be a solely positive experience:

> I've had a lot of teachers say, I mean if there's only like two or three blacks in my class, [that they want to help]. And I've even had one teacher who held the blacks after class and was like, "I really want my black students to do well." You know I was surprised she said it, you know, she's not a good teacher.

This student notes differential treatment that seems to favor black students; at least, some white teachers seem sincere in trying to help the black students do well in their classes. However, this extra attention has a special treatment aspect and may communicate to the black students, and to white students who become aware of it, that in the view of some faculty members black students are expected to do less well than whites, thereby stigmatizing the black students. Indeed, surveys on several college campuses have found that many black students report that white professors expect them to be less successful in academic pursuits than white students. A survey of black graduate students at Michigan State University, for instance, found that more than half knew faculty members who had differential expectations for white students and students of color.[11]

Some of the students in the focus groups gave accounts of negative experiences with some white instructors that they viewed as discriminatory, as in this case:

> It seems like ... old professors are usually more, more, I don't want to say racist, the word isn't racist, it's more obvious that they are not as open-minded as [others]. ... Like when you ask questions in class. If I was to ask a question, and a white person was to ask a question, the teacher will go into detail. But with me it's like, "Well, you should have gotten it."

The parallel here with some research on women students is interesting. For example, Roberta Hall and Bernice Sandler have reported on the "chilly classroom climate" for female students. They found that male teachers often use sexist humor, language, and disparaging remarks about women's abilities and do not draw women into classroom discussions as often as they do men.[12] Classroom obstacles for women or students of color can be blatant or subtle, even subtle enough to be imperceptible to outside observers. Some contemporary patterns of discrimination on college campuses are so hidden, novel, or subtle that students may struggle for the words with which to describe it. One University of California (Berkeley) report noted that black students there sometimes do not have "a textured and nuanced language to fit the newer and more subtly perceived forms of discomforting racism" and thus often self-censor instances of racism "before they can give language to it."[13] In one group discussion there a black professor asked a group of black students what they meant by racism. One student said in frustration: "You know, you know . . . they just act like you don't belong here."[14]

In our parent focus groups a few parents commented on this unwelcoming attitude at SU. One father spoke of a family discussion about SU:

> A friend of ours, their son is going to come out of there, and they're the ones that said, "No you don't want to go there" because it is racist. My wife went there for one semester going at night, and I can see how it is there. [What could you see that made you know that?] The attitude of the teachers. The attitudes of the people that were there. You can feel when someone wants you somewhere and when they don't want you somewhere.

Social groups are rooted in the "we feeling" of their members, an emotion conveyed through expressions of solidarity, social integration, and cooperation. A pivotal finding of our research is that the marginalized social position from which black students often interact with their white peers and with white faculty members is defined in everyday interactions and encounters. Every day the African American students go through a series of interpersonal exchanges on campus, interactions from which they learn how they are viewed and how they must act and react.

These students do not react solely on the basis of one negative exchange but use their intellect and individual and collective memories to make sense of what is going on around them. The following statement illustrates how one black student came to make sense of a singular incident, integrating it into a stock of knowledge that would help him understand future incidents:

> Another incident that I was involved in was trying to . . . subscribe a class. And the professor was white, and she gave me the impression fully—I mean quote, unquote "indirectly"—that I was not quite wanted in there. I was number one for the entire week waiting to get into the class. And I was attending classes, participating and what have you, and there were about two or three other white guys that was numbers two, three, and four on

the wait list. And I asked her if she would oversubscribe me, since the waiting list came in and I did not get the class. And she started hitting me about how she is all busy, she's got so much other stuff to do, that taking on additional student would become a problem, and that grading an extra paper would just be too much. As if I'm really asking her to bend backwards, et cetera. And what I was told a couple of weeks later when I did not get the class is that another guy got in. And the only way that he could have gotten in would have been through a [over] subscription because the wait list was gone. And I was number one, so if anybody was getting in through the wait list it would have been me.

But to hear that another guy got in, boom, that just let me know what time it was. And it just goes to show that when you think things are not going on, things are definitely going on. And it's a shame because we all need this kind of stuff in terms of trying to provide positive momentum to try and get the job done. These are things that build up rage. And then certain people have a problem controlling inner rage, and they do things perhaps that they may regret.

This student describes the painful effects of a situation of anomie, a situation where one cannot trust the existing rules to be applied in one's case. It is likely that his prior experiences on campus, and those of his friends, lead him to believe that discriminatory "things are definitely going on." After using the first person singular throughout most of the account, he concludes in an impersonal voice that describes the effects such incidents generate. This shift in language is a device to put some distance between him and his feelings. He apparently shifts to a description of a general black situation, but the rage he attributes to "certain people" is no doubt his own.

This account points toward the significant impact that racial barriers can have on the health and well-being of those targeted. Research studies have found rage over recurring racism to be common among African Americans. This rage, when repressed, can create serious health problems, such as hypertension, and can explode at inopportune times. According to a 1993 Princeton University report, students of color there frequently react to recurring discrimination "by storing up their responses. This often leads to a kind of accumulated rage that evokes strong reactions in instances which would not seem to warrant such a response." In turn, the report notes, such an overreaction reinforces whites in their notions that African Americans and other people of color are thin-skinned and volatile.[15]

This accumulated rage over racism is central to recent discussions of black and white Americans. Recently, the arch-conservative analyst

Dinesh D'Souza has argued that racism is disappearing from U.S. society and that middle-class African Americans have a rage that indicates a "questionable grip on reality" and a frustration over "pursuing unearned privileges." In his view the rage is unjustified and unrelated to continuing racial barriers these middle-class African Americans face in this society.[16] In contrast, in a very perceptive analysis of black rage, the scholar bell hooks has shown that it is useful for a white-dominated society "to make all black rage appear pathological rather than identify the structure wherein that rage surfaces." In her view, black rage is very much grounded in persisting racist barriers in U.S. society. While this rage can lead to pathological actions, it can also lead to constructive actions that empower African Americans. What she has in mind is the way in which rage can become "a passion for freedom and justice that illuminates, heals, and makes redemptive struggle possible."[17] Regularly, in our student and parent commentaries we see this passion for freedom and racial justice, a passion that has significant educational relevance for all students and staff members on contemporary college campuses.

The situation of anomie, of unclear norms, described in the last account may be more widespread than one might think on college campuses. A major factor determining satisfactory progress toward a college degree is fair grading and evaluation by the professoriat. Whether one is a white student or a student of color, one has the right to expect grades to be based on the same standards. Certainly, the image of the university as an especially open and tolerant place might lead students to expect that grading will be done impartially and without restraint on freedom of expression. However, these conventional academic guarantees are often not enjoyed by black students. Research surveys at State University and on other campuses indicate that from a fifth to half of African American students report they have received unfair grades because of their skin color. A recent study of the experiences of black graduate students at Michigan State University found that a third knew faculty members who graded students of color lower than whites, and thirty percent knew faculty members who gave less help to their students of color than to white students.[18]

Both in their general discussions of the university's racial climate and in their specific responses to a question about instruction, the black students in our focus groups reported on their specific encounters with university instructors. One student noted the actions of a white professor with a bad reputation among black students:

> I had a professor in a humanities department . . . just being wrong toward black students and grading them incorrectly. Wrong,

everything, people always going up, [complaining] can't get the man out. Can't get the man out, "Nothing they can do about it." He's still there, still teaching, still has the same problems.

Discussing a graduate student teacher for a university writing course, one black student reported a similar problem:

> In a writing course this guy—he was a graduate student and I guess he was the TA—and he was teaching the course. I was the only black student there. And this course [means] getting to write like six or seven papers, et cetera. And I love to write, and I think that expressing myself on paper is something that I don't have too much of a problem with. And I was, in serious papers, [doing] even perhaps more than he requested.... The effort and the detail that I put into these papers, you know, is not being commended. It's like he was giving me C's. And everyone else was getting A's and B's. And I had to confront him about it. Because what I did is I read a couple of the A papers just to see how some of these students [wrote]. And ... I realized that there was some sort of imbalance in terms of how they approached this, and sometimes [they were] meeting half the requirements. And I'm taking all the requirements and more and putting everything in a cohesive-type form, everything, and getting a C.... So I met with him once, and we had to really break it down, because I was like [I want an] explanation of why I'm getting a C on all these papers one behind the next. And I really got tired because he really couldn't provide me with good sufficient answers as to why this paper was a C paper. You understand, I was like, "what's going on." And it became a bit ugly, but at the same time I felt good about pressing the issue.

At every U.S. campus many students get bad or mediocre grades. However, the critical element in this student's account is not the grade itself. Examination of his peers' graded work led him to the conclusion that the criteria applied to whites were not applied to him. One key dimension of this case is the instructor's inability to provide answers that explained the modest grades on the black student's papers. Fair grading criteria and honest explanations are important for all students, but especially for African American students who are veterans of campus and societal unfairness. Interestingly, most black students seem willing to give white teachers the benefit of the doubt wherever possible. Differential grading practices constitute racial maltreatment in that they seek to affix to black students the label of weak achievement or failure. As a result, academic transcripts will not measure accurately the black achievements.

Another male student was able to discern the likely reason for certain grades he received:

> I wrote a paper in a humanities course about how Africa was a civilization long before other civilizations. . . . I know other people who wrote, you know, similar things . . . black issues . . . and the teachers like really got on them for that paper. . . . I don't know what it is about the teachers but they really come down on you for attempting to write papers, something, you know, that has to do with [black] topics. If it's controversial, it's not good. If you're not writing about peace and love or whatever, or something that's just neutral, it's not good. . . . [And how is that manifested? How do you know that's what is going on?] I mean you can see it . . . if your write some papers, you're writing, you get B's, B+'s, A's. And then all of a sudden you write this paper on Africa, and you get a C-. You're like "What! How did this happen?" Or you know when they try to invalidate your material. "You can't say this, you can't do this." All of a sudden, "You can't do this in your paper." You know, Where did this come from? If I wrote about how great Abraham Lincoln was, I probably would have gotten an A. But I'm writing about Africa; I'm getting a C-. It doesn't, you know, it just doesn't click.

All students who write on creative topics run the risk of displeasing teachers who are not informed on such topics or who have a different perspective. However, at a predominantly white institution, it is too often the views and knowledge of African American students in regard to certain historical, political, or racial matters that are deemed inappropriate or odd by certain white instructors. Many black students like to do research on and write about topics such as the history of Africa, a continent that evokes strong positive emotions in many blacks and negative stereotypes in the minds of many whites. Most critical here is the intellectual censorship of topics of importance to black students, a censorship that again makes them feel like aliens in white territory.

Contesting grades can bring into play other white racial concerns and stereotypes, as in this example from a male student:

> I'm in [names a course] right now, and I'm doing pretty good in it, but I have another friend who's black who's not doing that well. And the teacher, he's kind of an ass because like, my friend, he went up to him and was asking a question, "Why did you put all these circles on my paper and grade it this way?" And then the teacher says something like, "Well, come back. I think you're not in the right mood to discuss this." He was like the way I am now.

> Not like yelling or nothing, but just asking him a question. He
> says, "I don't think you're in a mood to discuss it. Come back
> after you've calmed down a little bit." [Moderator: Do you think
> it was racially motivated?] I think so.

Again, the position of black students in the campus social structure is
made clear. The teacher's dismissal of the student's question is based
on the way the professor read a black student's demeanor. This white
teacher devalued the black student's question, and the injury was
compounded when the teacher suggested the questions were rooted
in anger or agitation. As college teachers ourselves, we are aware that
students are sometimes not objective about the grades they receive
and often want to discuss them. Yet, here this common situation was
apparently not read as ordinary by the white teacher. Instead it seems
the student was stereotyped as a threatening young black man.

The perception that college rules are not applied equally to whites
and blacks was clear in some discussions of grades that took place in
the parent groups. One mother spoke of a friend who faced impersonal treatment and differential grading along racial lines:

> ... thinking about a friend who went there. And she had a good
> feeling from high school. And then she said the classrooms were
> so large she was lost. And she would try to talk to an instructor.
> She didn't get any really response for help ... she was not
> directed properly. And then she knew of white students who had
> lower test grades than herself, but on their transcripts [their
> grades] were higher then hers.

Another mother commented in a similar fashion:

> A friend I had a number of years ago had attended [State Uni-
> versity]. I think one of the things that she felt slighted with [was]
> the grades. She felt that she didn't get the grades that she should
> have gotten. And particularly [in] English courses.

Grades are part of the performance record that becomes central to an
individual's academic history, one that follows a student well beyond
the university. *Recurring* accounts of grading problems at predominantly white universities raise questions about the integrity of the academic system. The last few accounts demonstrate how professors'
grading practices can become a problem for black students when they
are rooted in inconsistent standards for class performance.

The father of a successful student presented his view of the special
aptitudes and discipline needed for black students to make it at State
University:

> Because my kid was there, and I want to give you first hand experience. He was successful, and he would have been anyway. He's an introvert; he's a scientist. His [professor] could push him in a corner, and he'd come out all right. But the average [black] kid cannot. He was focused in a corner; he stayed in a laboratory. He'd do the studies, and all the lab on his own. And he didn't need a lot of [help]. We would talk about his school, "Who is assisting you? How is this working?" And just in our discussion in conversation, I could see that if he didn't have the aptitude and discipline to go forward, he could very well fail.

Social neglect or isolation on a majority-white college campus is more difficult for some students than for others. The implication of his commentary is that some instructors neglect or isolate black students. On such campuses the average white student has more chances to "make it" than the average black student, who, because of campus and societal racism, may need extra support and encouragement from faculty members.

Thinking along similar lines, one mother commented on her son's problems with support at State University:

> I don't think that they have the same support system ... at the State University, that they would at a historically [black] college. I don't think that the teachers or the professors are as interested or [that] they ... give them the certain help that they need. That's how I see it.... And that's why I did not want my youngest son to go there.... His brother went to a historically black college; and I tried to get him there.... So then he said, "Well I'll go to the university, Mom, because I know I'll do well there." So that's where he's at. I don't know whether he likes it or what, but he's just there. I don't feel good about it, but you know, that's it.

Later in the discussion, she added:

> As I've said before, they [SU] don't take the time to be to the student what they should be.... They don't listen; they don't care. They don't take the time to guide them and direct them. [Moderator: How did you know that?] ... Because I had some friends whose children went there before my son went, and they told me that these things happened to their children.

Aware of the agony black students frequently go through at predominantly white colleges, this mother tried to get her son to go to a historically black college. Our interviews suggest how black colleges and universities, although declining in number in recent decades, are frequently viewed as places of strong individual and educational support and as refuges from the vagaries of white racism. In our groups, as well as in other research studies we have cited, many black parents and students indicate that at predominantly white universities black students often do not get the same kind or amount of attention that white students receive or that black students receive at historically black colleges. The parents' and students' conclusions are not unsubstantiated, but are based on a familial and communal stock of knowledge about the racial slant of certain educational institutions. Such knowledge is usually grounded in the experiences of numerous black individuals over some period of time.

Problems with White Coaches:
"It's Always Little Incidents That You Have to Read"

While black students who are athletes may get some privileges that other black students do not receive, this does not mean they do not face negative stereotyping and other negative treatment. One student noted how he and his fellow black athletes suffered at the hands of white coaches and players. In his account we see how his father helped him think through white actions:

> There is racism on the team and with the coaching staff. I can see it within the coaching staff itself. You know, when I first came to school I didn't understand it, and my father and I didn't realize it. And after the first year of being in this university, and the second year, he said "I can see you realize what white people are trying to do to you, how they try to manipulate you and everything." And . . . there are some guys on the team that are racist, and they make black-white jokes. They make them as jokes, but you know almost every day of this whole season that somebody will say something about white and black. And I can understand that they really don't like us on the team. Like the new coaching staff has come in, and they'll bring a lot of blacks in. And the old coaching staff will bring a lot of whites. And they weren't as good athletes as we were, and the [white] guys on the team now are like saying the football team will be the next [names a black university]. Because on away trips we take lots of people, and I would say most of us are black now. But before it was like almost everybody was white. . . .

Later in the group discussion the same student added:

> And like coach [gives name], I came to the program under him and everything. But that's when I was young, and I couldn't see

everything. But I mean he made comments towards other teams. Like we were playing [names another university] two years ago in a city near here, and he was saying when we play that college, you know, they're going to have a lot of brothers on their team, and he was like, "They can run." And he used to make a racial joke like if they're black they can run and everything. Then the white guys thought it was real funny, you know, that they can run. But no one that was black really thought it was a joke and everything. So it's always little incidents that you have to read beyond what's really happening. So you can see that it's race.

This student suggests in additional comments not reproduced here that because of the desire to retain scholarships black athletes mostly suffer these jokes and comments in silence. Ironically, this account of a negative racial climate comes from an athlete, a student whom the university recruited and who will represent the university. The climate again is one of "we" against "them." Racial stereotyping is so much of part of U.S. culture that white coaches and student athletes at predominantly white campuses often do not view racist comments and joking as offensive. Sometimes this "joking" can be very serious. For example, in 1993 the *Chronicle of Higher Education* reported that several whites on a University of Minnesota (Morris) wrestling team, with the knowledge of a white assistant coach, set up a surprise gathering for two black athletes on the team. As a prank, the whites took the blacks to a remote location where other whites on the team greeted them in Ku Klux Klan garb.[19]

Friends' accounts and mass media reports of incidents involving white coaches have contributed to the negative views of mainly white universities among parents in local black communities. For instance, one father, who had majored in physical education in college, recalled an incident he had seen in the mass media in which the white coach of a major university's athletic team had refused to shake the hand of a black coach whose athletic team had beaten his team. This account illustrates how past events become part of the persisting image of predominantly white universities among black Americans today. The publicized conduct of the white coach made him seem a sore loser. Beyond the personal consequences, moreover, his conduct undermined the sportsmanship often thought to be central to college athletic events and created an incident that became part of the collective memory of black communities.

The racial implications of an incident involving a student athlete were discussed in the parent groups. One mother noted that she was not really into sports:

However, I do remember when the [black] guy who got this contract was taking drugs. That's when it really came into play, when it was really noted that these [black] students were being used, and I'm saying used, for the purpose of playing major sports and bringing money into the school.

A parent in another focus group commented on an important aspect of this incident:

The second thought that I put down had to do when you asked if there was something of a racial nature, it always comes to my mind was the way this black athlete was vilified by the school. They played him off to be some dumb jock who, if he wasn't good at his game, then he would have never been there. When in fact he had progressed as well as most students who do not play under the microscope that he was under.

A father in a third focus group pointed out yet another issue about the incident:

Another thing was when that athlete had been on drugs there. And I didn't like the point where to me, the coach should have known. I've played sports and your coach is like your father. He knows what's going on in your life and they didn't pursue him and what's going on. And I always had it in my heart I felt that he knew about these drugs that this boy was doing. And they did not pursue it. They just gave his money, and they let him go. . . . And it just gave me a lot of negativity about State University.

In Chapter 2 we observed how an incident involving drugs can precipitate parental fears about what their children might face at a predominantly white university. In the comments above we see how a drug incident was seen by these parents as a sign confirming their fears that at SU black young people are not be nurtured and supported the way that all students should be. The white condemnation of the student is seen as excessive, distorted, and indicative of a lack of caring, especially for student athletes who are viewed as exploited by athletic programs.

The Case of Black Faculty Members:
"The Teachers Weren't That Black"

The desegregation of college and university faculties has come slowly in the United States. In the early 1950s even the liberal University of

Chicago turned down a prominent African American scholar, E. Franklin Frazier, for a faculty position because "the wives of white professors would object."[20] As late as 1958 there were only 200 African Americans teaching full-time among the many thousands of faculty at predominantly white colleges and universities. It was not until about 1970 that these colleges and universities felt mild pressure from the federal government to hire black faculty members. Even by the mid-1980s black instructors made up only 2.2 percent of the faculty at predominantly white colleges and universities.[21]

The prevailing whiteness of the SU campus quickly becomes clear to new students in the scarcity of black instructors, who make up a very small percentage of the campus faculty. The relative shortage of black faculty comes as a blow to many students, as this young man explained:

> And when I got here like, the students weren't black. The teachers weren't that black. And it was like I go through this science department, and there are no black teachers or no black TA's even. I mean there're none; and at first it really screwed me up. I'm walking around, and ... it just didn't seem normal. It seemed like I commute into this place, and I'm like in the twilight zone where there's no one I could possibly relate to in the whole department.... But it just made me feel like I had no hope to go through.

The "twilight zone" metaphor suggests the unreality black students often sense at predominantly white universities, as well as the personal wounds a white-centered campus can inflict. Having "no hope" to get through is a serious burden to bear on top of the usual difficulties associated with leaving home for college and becoming a university student.

Several focus group participants pointed out the utility of black instructors for informal counseling and support rooted in the collective black experience. One young scholar expressed it this way:

> Coming into the State University, one thing that I would have loved to have happen was to have more relations with black professors, and [in] the courses that I have to take. I consider it a sort of negative to not have that guided factor out there teaching you.... If you just know somebody up there that went through struggles and tension and pain, and he is actually teaching you. And if [you] can see a black sister or a black brother out there teaching you, it would just make me want to try harder. When I go in the classroom for school, and I have to look up, and I realize, "Well, this is what it's coming to." I'm not saying that I'm

not going to try because I'm going to try my hardest all the time.... [He adds a comment on white and black instructors later.] You tend to feel sometimes that they're not quite going to look out for you as much as if you had perhaps a black professor out there, who might be willing to give you that extra listening ear towards some of your personal situations, et cetera.

The presence of African American faculty is one antidote for the condition of hopelessness many black students describe. These faculty members are perceived as having suffered some of the same tensions and pain faced by the students, experiences that even the most sympathetic white instructors cannot be expected to have.

One SU student was surprised and excited in finding a black professor teaching her course:

I have an adjunct professor this semester who's black. He's not on the staff; he's just like he's adjunct. And it freaked me out, because I didn't expect it. I walked into class, and you look, and it's like "whoa." You know? I'm like excited, and other people are like, "Why is she so excited?"

From the point of view of the black community and of black students, the importance of black faculty was accented in another student's comments:

For example, they were supposed to have a conference on something about if blacks were more genetically [different].... And I'm not quite sure [about] everything that happened, but I think a lot of the people who protested it were black faculty members specifically, who understood the basis of the research.... And it really wasn't until after the school had decided to like succumb to the pressures and not have the conference here that a lot of other people were informed about it. So I think unfortunately that move had to be made by black [faculty] members within the school. And the school itself didn't say, "No, we cannot be the site...." Because they were going to sponsor it, I mean, if nobody had protested it.... But I think that over the past four years there has been a lot more unity, or maybe I've just have become a lot more aware of the unity between like the faculty and the students and things to that effect.

Black faculty members are often seen by black students as necessary leaders, even where they do not wish to be. In this case, black faculty members and students had a common ground in opposing academic activities that were questionable from a black perspective.

In the group interviews a few parents also spoke about the importance of black faculty members. After explaining that her experience with white professors had left her with the feeling that SU was a "cold" place, one mother commented on issues linked to the absence of black professors:

> I have friends who go to State University [who] are trying to work on their master's degree just because it's convenient. Because they work, they have careers and they want to get a master's degree. And, you know, they feel that there's racism like I was telling you about. . . . [Later she added] And, I don't see that many blacks on campus. At least when I was there, I didn't see that many blacks there. And of all of the four professors that I had in my department, none of them were black. I did not see any black people, really, except a few people that were in my classes. But I did not see any black professors, so I didn't know if they had any or not. But visibly, it is a very white-looking campus.

We have seen that "white-looking" is a key dimension of the space at SU. Certain recurring messages for black students and parents signal that SU is a place where they are unusual and unwelcome. In the group interviews most participants seemed to be saying that the recruitment of black graduate students and faculty members is a critical part of the corrective action that would be necessary to make this predominantly white environment much more hospitable.

The Difficult Position of Black Faculty and Staff: "You Are an Associate Professor, and You Work for the Dean"

For all the importance that black students and parents attributed to the presence of black faculty, they were not naive about the role that they could play. Some in the parent groups dealt critically with remedial measures being taken by the university, including the hiring of black staff members. These token efforts were viewed as inadequate to solving the range of individual and systemic racial problems. One father noted that

> I was there months ago. . . . The change is that you have big black people in places that are supposed to be to help you, in equal opportunity offices and so forth. [But they are] really there just there in name only. Well, you know the typical environment— you are [an] associate professor and you work for the dean. You're not going to do anything to cut your throat in getting your promotion and so forth. It's less than tokenism. The people

are sincere and so forth, you pull them aside and talk to them, and they'll tell you what it is. But how do you break through that?

In such cases, the apparent tokenism is not even tokenism in practice. The black parents are sensitive to the problems of black faculty members put into relatively powerless positions where they cannot speak out aggressively on racial issues. Pressures on faculty of color to fit into the white campus atmosphere are great. For example, a 1993 survey of forty-two mostly black, Latino, and Asian faculty members at the University of Nevada (Las Vegas) found that forty-three percent of those replying to a question about assimilation said they had to abandon some or all of the important parts of their cultures to be successful in their university departments. Two-thirds of those replying to a related question reported that they sometimes or all the time felt pressure to ascribe to white colleagues' values. Moreover, thirty-five percent of those replying to a question about decision making in their university unit said that they were excluded from the decisions some or all of the time.[22]

Putting a significant number of black faculty into positions of power is very important for black parents and students. One mother noted how she felt about the recent hiring of a few black professors at State University:

> Negative .... In their key positions, then, I know two people came from a black university to State University. And they're in top positions, so maybe they can work with each other to do the things that they want. [To] try and act like they're helping you.... Then I know about five that [left] the State University because they felt things weren't going right with them as far as benefits and how they were being treated. And they left.... The change from what I see is not better.

Earlier in the group discussion the same parent had commented about

> All this kind of stuff you read it in the papers about the university. And a few years ago I remember ... they had just hired a black administrator, somebody in a high position, and they kept talking about this thing as if he were the only black person in the world.

A father commented on the same appointment:

> There have been some changes that we've seen that have been cosmetic anyhow. [Moderator: Like what? What do you mean by cosmetic?] You have a black administrator over there few years

ago, you've had a black administrator? . . . The [black] enrollment
is up, but I can't say that the graduation is up.

The parents recognize the changes in recent years at SU and approve
of having more black faculty members and administrators. But, as we
have noted previously, they and the students are wary of a tokenism
that means little real change. Indeed, the "minoritization" of certain
university programs or positions is usually a cosmetic process in which
a few black professors or other staff members are placed as legitimiz-
ing tokens that make the institution look good in regard to racial
diversification. Black faculty members and administrators provide, as
some of them actually say, a kind of "fire insurance" for the white
administrations of these universities. Yet their token positions usually
offer them little power to effect significant changes in the campus
operations or racial climate.

The situation on predominantly white campuses can be very rough
for black faculty and staff members. One survey of several hundred
black faculty members at mostly white colleges found that a substantial proportion thought that racism was the important barrier to black
employment in their educational institutions.[23] Another report on the
quality of life for black faculty at predominantly white colleges found
that, where the number of black faculty members is small, "the burdens of institutional and individual racism weigh heavily. The psychological safety associated with numbers is not available to persons who
work in these isolated situations."[24]

The difficult position of black staff members was made clear in a
recent interview we conducted with a female African American educator who has taught at two mostly white colleges in the 1990s.
Reflecting on her own recent college experiences, which also took
place at a mostly white college, she commented on remarks made by
white faculty, staff, and students:

> The difficulties came, however, in ignorant racial remarks, and
> the comparison of my success with the media's hyperbole of my
> people's failures. I was seen as a "credit to my race" for my many
> accomplishments and academic success. I was often asked to speak
> for my entire race, and covertly asked why other inner city black
> youth didn't pull it together like I had.

Continuing her interview, this educator related how she encountered
overt racism in the form of a mock slave auction set up by a group of
white students to raise money for religious purposes:

> This was one of the most painful racial experiences that I ever
> encountered. A group on campus decided to do a fundraiser

which would allow professors to bid on students in a centralized location (the cafeteria) to do grunt work for them. In return the students would use the money raised to do ministry. As staff and faculty began to jestingly poke and pick at students on the auction block, onlookers began to cheer and shout demeaning epithets that I interpreted as being characteristic of white masters toward black slaves. The few black students that were present in the cafeteria looked on as I did in horror and disbelief. After all, this was an academic and religious institution. After stuffing down my lunch and trying to downplay my initial outrage, I questioned other students to get their perceptions of this recent event, in hopes that collectively we could confront the college president and participating staff with this grotesque display of the many improprieties suffered by persons of color and the poor. To my dismay no one had much to say about it: "What was the big deal, the money was being used for a good cause!" Perhaps my voice of justice was silenced because I was a newcomer, or maybe because I was so young, but whatever the case my concern never went much further than my immediate colleagues.

Next in her account she explains that after graduation, she went on to get a graduate degree elsewhere. Later, a white administrator at her undergraduate college called her with a job offer, which she took. As the only black staff member, she soon ran into the same type of racism:

After being warmly accepted by the students of color, I became an advocate and outlet for many of their frustrations. Upon my second term at the institution, a close colleague of mine vivaciously announced, at a staff meeting, that her students were planning a slave auction as a fundraiser for outreach! As other staff members openly gave their approval, I braced myself for the confrontation that I knew had to take place. History would not repeat itself, at least not without some kicking and fighting by this black woman. As the flyer for the event displayed an African bound in chains on an auction block, I knew that my freshman feelings of outrage were not an exaggeration, nor was my rekindled hurt and anger unjustified.

After speaking with her supervisor about what she saw as "the atrocity of such an event," and having gotten some support from him, she approached the well-educated white colleague who was setting up the fundraiser with the students:

Confidently, I approached my colleague sponsoring the event, and conveyed the dehumanizing elements of such an event, not expecting any resistance, nor what came next. She stared blankly into my face as if to say "What's your problem?" As I tried to constructively share my personal encounter as a freshman and the detrimental effects of such an event on everyone in the community, she retorted with, "Slavery has been over for hundreds of years, no one thinks of it in terms of black and white any more, so why make a big deal of it?" Had she heard anything I said? And why didn't the man on the flyer have straight hair instead of an Afro? After talking to her a few more minutes, in vain, she finally agreed not to hold this profitable event "if it bothered me!" If it bothered me?! I could have hurt someone at that point, so I turned and walked away. I was at least pleased that the event would not take place, even if the people didn't understand why it shouldn't. I was successful, with the help of my supervisor, at getting any future slave auctions banned on campus.... Although some backlash came from students who had to think of a more creative way of raising money, and staff who thought I was playing the victim role, I felt a small victory had been won.

This educator's experiences echo those of the students and parents in the SU focus groups. In this example some whites, both students and professors, thought nothing of holding a mock African-slave auction. For them, it appears to have been just another fundraiser. Yet, slave auctions are among the *most* demeaning and cruel events in the family and community memories of African Americans. While in the mind of some whites, slave auctions are not important and happened "hundreds of years" ago (an exaggeration, since slavery existed just 130 years before the statement was made), in the black educator's mind they are oppressive and still vivid memories and a cause for outrage. This personal narrative illustrates how the same historical events can evoke very different feelings and memories, and have quite different meanings, for black and white Americans. For most whites involved, a mock slave auction is an opportunity to have fun and raise funds, ironically in this case, for religious ministries. For the black students and staff, however, it is the cause of more frustration, anguish, and painful memories.

Like many whites in similar situations, the white colleague here appears not to have understood the black staff member's position, and she dismisses her concerns with the comment that "no one thinks of it in terms of black and white any more." This white assertion places the black staff member outside the circle of people who think correctly about U.S. history. In effect, the white protagonist tells the black woman that her "place" in campus space is marginal. A white person fails to recognize the feelings and understandings of an African American. The white staff member agreed to cancel the slave auction, but only because it bothered her black colleague. By this act she granted her black associate as an act of personal favor something to which the latter had a legitimate expectation—and something the white protagonist herself should have ruled out as a matter of historical knowledge and moral conscience.

Conclusion

In this chapter we have focused on what is perhaps the most central social and intellectual exchange in higher education—that between professors and students. The voices of black students at predominantly white institutions are worth attending to because they come from an important group of the consumers of higher learning who are, at the same time, part of its distinctive product.[25] In this age of large college enrollments and of computerized, bureaucratic processing of students, higher education still rests at base on the regular interaction between teachers and students.

Students, black and nonblack, occupy distinctive positions in the social structure of a predominantly white campus, and these positions are defined and redefined within a complex web of interracial relationships. Social scientists have long described many human realities as being socially constructed. What is taken as socially "real" is at heart a collection of shared understandings, but these understandings have a past and a future. Social meanings generally transcend particular individuals at one point in historical time. Because of these individual and collective understandings, the world around an individual becomes socially structured and personally predictable. Individuals and groups accumulate memories and stocks of knowledge that help them in the process of making sense out of the world around them. When human beings become part of a new physical and social environment, such as a college campus, they must interpret the signs and symbols, as well as others' behavior toward them, in order to know "their place." As we have seen, the voices of the black students and parents describe not only their interactions with whites, but also the social structure of the university campus as it is lived and processed by these key actors. In the student and parent reports we often observe the social positions defined for black students in what is still fundamentally white educational territory.

The SU students' experiences with white faculty members suggest that racial insensitivity and inequality are well-institutionalized in what may at first seem to be an unlikely place—the presumably tolerant halls of higher education. Yet, the long history of racial restriction and exclusion at traditionally white colleges and universities provides ample reason for expecting racial insensitivity and inequality to be present today at such places. Over the course of U.S. history, one generation of white male professors has, for the most part, been succeeded by another generation of white male professors. Today, most college professors continue to be white men of European background, and the majority seem more or less comfortable with their racial privileges. Few, indeed, wish to actively intervene to root out racist barriers in academia. In addition, the intellectual discourse at traditionally white colleges and universities is for the most part parochial and restricted by subtle or overt Eurocentric interests and biases.

On predominantly white campuses across the nation, African American students who come to see that some, or many, of their white professors are insensitive, prejudiced, or discriminating are less likely to go to them for advice. They know that they will not get the recognition and respect they deserve. They are not likely to adopt these instructors as role models. As a result, many black students dissociate themselves from the important reference group of white scholars and have no real option but to create a support structure of fellow black students and, if they are available and willing, black faculty members. Not surprisingly, a campus situation of pervasive racial hurdles and impediments can affect the academic performance and success of many black students. As we have seen, SU is not unique; the difficult struggle for academic survival and success has been reported by students of color at many predominantly white colleges and universities. Indeed, students of color who were recently interviewed at Princeton explained that persistent racial bias on campus affected their "rapport with members of the instructional staffs—both faculty and assistants-in-instruction—so that their studies are not as satisfying as they would like."[26] Under such circumstances the black attrition rate often increases, and the severe costs of campus racism again become conspicuous.

5

ADMINISTRATIVE BARRIERS TO STUDENT PROGRESS
"Blocked at Each Little Turn"

Modern universities are complex organizations made up of large numbers of faculty members, academic administrators, and an array of support personnel. Their bureaucracies are governed by numerous academic, financial, and other administrative rules, many of which touch on a college student's life. Academic rules govern the courses taken and the grading system. Financial rules and related administrative regulations establish the cost of tuition and fees and how they are to be paid. The creation of student organizations, the determination of projects that students can undertake, the definition of university facilities students can utilize are all regulated by college administrators. The number and complexity of rules that govern U.S. colleges and universities are such that many specialized employees are required to interpret and enforce the rules for faculty, staff, and students.

In the process of dealing with the large array of staff members on a large university campus, African American students periodically encounter problems with racial overtones. On the exit questionnaire given after the group sessions, the SU students were asked a general question about this issue: "How often have you been mistreated by a white administrator or clerk at this campus because of your race?" Nearly half said once or twice, while eleven percent said several times. Thirty-six percent indicated that they had so far not suffered racial mistreatment by these staff members.[1] Significantly, the percentage of students facing discrimination by administrators and staff at State University was higher than that at another major public university in the South, where a research study by the first author found that a quarter of the black students reported racial discrimination from campus staff.[2] These data, taken together with references to similar problems at other campuses in the "racial climate" reports cited in this and previous chapters, indicate that staff members frequently create unnecessary racial barriers for black students on predominantly white university campuses.

In this chapter we are concerned with the concrete character of racial obstacles presented by university personnel. In their everyday rounds on campus, black students come into contact with a number of different types of white staff members, including academic advisers, clerks and supervisors, dormitory staff members, and campus police officers.

Academic Advising: "They Just Neglect to Tell Them"

Among the most serious challenges facing predominantly white colleges and universities is the transmission of academic and other campus information to black students and other students of color. Sound academic advising is decisive for the academic careers and graduation of all students. Few students have the time or skills to learn all the important rules of the college catalog. In some cases the academic advisers for students are faculty members who do part-time advising; in other cases the academic advisers are full-time staff members hired for that purpose. The academic adviser is one of the human contact points for college students. A good adviser can start young scholars out in the right direction and aid their navigation through vague or complex college requirements, while a poor adviser can wreck student academic careers by giving erroneous or insufficient advice. If advisers provide recommendations that put a student into the wrong courses, or if advisers do not tell students about the requirements that affect them, then students may suffer needlessly, wasting time, energy, and money.

On the predominantly white campuses with which we are most familiar, the corps of faculty advisors is almost all white. In addition, the professional advisory staff is in the majority white, but does include some advisors of color, many of whom were brought in recently to work with special groups of students, such as athletes. When black students were finally admitted in significant numbers to major universities in the 1960s and 1970s, scattered "offices of minority students" were established in some of the academic units on these campuses. These offices were seldom seen by university administrators as more than a recruiting device or a modest supplemental resource for students of color in need of advising. Today, these offices tend to be understaffed and underfunded, and they are frequently headed by one of the few African American faculty or staff members on the campus. Moreover, over time these special "minority" offices have often become the primary places where black students and other students of color can get adequate academic counseling and personal support. Nonetheless, on many predominantly white college campuses, the advisors of color are not numerous enough to make a major difference in the campus-wide advising system; most of these advisers are not placed in specific academic departments where much of the day-to-day advising need is concentrated. As a result, most of the departmental advisors whom students of color encounter over four or five years of college do not share the student's cultural backgrounds or concerns about racism.

In addition, many students of color miss out on much informal information often accumulated by college students themselves about the norms of programs, departments, and campus facilities, because they are less likely to participate in the dominant white cliques, fraternities, sororities, and student organizations. This is not to say that black students and other students of color do not participate in campus organizations, including groups they create, but only that their lack of full participation in numerous traditionally white campus organizations may limit the information they have to navigate university campuses.

In the accounts of the students and parents in the focus groups, it is not always clear whether the academic advisers discussed are faculty advisers or other staff members; we group the statements about advisers together in this section. A few students commented on having a positive white adviser, either a faculty member or a staff member, but a number had negative accounts. Academic counseling for black students at State University can involve subtle discriminatory treatment, as reported in this account:

> Some of the things that happen are really subtle though. For example, I have yet to have good advice in, on this campus, because I don't know who to go to. I have a white adviser, and I have yet to have good advising from him. And I know it's racial because you can tell by the way they look at you sometimes.

Encounters between advisers and students constitute what Erving Goffman called a "focused interaction." Adviser and student in effect agree to sustain for some time a focus of cognitive and visual attention on a joint task usually defined by a student's query.[3] These face-to-face interactions can include an array of glances, gestures, and verbal statements that participants generate, sometimes consciously, sometimes unconsciously. Such signs allow people to reach conclusions concerning the nature of the interaction they are having. In this account the "look" the student received leads him to the conclusion that the adviser's failure to guide him effectively is related to his racial images or prejudices. White advisers are no different than most whites, for most have limited experience interacting with African Americans and thus may react in terms of discomfort or stereotyped images. The black student in the interaction, however, is likely to have had many interactions with whites and is thus able to interpret the reaction, with a fair degree of accuracy, in racial terms.

Racialized "looks" from whites are a common experience for African Americans of all ages and in many different settings, especially in settings which have been dominated for a long time by white Americans. In an earlier chapter we noted the hostile glances and discourteous scrutiny that blacks sometimes receive from SU's white students. These looks, which at the extreme take the form of hate stares, are an old problem for African Americans.[4] Whether they are hostile, strange, or discourteous, the white looks function somehow to question the presence of black students in a "white space." Such scrutiny may appear to be of minor significance to white observers with no history of these recurring experiences. Yet for African Americans in white settings the strange or hostile look often has a lasting impact.[5]

One black student went into detail about the signs she interpreted as discriminatory from a white adviser in her particular college within the university:

> I had an appointment with the adviser. And I was waiting there for a long time because the person that was there before me had been there for a while. And the secretary had told me . . . that the person had been there for over an hour. So I had all my stuff very organized ready to go in for my appointment. And so when I went in, it was a white adviser, of course. And they were just like, "OK, what do you need?" And I explained my situation, but they didn't advise me. They were just like, "Do this, do this." It was not, "How do you feel about this? How do you feel about that?" And it was over within a matter of fifteen minutes. . . . The person before me was white, and they spent an hour speaking with them. And it came to a situation where I had to go to the college office

—there's an office for minority students—and I had to go there to get special attention just because [the white adviser] didn't want to take the time to go over . . . [my complex situation].

The interactive signals this student interprets are less subtle than a look. The information that the white adviser communicated was more than just the academic advice. The student had evidence of disparate treatment: The white adviser gave cursory advice and did not take nearly as much time for the black student as for a previous white student. Whatever the adviser's motivation was for this cursory treatment, by providing an autocratic verdict without listening carefully to the student the adviser communicated at the very least discomfort with the student and her academic problems. Here we see how important it is for mainly white colleges to have numerous advisers who can deal with African American students and other students of color in a supportive manner. The last commentary, together with similar accounts by other students in the focus groups, points up the importance of the offices of minority students on predominantly white college campuses. Although these minority offices are frequently not adequately staffed and funded—indeed, their administrators often seem to be "ghetto-ized" or embattled—they provide critical academic and social support resources for African American students and other students of color.

In his comments in one of the student focus groups, a male student offered a contrast between good advising and poor advising:

> I have had a white adviser when I first came here. And then when I joined a sports team, they had made us go to another, another adviser, and she was a black lady. And she, you should see the difference in general. . . . The white person was more or less like, "OK, you got to take this, you got to take this, this, this, this." You know, "Peace." Meanwhile, I'll say it, but I don't know if you [had her]. . . .[Another student: Yeah, I had her, she's good.] She's nice, she sits you down, you know, "Hi, how're ya doing?" And makes you feel at home and welcome and everything. Doesn't make it seem like it's a big rush. Because I find that a lot; the other advisers are like, "OK, I've got to do this, I've got to do this. I'm in such a rush." . . . She's just a totally different person.

Again, a student notes that the *quality* of the advising is very important. The contrast here is between being made to "feel at home" and the provision of too-quick answers. In this fashion some white advisers signal that what black students have to say to them is of no great importance. The failure of a white educator to recognize a black student's concerns as worth careful attention can have a critical effect on self-esteem. From the black student's perspective good advising involves not only the amount of time devoted to student concerns, but also the impression given that the student is welcome and that the adviser is willing to listen.

One student in our focus groups provided an interesting insight on the ways students resist some of the damaging effects of a weak university advising system:

> They had a whole bunch of students come in for orientation and stuff. And at nighttime we would try to get the black students together, just so we can give them the opportunity to find out what's going to go on, on campus. You know, how school will be, what type of expectations they had. And they were telling us that their advisers were giving them some garbage advice, that they were giving them the worse advice ever. And we were like, what you don't have to take. The advisers made it seem like they had to take this—it's either this or it's nothing. . . . They didn't advise them that . . . there are ways to get around doing certain things. And the adviser was horrible. And we were sitting there like: What they didn't tell you about this class, you know, like it's a class . . . for minorities, for [minority] students. But they never told them about that class. I don't know if it slipped their mind, or if they just didn't want to tell them about it. They just neglect to tell them about so many different aspects.

In the last few comments several African American students shared the same experience with white advisers who manifested little interest in their academic needs or problems and responded in a mechanical way. The white advisers and black students somehow failed to connect. As a rule, the responsibility for this failure falls squarely on the shoulders of the adviser, because they are, or should be, trained professionals. Clearly, black students often react negatively to an insensitive or autocratic style of advising.

This last account shows that black student networks can serve to convey information white advisers may neglect to communicate, thereby substituting to a degree for traditional campus networks not readily available to black students. This account also makes evident how black students develop ways of countering ignorance, insensitivity, and prejudice. They often do not simply stand by and suffer, but incorporate into their life strategies an array of tactics designed to cope directly with racial difficulties and obstacles. They develop personal and group strategies for countering instances of racial callousness and antiblack hostility in everyday settings.

Hostile or insensitive white advisers probably cannot anticipate or imagine the problems or needs of African American students. However, the fact that the established advising system often fails to work for black students is not just a matter of some advisers' stereotyping or insensitivity. It is often a matter of inadequate experience on the part of white academic advisers or of the inadequate training provided for white advisers at many mainly white universities. For most white advisers, their own college experiences did not prepare them for face-to-face interaction with black students, and their university training also may not prepare them well for empathetic listening and understanding.

Getting Information:
"They Generally Were Kind of Disinterested in Me"

The difficulties in getting accurate, timely, and appropriate information are not restricted to students currently on the campus. Potential students are affected as well. Several black parents spoke about the negative character of direct contacts with university staff in regard to certain academic programs. For instance, one father commented on the flyers that State University sends out to solicit enrollment in its business school:

> Several years ago, when I was enacting my MBA, State University sent me a card in the mail. And I figured "why not," so I filled it out and sent it back in. Then I received a letter in the mail to go out. . . . And I went there and met I guess the lady who sent me the card. And I told her what I wanted to do, what my interests were, I was working, I was married. And never heard from her ever again. I went on somewhere else to get my MBA. . . . But at the time I never heard anything more about it. She met me, she read my resume, the whole nine yards, but right after that the contact ended.

Commenting on similar problems, another father mentioned his trip to the admissions office:

> I went to the admissions office . . . and the person who was at the desk was only one person, like a student aide, and I stood there quietly because they were on the phone and they got off the phone. And then they generally were kind of disinterested in me, not talking to me at all, not knowing that I had a scholarship, that I could go to school, and I just kind of laughed and left.

African Americans frequently report a lack of responsiveness on the part of white officials and clerks with whom they must deal. Because it is often subtle, an outside white observer might not view it as discrimination but rather as bureaucratic incompetence or indifference.

However, other research studies have demonstrated how the cumulative encounters of black men and women with white-controlled bureaucracies make them experienced in coping with this type of mistreatment and very attuned to the subtle and blatant signals of such racial rejection.[6]

Even in the case of "pure" bureaucratic impersonality or callousness, moreover, there is often a racial impact for African American students at universities that are white-normed and white-centered. For example, a University of California report noted that large institutions are impersonal for all students, but that the impersonality is "heightened for anyone who . . . experiences his/her situation as marginal."[7] In such situations normal student problems can become even more burdensome and difficult.

When asked if she thought the opportunities for black students were different from opportunities available to whites in the state's university system, one mother whose child went to State University made this comment:

> The student who really wants to try to find out where monies are available to help themselves to get through school financially, they meet little barriers, little stumbling blocks, i.e., they go to a place and the counselor or the person who has the information to give to them won't do it because this is a black face looking at them. And then when a nice little white comes along, they have all kinds of wealth of information to pass on to the student. And sometimes it's so subtle that the kid can't honestly say, or specifically state, that this [discrimination] happened to them because they really don't know it. It's later that you find it out, but it's too late. And this is very subtle—sometimes it's subtle, and sometimes it's not. But I find that I see that happen an awful, awful lot that the kids are barricaded or blocked at each little turn they make, unless they happen to come across an African American counselor or student or someone in the position to help them. . . . It's so subtle, and insidious that its really criminal.

Problems with financial aid are not unique to State University. In 1994 the U.S. Office of Civil Rights investigated complaints by students of color at Brown University who reported being rudely treated and discriminated against by staff in the financial aid office on campus.[8] The injury inflicted by this staff behavior is grievous because on modern university campuses financial and similar information is valuable and often necessary for survival and success. The experience of being "blocked at each little turn" can be serious, as it may lead to a student dropping out of school. This in turn can bring serious consequences not only for the student but also for his or her family and community. The serious character of the injuries of these white blockades are signalled in the parent's adjectives "insidious" and "criminal."

Note again the positions of the black and white actors in the social space of the university. In the last several reports the black students and parents indicate that they face abuses that are routine or accepted behavior on the part of certain whites. Numerous white advisers, like some white students and other staff members, appear not to give a second thought to their actions in regard to black people in their daily rounds at the university.

The Curriculum:
"This Wasn't a Good Class to Have"

Academic advising involves discussions of required courses every student must take. In recent years there has been much discussion of the need for multicultural or cultural diversity courses at universities, but most predominantly white colleges and universities have made no movement, or only a token movement, in that direction. In addition, although there are still numerous African American studies programs at various colleges and universities, many of these have faced some opposition from whites on and off campus. This opposition has grown in the backlash of the 1980s and 1990s. In a number of colleges and universities these programs have been reduced or discontinued, and at many colleges and universities the courses are not seen as academically valuable by a substantial number of white administrators and faculty members.

The situation at State University reflects some of these trends. Certain African American courses have not received the same academic standing as those in other departments, according to one student:

> It's like the university requirements, and stuff that you have to take. And you have to take two "higher-level studies" [courses]. And I asked [an adviser], I said, "Well, how come they don't have African American studies classes in the higher-level studies?" . . . This is the new program that they made up. They had them in the old [requirements], but now in the core they don't have any African American, upper-level studies. And she was like, first she was trying not to answer the question, and then she just kept going on. . . . And finally I asked her again, and she said, "Well there's this review board, and they review the classes. And I guess they might have just thought that wasn't a good class to have." . . . But it's just like the administration. Because they had all kinds of American studies. All kinds . . . like crazy classes they have. But

they had no African American studies. That's one of the problems
I had. That's with the administration.

There may or may not have been a legitimate academic reason for the
change in listing African American courses for this requirement. In
any event, the student did not get a reasonable explanation from the
adviser. Rather than offering to find out why there had been a change,
the adviser chose to legitimize the status quo. In the process she conveyed to the student that the African American studies courses, which
relate to the student's own cultural heritage and background, are not
important. Instead of engaging the student in a dialogue to explore
the student's concern, this adviser acted defensively. Such reactions by
white staff members can alienate African American students and make
them feel even less comfortable on the campus.

Yet again there is a suggestion here of the marginalization of African
American interests at predominantly white universities. As we noted in
the case of offices of minority students at these universities, many
white administrators put little effort into responding to the intellectual
interests of African American students and their home communities.
Even in the best of circumstances, the creation of modest African
American studies programs has usually signalled that white administrators wish to meet the pressure to broaden the curriculum, not with
internal changes to expand traditional courses, but with a few "minority" courses offered in what turns out to be an academic "back alley."[9]
Sadly, many African American students come to accept this marginalization as the best they can expect on their college campuses.

Everyday Activities on Campus: "He Doesn't Belong in Here"

Large universities have many staff members working to keep the institutions operating smoothly. Among these are dormitory managers,
residence hall assistants, cafeteria managers, cleaning personnel, and
campus police officers. The participants in our focus groups shared
their experiences with some of these university employees, as in this
account of a male student:

> But I feel like a racial thing that I've always thought about is if
> blacks have like a party in the dorms or something. A lot of the
> RA's [residence assistants] are white, so when the RA hears about
> there's a party in there like at 12:30, One o'clock, they want to
> stop the party. But yet if it's a white person having a party in their
> dorm that party will go on till [all hours]. . . . It's happened this

year. And I've heard music, partying at like four o'clock in the
morning. And it's the white people. A black party just gets going
at one o'clock. . . . I used to live in [a certain dorm] and we used
to have three floors [with] a party in it. Once they found out
about that, you know [at] one o'clock when everybody's getting
in there, everybody would just be getting in there. They come in
and want to stop it. I just feel it's wrong.

What provokes a sense of being wronged in this instance is the evidence of differential treatment; the rules applied to black students are
different from those applied to white students. The details on the timing and stopping of a black party communicate a feeling of not being
understood and of whites negatively reacting to certain black student
activities. Evidently, some white staff viewed the black students' parties as more of a serious disturbance or security risk than the white
student parties.

One male student noted the role of stereotyping in the treatment of
black men in the dormitory:

I was living up [in a dorm], and this guy across the hall from me,
this black guy—he's a good friend of mine—he had a bunch of
his [black] fraternity brothers up. Well, I don't think he was a
member at the time. He was pledging . . . he had a bunch of
friends up, and they . . . had a little party. We kind of had our
doors open, and we kind of went in between the two rooms and
that type of stuff. And this RA came through and saw this beer
can sitting on my desk. So he asked me for my ID, and I told him
I was under age. So he told me to pour it out. Well, it was already
empty. So like a couple of guys, the fraternity guys, they went out
into the hall, and they were sort of kind of giving him a hard
time, but like, so the RA wrote us up. And he told them that he
feared for his life. . . . And they had the police come in and talk to
the residence director . . . and all this and that.

Note in this case the black pain and anger over a white RA's overreaction to a dorm situation that black students defined as playful and
party-like. Instead of tailoring a modest response for the suspected
infraction, the white RA defined the situation as seriously threatening
and called the campus police. Here and in similar settings, the dorm
atmosphere is racially charged because of the stereotyped images and
cultural orientation of the dominant white group. Apparently, the
image of the dangerous black male, so extensively perpetuated in the
U.S. media, fueled the overreaction of the resident assistant.[10] Even
everyday dorm interactions can be shaped by racial perceptions much

like those of whites taking similar actions in racially desegregated settings outside the university. Moreover, the encounter here is reminis-
cent of incidents described by anthropologists where white Americans
come into different cultures on other continents and misinterpret the
behavioral signs of those who reside in the cultures, sometimes with
tragic results.[11] The institution and its higher-level administrators are
also implicated, for a number of the student accounts reveal that some
white staff members are not sufficiently trained to deal with cultural
differences on campus.

In several student accounts of interaction with university staff the
role of racially defined space on campus becomes conspicuous. The
way in which black men are viewed as intruders into white spaces is
suggested in this comment by a black athlete about his friend's treatment at a dining hall reserved for certain athletes:

> My friend John was on the football team, but he graduated. And
> John's black. And we came from playing basketball, so we went
> to eat dinner. And he wasn't supposed to eat over there, but he
> was just sitting over there talking to us, right. . . . The lady who
> checks us in she was white and everything. And the manager he's
> white. . . . And she went and told him that John was over there
> . . . and we were eating. And he came out, and he was trying to
> make John leave. . . . And John was like, "Well, I'm just sitting
> here and everything, I'm not eating anything, I'm not going to
> take anything." And he [the manager] was like, "No, you've got
> to leave." . . . Then I got into it because . . . [there were] two
> white guys in there that didn't belong in there—you know, their
> names weren't on the list and everything. And I said, "If John has
> to leave, why don't you make those two guys leave?" And he
> said, "Well they're not doing anything wrong." I was like, "Their
> names are not on the list. They don't belong in here." He said,
> "Well I'm not aware of that. . . . That is not of my concern, my
> concern is of him because she came and reported to me that he
> doesn't belong in here." So John had to leave and everything, and
> I was upset. . . . I didn't think that it was right. . . . And this went
> on for about ten minutes, and after John left, he never even went
> over there and asked those two guys did they belong in there or
> anything. . . . And so that made me feel real bad, to see again that
> everything is racial.

The student's conclusion that "everything is racial" is probably not the
view of the campus held by most whites, including white administrators
and faculty members. However, for black students the *recurring* evidence
of disparate treatment makes that conclusion unavoidable. Interrupting
everyday activities, the unfairness here seems to include the perception

on the part of white staff that the offending black man is a special type of intruder. The humiliation of seeing a friend forced to leave a place under such circumstances is painful and delivers the message that one's skin color determines one's treatment in campus settings like a dining hall. Again and again, these white messages convey information on the real social structure of a majority-white campus.

Negative Encounters with the Police: "They Brought Dogs and That Scared Me"

Recent research studies have shown that police malpractice and brutality are common problems facing African American men and women as they travel the streets of our towns and cities.[12] This police malpractice is not confined to black residential areas. African American faculty, staff, and students at predominantly white college campuses across the nation report campus security or local police harassment. Police harassment of black students has been reported at colleges as different as Northwestern University in the Chicago area and Mesabi Community College in Minnesota. A black faculty member at Vassar College recently noted that black students do not feel comfortable on campus, in part because they are singled out by security personnel for special "carding" and because of the lack of black faculty and staff members on campus.[13] At Princeton black male students reportedly are careful to carry backpacks or wear college caps to forestall being harassed by campus police, and at Harvard administrators have recommended to African American students that they carry identification to prevent local police harassment.[14]

Black male students sometimes become prime suspects for officers investigating campus crimes. For example, late in 1992 a white woman in Oneonta, New York reported that she had been attacked by a black man with a knife. Responding quickly, the police asked administrators at the State University of New York (Oneonta) for a list of all the black and Latino men there. The local police used the campus list to interrogate the students wherever they happened to be, even in front of employers and friends. According to long-term residents of the area, the local police had a history of racial harassment. The sociologist Ruth Sidel has noted that the university's release of the names of the students violated their privacy and right to be presumed innocent, as well as the Family and Educational Rights and Privacy Act.[15]

On our exit questionnaire eighty-six percent of the students at State University reported that they personally had not been mistreated by a white campus police officer because of their race, but eleven percent said that they had been mistreated once or twice and three percent said "many times." The responses to this question marked the only case where a major white group on the campus reportedly had not caused a large proportion of the African American students serious problems. Moreover, this proportion is similar to that found on other large public university campuses.[16] One reason for the relatively low percentage may be that white campus police officers, unlike white professors and advisers, are not members of the university staff that many students deal with on a regular basis.

Nonetheless, campus police officers and other security personnel have caused some African American students serious problems. One male student discussed a problem with campus police officers checking identification of a car full of black students:

> This was back in my freshman year. A bunch of us had gone to the movies over at [local theater]. And we were coming back on campus. And this was at the time where they had started the policy where, if you're coming on campus, you have to show your ID. . . . I think it was like the first car coming up, and they stopped us. And I didn't know I had to show my ID. And then they walked down to the front of the car, wrote down the license plate number, walked out to the back of it, and they gave my ID back. It looked like the next two or three cars, . . . [they] didn't stop [them] or anything to see their ID.

The student then noted that the next several cars had whites in them. His distress came from police singling out blacks, or black males, for too-close scrutiny and rigorous enforcement of regulations that were waived for whites entering the campus.

Reflecting on campus social life, another male student discussed the differential policing of black student parties:

> This is [a] kinda subtle type too. But I know when you go to a black party . . . you have eight police there plus a police car outside, plus student aides right there at the party. But yet you go down to the [white] frat row, and they've got no type of security there. . . . And they end up having a big 300-people fight, and something like that, and then they are so wild. Me and my friends went to one of those white frat parties, and they are so wild it's ridiculous. And black people do not act anything like that at their parties. . . . There are a few fights at black parties . . . but it's funny how you have all the security at the black functions and nothing at the white functions. And that's, that's a subtle form of racism right there.

Another student added that brawls at white fraternity parties get little publicity. On many college campuses, numerous white fraternity parties have received "boys will be boys" toleration from administrative and police officials. Interestingly, judging from media reports, they, and not the black student parties, have caused many serious problems for campus administrators in recent years.

This disparate treatment by local white security personnel is not new to State University's campus life. One father in the parent focus groups commented on black parties he once attended at SU:

> I'd say from my experience . . . and I used to go there when I first came out of high school; I came to little parties and them things. And people still say the same thing. You see an influx of police and dogs out on the grounds and everything. You know how you will see a lot of police. And when black people, when teenagers see that, it's going to cause problems. And I know that sometimes when they have rock shows, white shows, [there aren't] as many police. . . .

Differential treatment by the police is not a matter that is taken lightly by black students or parents. These student and parent commentaries show how excessive security at school functions where black students predominate can create a "siege" mentality among the students, one that may have a lasting impact on their view of policing and the criminal justice system.

Another black student spoke about the extra police officers brought in for the music concerts of particular interest to black students:

> We do concerts and . . . we have to sign special registration forms for all concerts. And campus police have to sign off on it. And we had a white music group, and we had a black music group. OK, they were like: white concert, musicians, heavy metal thrash, about twenty officers, standard security. [For] the black rapper's concert, they wanted thirty-five cops. I'm like, first of all, the [names auditorium] is about four steps from the police station, so there was no need for [so many]. If they needed extra security they could have just walked outside and yelled help, and ninety [would come] straight. . . . I could understand five more security guards, but fifteen more security guards . . . ?

Special surveillance by police officers was reported by several of the students who discussed campus social life. In their minds, yet again, these whites associated black social functions with a potential for trouble or violence. This perception led whites to impose exceptional security requirements in the form of additional officers. White student functions, including those with records of rowdiness, reportedly got less, or sometimes no, close police surveillance. At many universities, student organizations have to pay for security for parties that occur at off-hours or during weekends. Thus, black student organizations must pay for extra officers at a time when the cost is higher than normal. Such increased costs can decrease the number of events and the ability of the students to raise funds for other purposes. Moreover, a related problem for African American students is that their organizations usually do not have the financial support or resources of the traditional white organizations on campus. Limited funds mean fewer events, and fewer events mean a less comfortable campus atmosphere, especially with regard to social comfort. Fewer events also mean that black students do not have the same freedom of expression in terms of the range of social and political events that white students can muster.

During one focus group's discussion of the racialized character of campus policing, the callous actions of some campus security personnel were accented in this detailed commentary from a female student:

> A black students' group had a party. And now, when black students have parties at the student union building, you have to buy tickets downstairs, then you have to go up stairs, get searched with metal detectors. . . . Oh, along with your ticket, they put these things around your wrists, and it was a plastic cuff. . . . And they put it on, and you can't take it off without cutting it. You have to cut it, you can't break them like you used to. . . . So plastic cuffs, they put it on me, O.K. So I got searched and whatever, and I got in there. And then I was like playing around with this thing on my arm right so all of a sudden it went too tight. My hand is turning purple. . . . All these like football players trying to like pull it off my arm, so all of a sudden my arm starts bleeding. I cut myself so I'm freaking out. And everybody says, "Run downstairs, get it cut off." So I'm like, "Please cut this thing off my arm," and I said "it's bleeding." And they're like, "Oh, my God, oh my God." So they get it cut off my arm, it's probably . . . around two o'clock.

After this painful incident, she then recounted going back upstairs to the party:

> They've already seen me leave; I've created an incident here; everybody's looking at me from upstairs. So I get ready to go in, and the guy goes, "Where're you going?" The policeman, a white man—(And that's another thing, why are all the policeman in this state that have to regulate these parties, in the first place . . . always white? It's like, can't you find some black ones for the night, some security [guards]?) They hate being there, so he said "You can't go anywhere without a band on your arm." And I was

like, "You just saw me." And he said, "You have to have a ticket and a band." I said "I have my ticket stub, you know, I'm all right." . . . I said "My arm is bleeding." And he's like, "You can't go back in there.". . . so he put another one back on me. And it freaked me out. I was like, "What's wrong, why?" And then when I got upstairs, and I told the one guy that was sitting there . . . it's bleeding, he was like, "Well, why did you put it back on?" I said, "Because that man told me I couldn't get in there without it." And he's like, "Well you're bleeding; you shouldn't have put one back on." He said these are plastic cuffs. He said we use these, we use these cuffs at the police station. . . .

The personal impact of mistreatment and insensitivity is evident in this account. The student's pain includes not only the physical injury inflicted by the cuffs put on by security personnel but also the callousness of the rule enforcement. Also, the broader issue of the lack of black security personnel is underscored in her commentary to the focus group. While the direct victimizers in these student accounts are campus security personnel, higher-level university administrators appear as background participants because they allow, if not mandate, the differential policing. Indeed, this and similar accounts from the students suggests that some white officials on this campus give special attention to the control and restriction of African American students. As we noted previously, this special surveillance is common at predominantly white colleges and universities across the nation.

Security problems on campus are compounded by problems some students face when they leave the campus to go to nearby clubs, as in the example from a female student:

[Blacks] tried to have a club . . . [on a nearby street off campus]. Not as close to the school, but it was still part of our area. It's called the "Western." . . . We were just there. And we were waiting, and it was the same type of atmosphere. . . . It was the town police. . . . And they came out, and I mean the club was over. And black people have a tendency to gather after events so we gathered—and this has happened at . . . [the local club]. They brought dogs and that scared me—I've never seen that before in real life. I mean you see it on TV. It reminds me of the sixties. . . . I'm like, "Oh, my God." Nobody's doing anything, but leaving. Like most of us didn't have cars, so we piled up in cars. And they had the dogs out there. It was a club you know. What do you want us to do? That freaked me out.

This police overreaction recalls in the student's mind police brutality of the past—the police dogs used on sixties' civil rights demonstrators.

Legal segregation ended, and the civil rights revolution occurred, before most of the students in the focus groups were born. Yet, this present-day encounter with local police officers resonates with the collective memory of African Americans. This student made mental connections between her situation and certain racist events in recent African American history. The phrase "that freaked me out" makes her anxiety and distress clear. Again, there is a psychological state of siege as black students face "the white law" in a campus environment that should be friendly and hospitable, but isn't.

This account suggests that near-campus spaces may often be no more hospitable for African American students than a white-dominated campus. Recently, at the Indiana University of Pennsylvania black students pressed for a boycott of a commercial mall where black students were reportedly harassed. In one incident, a black student waiting for a bus was arrested by local police, who called him "boy" several times.[17] That problems with whites just off campus are common is underscored in a mid-1990s survey of black students at a large, mostly white Southern university. Four in ten of the black students there reported having encountered discrimination by whites off campus, many in the first few semesters.[18] Moreover, in a 1993 survey of "ethnic minority" (mostly black, Latino, and Asian) students at the University of Nevada, over half said they had faced discrimination by people in the local community.[19] Not surprisingly, many students of color come to feel unwelcome both on and off their college campuses.

Conclusion

African American students at majority-white educational institutions periodically experience racial insensitivity, hostility, and discrimination perpetrated by a range of campus personnel, as well as off-campus shopkeepers and police officers. As we see in our student and parent accounts, the role of the perpetrator is played by whites who fail to pay serious attention to what black students have to say, to what they are doing, or to their personal or group circumstances. The police officers who disparately check cars occupied by black students, the dining hall manager who notices only the illegitimate presence of a black man and not that of white men, the officer who insists that a known student must wear a painful arm band, and the advisers who respond differentially and with inadequate advice—these whites share in a failure to pay attention to black students as human beings equal to whites. The motivation of the whites is likely quite varied, and may range from ignorance and racial insensitivity to blatant racial stereotyping or hostility.

Yet again, the concept of human recognition—which encompasses the idea of visibility and which is denied by invisibility—is an important tool to use in thinking about these examples of racial interaction. In the student encounters with white staff members, we again observe a lack of recognition of the full humanity of the black students. For instance, when white advisers fail to recognize the legitimate questions of black students, they typically fail to explore student concerns adequately and give intelligent or appropriate advice. Even more destructive is the realization on the part of the students that they are not being validated as really belonging to the university community or as sentient, intelligent human beings with significant concerns. The lack of human recognition the students detect in some white peers, teachers, advisers, police, and other campus personnel is serious, for it teaches major lessons about neglect, exclusion, or self-worthlessness.

In addition to the damage to the students' self-esteem and self-identity, there are other tangible costs. We have seen how racially biased or insensitive academic advising is damaging to African American students. Take the example of channeling. At many colleges and universities, African American students, as well as other students of color, are sometimes directed away from certain academic disciplines, such as the physical sciences or engineering, by their advisers because of racial assumptions and stereotypes. This problem with channeling is reportedly common on white-dominated campuses. For instance, students of color recently interviewed at Princeton complained of academic advisers who suggested "they should not take certain courses of study or aspire to certain professions because members of their ethnic group generally do not have the skills to excel in that area." These Princeton students also said they faced "academic advising and work assignments" that channeled them into courses of study that dealt "solely with minority issues."[20] Such actions by university faculty and other staff members have the effect of further marginalizing the black students.

Not all staff actions which have harmful effects are motivated by racial animosity or stereotyping. Some are the consequences of university campuses being large, bureaucratic, and impersonal. Although all students at large institutions face being treated like numbers, the destructive effects of impersonal treatment are accentuated for students who have had recurring experiences that accent their racial marginality on campus. Advising mistakes can seriously impede the progress of, or affect the retention of, African American students, since as a group they have fewer economic and campus information resources than do white middle-class students. In addition, because they are less likely than white students to have college-educated parents, black college students often do not have as much prior information and advice about coping with the educational problems of a college environment.

On most predominantly white campuses there seem to be few signs of change. White administrators at the universities we have studied do not meet collectively and regularly with black students and faculty to seek ways to break down white ignorance, insensitivity, and discrimination on campus. As a rule, whites in authority at most chiefly white campuses do not meet with their black constituents on problems of campus racism until there is some type of campus protest. The case of Rutgers University president Francis L. Lawrence illustrates this point. Lawrence's comment that African American students do not have the "genetic hereditary background" to do well on SAT tests was protested by African American students in a number of campus demonstrations early in 1995. Otis Rolley, the black spokesperson for the Rutgers United Student Coalition, the umbrella group for the student organizations responsible for the campus protests, told a reporter, "The important thing in all this is that students do not have the power or a voice that is heard so that they can control racism. So occasionally we have to take over buildings and gyms simply to be heard. We are invisible, understand, simply because people refuse to see us."[21]

6

ISSUES OF RECRUITMENT AND RETENTION
"If They Do Anything, It's to Encourage You to Leave"

The Challenge

As a rule, the problems of recruitment and retention affect African American students and other students of color at predominantly white institutions to a considerably greater degree than they affect white students. We group recruitment and retention because they constitute stages in a process that all college students follow. The process begins with some type of self or university recruitment. Then, after admission to college, comes the stage of retention of a student for four or more years, retention that depends on a student's performance and on related factors of academic and social support. If students are retained, they graduate and begin to enjoy the substantial privileges U.S. society generally grants to those with college credentials.

The percentage of black high school graduates going to college increased from the late 1960s to the late 1970s. By 1972 some twenty-seven percent of black high school graduates were enrolled in college, compared with the somewhat higher figure of thirty-two percent of white high school graduates. By the late 1970s the proportions enrolled in college were nearly the same. However, over the 1980s and 1990s the racial differential widened. In 1993 some forty-one percent of whites and only thirty-three percent of blacks were enrolling in college.[1] In addition, once in college, the retention rate for African American students is considerably lower than that for white students. Recently, Arnold Mitchem, executive director of the National Council of Educational Opportunity Associations, reported that among students enrolling at four year colleges and universities the graduation rate after six years was fifty-six percent for whites but only thirty-two percent for African Americans. Moreover, reviewing the colleges in one large state, Illinois, he noted that the college graduation rate for students of color eight years after high school was half that of whites.[2]

Explaining the problems of black participation in higher education, some analysts have accented the rising costs of a college education and the significant decline in financial aid, both factors that disproportionately affect families of modest means. Other commentators point to the alternative of good jobs in the military. Yet others emphasize the allegedly anti-educational values of black individuals, families, and communities. As we noted previously, some prominent white analysts have argued that the reasons for black educational problems lie substantially within the black family or black community.[3] Significantly, most white analysts ignore or downplay the role of white racism *within* predominantly white colleges and universities in creating and sustaining educational hurdles for African American college students.

In contrast, many African American leaders and community members are critical of the commitment of whites, including white administrators, to recruit and retain black students at traditionally white colleges and universities. In a survey of more than two thousand black students at twenty mainly white colleges in Southern and border states, researchers found that most questioned "the commitment of administrators to their success." Less than half felt the administrations at their colleges made an effort to recruit black students or to help black students once they were on campus. Moreover, only a quarter felt that counseling and advising services were especially sensitive to the needs of African American students.[4]

Recruitment: "For Sure the Athletes"

Judging from student comments in the focus groups, most students were not directly and personally recruited to State University by white alumni, officials, or faculty at the university. In assessing their reasons for choosing State University, the black students did note a variety of factors, such as cost, location, and sports, which helped convince them to matriculate there.

Some of the students in the focus groups noted how sports programs enticed black athletes to the campus:

> Yeah, for sure the athletes, I definitely heard about that. I mean they practically, I hate to say it but spoon feed a lot of the athletes.

Disparate treatment of any kind creates hard feelings. Even when black students get admitted on athletic fellowships, this is not perceived by all black students as an unadulterated honor.

For those black students who were more or less directly and personally recruited, the results were mixed. One student noted the positive impact of university attention:

> When I was a junior in high school, they brought me up here to the school. You know, I went through all the departments, and I met the teachers. I met the president of the school and all that stuff, so that pretty much locked me into going here.

Another male student echoed this view:

> I could say I was recruited because when they came, they sent us a letter. They had minority day, right, and all minority students, black students, were all introduced to the university president at the time. [He] came out and was talking, talking about how we are supposed to be like the smartest class ever to get into this university based on GPA and stuff like that. They showed us around the departments and stuff, and they took us to one of the football games. . . . The thing that got me is that they made that effort to, because I really wasn't planning to go to this university until that time. . . .

Not surprisingly, recruitment strategies work best when the students feel that they are being respected and recognized.

In Chapter 3 we quoted a student who learned about the whiteness of SU's campus from a yearbook that her mother ordered early in her college career. In other comments in the focus groups several students reflected on impressions of the university's racial environment that they received from looking at photos and other material in university brochures. University brochures are important in the decision-making process of students who are not actively recruited, as this comment makes clear:

They didn't actively come out to my school, and say "I'm the representative of the university. We offer that, offer this." I mean they basically did that with the little brochure they sent you with the [packet] that you picked up at your high school.... [The brochures] they send are generic. There you only see white people—you only see one black person in the crowd.

A female student amplified the point about black reactions to the representations in university brochures:

And they'll put that [information on black students] on the literature, and then they'll get more of us to come here. You know, that's how they do it. Because I know when I saw the brochure, and I was looking through it, I saw like a couple black people here and there. Maybe like but one or two. They put two of us in there just to make us feel good. And I'll be turning the page and saying like, where are them black people? I'm turning the page and see a black one, and said, "Okay, start feeling a little better."

Universities are usually thought of as places where words are the coin of communication. Yet pictorial representations in college materials are also part of the campus culture, and they can signal how those in charge see the university socially as well as physically. The tack taken in these materials can make African American students feel, as the latter says, a "little better" about the choice to go to a mainly white university.

Most parents in the focus groups seem to have heard less about the university's recruitment programs than the students have. Many expressed wonder or frustration at the fact that they had not encountered or heard about SU's recruitment programs. When the moderator asked one group what they knew about the programs that State University has in place "to recruit and retain African American students," the immediate response was:

One father: Do they have any?
Group voices: I don't know of any.

The first considered responses to a similar question in another group went this way:

One mother: We should know about them [efforts to recruit] if they are, we should know about it. We should be able to say, they are doing a, b, c, and d, if they really wanted us to know about it. [Another parent: Is the media covering any of it?] That's my [view], you know. If they really wanted us to know, if they really wanted us to know, we should be able to tell you exactly what it is.
Another parent: Even if they are, it's not being exposed.

There were occasional exceptions to this pattern of no information about the university's outreach and recruitment programs. A few parents had heard of some honors or scholarship programs at the State University for students of color, which they regarded as a type of recruitment effort. In addition, one parent found a community-oriented program at SU, but only because of her own efforts:

> This summer I called the State University to find out if they had talented and gifted programs for children, if they had athletic programs for children, because I wanted to send my boy. . . . And they did have programs, but the people, when I called them were, "Well, how did you hear about this program? How do you know about this?" And the price of what it, was what we cannot afford. It was very, very expensive. . . .

This parent makes it clear that community programs can play an important role in interesting black youngsters to consider a predominantly white college, but they need to be publicized and reasonably priced if they are to be successful. At several times, the black students or parents made a point of noting the absence of a service orientation to black communities among white officials who head the state's chiefly white colleges and universities, even to those black communities that lie nearby. The lack of an aggressive and sustained outreach to black communities on the part of predominantly white universities is not unique to State University; it is a problem reported in black communities across the United States.

University plans to recruit African Americans are often undermined by the commonplace image of the university as a "lily-white" place where they are not welcome. One father made the point that recruitment plans are burdened by the weight of insincere practices in the past:

> When I was in high school, I went to a predominantly white school. In fact, there was eleven blacks graduating so it was like—we were just practically all, all white. And when the recruiter came to try to encourage people to go to State University, the guy that showed up, he was very serious: talking about the academics, talking about different fraternities and things of that nature. And sports wasn't the issue. I had work release so I had to leave. . . . I had the time to go to [another] high school to hear the same individual—I thought would be the same individual talking. A whole different package came. We're in a predominantly black school. . . . Different pattern, different dress, different goals, different aspirations—I'm saying, boy, is this the same school? And so I asked the man—he's about forty or so . . . "I saw this same

speech given over at [the mostly white high school], but it's totally different. Is there any particular reason why?"

This parent takes us back to the 1970s. Serious plans to recruit black students today must consider the burden of the recent racial past on black parents and communities. The presentations at the high schools were conspicuously different, a two-faced approach which not only suggests a less sincere effort at the predominantly black school to recruit students for academic programs but also shows how racialized events become firmly embedded in the memories of black parents.

Recent research studies indicate, not surprisingly, that African Americans spend much time thinking about and discussing the ways to improve conditions for people of color in white-dominated institutions. Indeed, African American parents seem very concerned about the meaningful and full desegregation of traditionally white colleges and universities. The parents in the focus groups made numerous suggestions for improving a predominantly white college's recruitment of black students. Some focused on the necessity for white officials to openly acknowledge and work with important institutions in local black communities. For example, one mother noted the relevance of black churches for university recruitment strategies:

> I remember reading something about a black recruitment within the past year, ... [Group laughter] but I think that where it makes its mistake is that it does not make its recruitment known widely, that it doesn't make itself known in the places that blacks go. And in our churches, you know, there should be some kind of recruitment there. In our high schools, there should be real recruitment there.

Another mother expounded on the significance of local schools in black residential areas:

> Maybe [SU could] form equal partnerships with high schools. There are some universities. I think [names another white university] has partnerships with some high schools. I know [names a mostly black university] has partnerships with some high schools where you can take some classes. So maybe if State University did that, or offered tutorials on the high school level where you could meet some of the students. And I'm saying of different ethnic backgrounds, to show you don't have to be African Americans to relate to African Americans on every level. Just to bring a greater presence into the community.

In one focus group a father noted the need for better advertising in the media serving black areas:

> Their PR [people] need to do better work for us in the advertis-
> ing field. Put something on the radio that the young people listen
> to, like a black radio station or something. Advertise on that radio
> station. Advertise on [names another] station or something. You
> know advertise on more Afro-American stations and let them
> know, "Well, hey, that's that school that such-and-such had a
> problem with. And I hear that black people are going there."

Interestingly, these parents are not cynical but suggest practical and
effective ways of reaching African American youth and their parents
with intensified university advertising and other recruitment efforts. It
is a sign of the self-centered or racially biased character of most white
recruitment programs that numerous African American parents in this
and other states have not encountered a white university actively
recruiting students through black churches or black radio stations.
State University has made some recruitment efforts in predominantly
black high schools, but in the parents' view this is not nearly enough.
The presence of university recruiters in more places where African
Americans congregate would deliver a message that State University's
officials wish to recognize and respect black communities.

Interesting too is the mother's brief suggestion that recruiters of
different racial and ethnic backgrounds might come to black communities to show that "you don't have to be African Americans to relate
to African Americans." She clearly had in mind nonblacks who could
be sensitive to the concerns of black communities. This idea, which
was accepted by other parents in that group, suggests two important
points. First, African Americans constitute an important repository of
multicultural values in U.S. society; many African Americans have a
broader perspective on issues of cultural diversity and of human rights
than do white Americans. Most seek a truly integrated society.
Second, white educational institutions which rely only on a few African American staff members to conduct their (usually modest) recruitment efforts in black communities may deliver this message to black
audiences: White administrators do not consider expanding campus
diversity enough of a university priority to spend significant efforts to
train whites to be sensitive and sincere recruiters in African American
communities. Moreover, multiracial recruitment teams would reflect
the reality of the campus, where recruited students will have to relate
to nonblack students, faculty, and staff.

Retention Efforts:
"Well, They Haven't Done Anything"

We have discussed earlier the fact that many white analysts of higher
education do not consider seriously the problem of racial discrimina-

tion in assessments of black student retention at majority-white colleges and universities. Most white analysts have missed the relevance of the white domination of campus culture and bureaucracy to the dropout (push-out) rate for black college students. Indeed, many conventional analysts go so far as to argue that *too much* is currently being done by university administrators in terms of affirmative action and scholarship programs for students of color on their campuses.

Black perspectives on these educational matters are typically quite different. For example, at the University of California (Berkeley), African American students have pressed hard for more black faculty and for stronger academic support programs. As one report there put it, the black students are "challenging the university with a view that if you go and recruit us to come here you also have a responsibility to help provide the kinds of support services that will encourage academic retention and graduation."[5] Like African American students at the University of California and similar universities, the students we interviewed had a markedly different view of racial relations on campus than that of many whites. They did not see much aggressive action on the part of university officials to deal with the persisting crisis of campus racism.

One focus group's first and collective response to the moderator's question, "But what is it that they've done to make sure you stay?" was "Nothing! nothing!" The general feeling can be seen in the comments of this young woman:

> I don't know what they do to keep us here. I think a lot of black students think like, "Dag, I'm a junior. I could transfer." . . . I mean I guess I should have left when I had the chance.

Another student then added: "You don't realize [it] until it's too late. They catch you."

In another group several students developed a line of discussion around their personal efforts and the intensive personal dedication involved in getting to the status of juniors and seniors, as is signaled in one of the first comments: "They haven't done anything. I think it's more of a personal thing why I'm still here." After several other students talked about their own determination and endurance, one male student underlined the point:

> It's like everybody else says; it's a personal thing. That feeling of accomplishment once you get that degree. That's all that matters.

A female student responded to him with "It's too late to turn back now," and yet another student concluded this substantive discussion with a very poignant comment:

I mean every time I walk into an exam I think of it as someone trying to hold me back. It's really a personal accomplishment for me; I think of it that way.

The students cite no evidence of major retention efforts by university personnel. A personal determination to succeed seems to be the primary reason that these young black men and women are able to endure racial and other hardships and complete their university degrees.

The comments of the African American students indicate that most feel little of the esprit de corps that white students seem to have in regard to the SU campus and its dominant culture. The black students are not building substantial positive memories of SU as a place that routinely facilitates their achievements and nurtures them in their personal and academic development. Indeed, several of the black juniors and seniors provided details on why they developed a "siege mentality" as part of their drive to endure and succeed. One female student elaborated on this matter:

If they do anything, it's to encourage you to leave. [Moderator: How so?] I think just the opportunities they offer for black people are just, you know, it's not enough to encourage you to stay. Basically I think that the black students that are still at this university, it's because of perseverance and because of what you want to do, and not because of their encouraging you to stay there. They're doing nothing to encourage you to stay there.

Strikingly, making it through a predominantly white college often becomes a personal crusade for African American students. The language used to describe their academic careers often includes words like "perseverance," "endurance," "battle," and "struggle." Their crusade, clearly, is not made easier by a racial climate that generates recurring thoughts about dropping out or transferring to a black college. The thinking of black students at white colleges and universities needs to be focused on the academic work at hand, yet many of these hardworking students must periodically think through the race-related dilemma of staying in or dropping out, a serious educational dilemma not faced by white students.

Some black students did underscore the importance of campus "minority" offices and policies that supported students of color. One young woman noted both the positive and negative aspects of certain programs for students of color:

They try to put it in the hands of the MSO, which is the Minority Students Office. So they try to put like, let them keep all the black people around. And it's like MSO can do things here and there, but they're such a small organization that it's hard for them to reach all the black people on campus. So some people just feel like they don't fit in.

Later in the discussion she added that there was a limited mentoring program. Most universities like State University rely substantially on "minority students offices" to serve the interests of the students so defined. While these university programs are generally viewed as helpful by black students, these usually modest undertakings do not address the broad range of needs of their target audiences.

Speaking at some length about black student retention, one student assessed critically the role of special programs on the SU campus:

> Retention, that's the biggest problem. They just got a report . . . specifically addressing the retention. Because it's like once they get us in there, they aren't doing anything to keep us in here. They just want us so, sitting here, so they can put it in their book: "Oh yeah, you see we have so and so amount of black people in this school." But once you're . . . in, it doesn't seem like they are doing a whole lot. I'm just talking about this university. There are specific departments, like the minority student office; they have a mentor program where they assign students, like, faculty mentors, and also some get student mentors to try to help them stay. There are other things like the black student organization—they have a . . . program you know that matches up upperclassman with incoming freshman to try to help them with their transition also. But, I think, I guess they are starting to try to do some more stuff than they have been in the past.

The student perception that whites "just want us sitting there" for the record reveals a serious weakness in the university's efforts to transform its structure as a white-centered university. University officials have failed to demonstrate to the African American students that their presence on campus is a matter of recognizing them as human beings equal in significance to white students.

Aid Programs for Black Students: "They Are Kind of Role Models"

In recent years there has been much debate about affirmative action programs at predominantly white colleges and universities. Some college administrators at such places have developed a number of modest programs to recruit African American students, and once they have matriculated, to retain them on their campuses. On some campuses one attempt at recruitment and retention is a modest fellowship or scholarship program limited to African Americans or to students of color taken as a group. However, the media discussions on this matter have been so distorted that in our experience many whites assume a much larger proportion of African American students on their campuses are receiving some type of special race-based aid than is the case. We have already noted white student comments to this effect at some colleges and universities. Yet this exaggerated notion is but another sincere fiction whites use to construct a world in which they are not culpable for racism or, at a minimum, in which there is no longer any need for new action to redress discrimination.

Significantly, in a recent year U.S. Department of Education statistics indicated that only about 45,000 students of color benefited from racially exclusive scholarship aid—about 3.5 percent of all students of color in U.S. colleges and universities.[6] In spite of the utility of these aid programs in making students of color feel welcome on campus, fewer than one in twenty get such college scholarships. During the early 1990s the George Bush administration investigated racially based scholarship programs with an eye toward eliminating them; this investigation was a major concession to the white myth that there is widespread "reverse discrimination" against white college students on financial aid programs. In addition, a Supreme Court decision upheld a lower court decision that knocked down a racially based scholarship program at the University of Maryland.[7] This and other conservative court decisions are likely to reduce further the already token number of students of color on special scholarships. Importantly, U.S. Department of Education statistics noted above clearly suggest that the real problem is not "reverse discrimination" in aid programs but insufficient scholarship and other financial aid for all students from low- and moderate-income families, including many students of color.

Indeed, this financial aid situation has worsened since the 1980s, as state and federal budget-cutters have forced many colleges and universities to reduce student aid programs. Recently, the Republican-controlled Congress has moved to make significant reductions in federal programs, cuts that will have a serious impact on students from low- and moderate-income families. In the 1994–95 academic year six million students received some $31 billion in federal aid, which represented three quarters of all aid provided to college students. Moreover, in 1995 about 3.8 million students got federally subsidized loans. Data on family incomes of student aid recipients indicate that half the federal loans go to low-income families, those earning less than $17,000 annually.[8]

In November 1995 a cut of $10 billion in college programs was part of a House plan for federal budget reductions, with a lesser cut of $5 billion embedded in the corresponding Senate plan. Estimates of the impact of such large reductions on various colleges and universities suggested that a fifth or more of college students might be seriously affected, and in some cases the proportions might be substantially higher. As of this writing, it is unclear whether these major cuts will actually be implemented. President Bill Clinton has said he will veto large cuts, and there have been protests from both students and college administrators across the country. Students have conducted demonstrations and petition drives against the cuts in states from North Carolina to Colorado and Maine. For instance, students at Lewis-Clark State College in Maine constructed a tent city on campus to protest the cuts, thereby suggesting that the aid reductions would create a new "Depression," particularly for students from moderate-income families.[9] The planned destruction of student aid programs will reduce even more the ability of students from low- and moderate-income families to attend college. And the impact will be greatest on students of color, particularly African American students.

Like other universities across the nation, SU has a variety of state and federal aid programs for its students, including programs for moderate-income students and a few programs for students of color. We asked the students and parents in the focus groups about their views of one small fellowship program for black students, a program designed to attract highly talented students to the university. (The student focus groups did not include any of the fellowship students.) In their comments some students in the groups felt that the fellowship program was too small and did not cover nearly enough students. Generally, the students felt that fellowship programs for black students had a good impact on other black students and should be expanded. Reflecting on the impact of such aid programs, one student articulated the view that the special fellowship students were much like other good students:

> I don't think it has any negative impact on the black students who are not [in the program]. Because I have some of them in my classes, and I mean they have the same brain wavelength. And you can study with them. And they don't know things that you know, and the same goes vice versa.

In the group discussions some students noted how the special fellowship students and other honor students become good academic role models for the others. One student expressed his view in this manner:

Definitely a positive effect because you see that the brother's making it, and it helps you out. It's like a peer role model. If you see someone else getting up, then you say, "Well, I can do the same thing."

One young woman agreed that the effect of the fellowship students was positive, but then noted how all the African American students can be role models in their communities:

I do think to an extent they are kind of role models. Because like, I volunteer with little kids and to them it's kind of neat because you do feel that they look up to you and it just, I don't know. Not necessarily that they are personal role models [for me], but for somebody else that they are.... But then at the same time you are too.

Another student then reiterated the point that all the black students are role models for younger people. Special fellowship programs for students of color draw attention to student achievements and can play some role in the encouragement of the black students' self-esteem. This social encouragement is frequently lacking, as we have demonstrated in earlier chapters, in the sociocultural milieu of mostly white universities. Without a few supportive programs like blacks-only fellowships, the majority of the black students indicated that they would feel even less welcome than they do now. As one young scholar put it: "It is a message like 'We don't want you here.'"

The views of black parents about the financial support programs were similar to those of the black juniors and seniors. While a number of the parents in the focus groups said that they were unaware of specific aid programs at State University, they were positively impressed with the idea of scholarship programs for black students. One father explained that the implementation of a program for black students would alter his view of a predominantly white educational institution:

The knowledge—now that I know that there's a scholarship program like that—it would be kind of make me put this university back [in consideration], when I would have just thrown it away, but back again. I'd say, maybe they're doing something.

Reflecting on the impact issue, one mother noted that some of the black honor students had served as important role models in a local community:

When I used to go to the honors ceremonies, that annual honors ceremony, there was a large number of the fellowship students who started mentoring programs in the community or tutoring programs. Their activity starts from their freshman year almost where they're involved with, not just the college community, their involvement is expanded to the community at large. And they're taking it to their home community and they're sort of beacons that people can look to and say, "Hey that's possible." So there is some value to the school and to the individual long before they get the sheepskin.

Another parent also accented the role that black scholarship students can play in the larger black community:

They could be also mentors for younger kids coming in because now children are going at the middle school age, or whatever, and visiting a university. And, you know, they're not being offered a sports scholarship, but they're there because of their academics. And, you know, we get a bad rap, but we have a lot of very intelligent black children out here. And a lot of them . . . run up against blocks when it comes to scholarships, and they don't know how in their mind they are going to go to college.

If they become active in local communities, black college students can give young children and high school students the idea that they too may be able to attend a majority-white university like SU. However, the last comment reveals that African Americans must still contend with the myths and stereotypes that white Americans hold about black intelligence and academic abilities.

White Views of Support Programs: "Whites Hate It Any Time They Do Anything for Us"

In the group discussions the black students discussed white reactions to aid and support programs for black students. Several hoped that whites who found out about black honor or scholarship students might change their minds about black people generally:

If someone finds out you did something—even the [white] girls I was living with would say, "Oh you're in the honors program?" Like they tried to be nice to me. I'm like, "Don't you try to be nice to me now, you fools." Then they think maybe you're not so dumb. [Another student: Right. Maybe you're kind of one of them. You're one of them.] Yeah, like maybe you can be with us.

The importance of human recognition is expressed in this account. In this case the recognition is for not being "so dumb." This honor student feels she is finally being acknowledged for her scholarly accomplishments by white students around her, although she questions their motivation. Changes in white students' ignorance about black students' intellectual accomplishments may lead some to alter their views and, perhaps, to some degree recognize the value of black students and associate with them.

In a parent focus group one mother began with a comment on the dangers of the white campus for black students, then later made a statement about the potential influence of the very talented black students on white students:

> We all have to go out and work in the white world, and so we might as well start in college. The child, if that school is right for them—it's not right for everybody—but the one that thinks that's where they want to go because they want to graduate from the school of journalism or business or whatever. Then I think the benefit is to them [the black honor and scholarship students] because they're going to get an excellent education. I think that if they can achieve there, the benefit is to other students that are also there.... And I think there's some benefit to all that. And the white students to interact and see that, yes, we're just as good as you are, OK.

In an earlier chapter we saw how the parents were concerned about the proper fit between a particular black student—and his or her talents and abilities—and a particular college or university. This parent links that idea to the choices of the most academically talented students, whose decisions once on campus have implications not only for themselves but also for the whites with whom they come in contact.

Still, a number of the black parents and students felt that special honors or fellowship programs for black students can create an unfavorable impression in the minds of many whites because of ingrained group stereotypes, a point one mother underscored:

> They hate [it] any time they do anything for us that's special—when it really isn't special.... It causes hostility and causes bad feelings and friction because the white kids resent that we're getting this special attention.

Also thinking about white reactions, one father emphasized how whites tend to tag successful black students as "exceptions":

> I'm concerned with your statement that these merit students are causing whites to break down stereotypes. To me all they're doing is creating themselves as an exception to the white folk.

> The perception still exists—they just no longer fit it. . . . They may be doing something individually, but whites are putting them in another category. Their perception of blacks has not changed. [Another parent: They need to educate, they need to have a special program to educate the white students. That's who they need to educate. Not us.] The whites will be the first to tell those kids, "Well, you don't fit the mold that I thought black kids are. You're different."

This father hints at the issue of black students' assimilating to the white campus culture. One research study at a mostly white Midwestern university found that black students who were successful in securing degrees in reasonable time tended to be the most assimilated to white middle-class culture. The majority of these successful students had attended white high schools and lived in white or mixed neighborhoods. The study reported that most of these black students had learned to value interaction with whites more than with blacks. Follow-up discussions with the black students found this was so because of the black students' assumptions about whites' information and knowledge about academic and professional success.[10]

Having to be much like whites in order to be successful in white worlds, including the world of the white campus, can have very serious consequences. The dangers from putting on the "white mask" can run the gamut from frustration to suicide. Indeed, a few years ago one of the nation's most talented young black journalists, Leanita McClain, committed suicide. The winner of several journalism awards and the first African American to serve on the *Chicago Tribune*'s editorial board, McClain commented in several of her writings on the painful problem of being black in a white world. African Americans in a white world must "consciously choose their speech, their laughter, their walk, their mode of dress and car. . . . They learn to wear a mask."[11]

Some of the students that we interviewed were concerned with the negative image many whites held about certain programs for African American students. One student noted the curious "wishes" expressed by some whites she met:

> I think that white people think that any type of scholarship given to black people is a handout and not an achievement no matter what they achieve to get that scholarship. Because I remember when I first got here most of my friends, the people I date anyways, were on financial aid, and white people always think that's a handout or our SAT scores are not as high as theirs. And we just got in. "I wish I was black," you know, "I could get into any school. . . ." You get that same type of attitude from [white] peo-

ple, and I think like the fellowship students look like another free ride for black people.

The inability of many whites to understand what it is like to be African American in the United States constantly encroaches on black lives. Even though most black college students do *not* get benefits from race-conscious aid programs, they still must bear the pain of white assumptions that black students are getting a "free ride." Other research studies, including our own, have shown that well-educated whites often believe, sincerely, that middle-class African Americans as a group have major economic and educational advantages not available to white Americans because of affirmative action and other governmental programs. This white mythology seems to provide many whites with a convenient way of believing that conditions have improved so much for African Americans in recent years that racism is no longer an important barrier in U.S. society.

Merit and Racial Privilege: Some Critical Considerations

In one group discussion of white attitudes, one student described an important conversation with a particular white student. Her account describes not only white prejudices about black Americans but also the sincere and sometimes strange fictions that many white Americans hold about themselves:

> We were talking about getting into Ivy League schools, and I was saying that most of my friends are like at Harvard and like that. I said, "They're all black and they're all at Ivy League schools." And they're like, she [a white student] goes, "I applied to Yale and Harvard." And she couldn't go. I think she got accepted, but she didn't have the money. And she goes, "Oh she [a black student] probably took my space," or something like that. So I said, "Oh. First of all she was the valedictorian of my school. She's smart whether she's black or white. She's smart. You're saying you think she got in because she was black." She said, "Well, yeah, that's probably why she got in." ... I said, "Well, why would you say that?" She said, "Well I don't know. I guess because black people get all these scholarships just because they're black." I said, "Well then just think of all the jobs you get just because you're white." I mean I've been to like a bank. I was at a bank and this girl was working there who hadn't even gone to college. I know people that have applied for the same position that had like at least some type of college degree, and they didn't

> get the job because they were black. . . . It's like all the things that
> are underlying, [that] white people take for granted, and then yell
> about black people getting stuff.

Even in ostensibly integrated university settings, many whites see the
very presence of black students as something of a novelty and the
product of considerations not having to do with achievement or
merit. In an interview for a University of California (Berkeley) report
on campus diversity, one white student was quite candid: "Every time
I see a Black person, not an Asian, but any other person of color walk
by, I think, 'Affirmative Action.' It's like that's your first instinct."[12]

Recently, students of color at Princeton have complained that
many white students think the former are there only because of "special admissions" and not because of their achievements. The students
of color, high achievers in conventional academic terms, found this
white attitude very surprising.[13] In addition, black students at southern and southwestern campuses have reported that white students
often see them as "affirmative action" students or as athletes, with no
allowance for other possibilities.[14] In the aforementioned Berkeley
report, African American students also reported that they had to justify being on the campus to some whites. In addition, one black student noted that his admission to that university was viewed by whites
at his high school as a result of affirmative action not of his achievements. Moreover, once he matriculated, he had a similar problem
with white students at the University of California campus:

> They try to water it down. . . . I came up here and another white
> friend, you know, he tried to water it down, [he said]: most
> "Black people get in, you know, under Affirmative Action"
> because they don't really get good grades, because they don't
> study or stuff like that.[15]

After interviewing African American students the Berkeley researchers concluded that constantly having "to justify one's right to be on
campus engenders self-doubt and defensiveness."[16] White comments
about black students getting special admission and other unfair privileges seem to be commonplace on traditionally white campuses. They
signal not only the racialized character of campus spaces but also the
sense of privileged entitlement to being at such places that many
whites have held for many decades.

On and off college campuses white status and privilege are often
mistaken for meritorious achievement. We opened this book with a
discussion of the comments of Francis L. Lawrence, the president of
Rutgers University, who reportedly told a faculty group that the

average Scholastic Aptitude Test (SAT) scores for African Americans were lower than those for whites because the former do not have the "genetic hereditary background to have a higher average." In the many public and media discussions of his remarks that followed, many white commentators seemed to assume that the higher SAT average for white high school students was solely or primarily a measure of merit.

In higher education much use is made of paper-and-pencil testing to certify young people as intelligent and able to do well in college. The majority of four-year colleges and universities use scores on multiple-choice tests like the SAT to admit students to undergraduate and graduate programs. Often ignorant of the serious racial and cultural biases built into these tests (and similar "intelligence tests"), many whites assume that the results of this testing reflect only individual merit and personal achievement. Indeed, many uninformed Americans interpret good scores on these tests not only as measures of superior achievement but also of superior intelligence. Such views are frequently coupled with the notion that black students, who as a group often average somewhat lower scores on these tests, are not as meritorious as white students. As a result, whites see the advantages that white students have in the admissions process at colleges and universities as being deserved and solely a matter of personal achievement.

However, the above-average scores of many white students on these tests reflect the accumulated social, economic, and political privileges of white Americans. Several research studies have found that there is a strong correlation between socioeconomic status and scores on SAT and similar graduate-level tests.[17] The sons and daughters of well-to-do people tend to score high on these tests, while the sons and daughters of blue-collar parents, especially of those with low incomes, tend to score much lower. Both the tests and their administration are biased against students from blue-collar backgrounds, who are disproportionately students of color. One can have a good idea of a family's socioeconomic privileges by looking at the SAT scores of its children. Indeed, not only the substance but also the language and testing situations of these paper-and-pencil tests generally favor those from middle-class white families with substantial resources, and often ill-gotten (in part because of past racism) economic wealth, inherited from previous generations.

Significantly, however, the emphasis of many white Americans on multiple-choice-test scores or grades as the best measures for academic admissions is not consistently accented. For example, if one examines the admissions practices of elite Ivy League universities like Harvard, Yale, and Princeton for certain key years over the last two decades, more whites were admitted on *non-merit criteria,* such as "alumni preference," than the total of all African American and Latino students admitted under affirmative action criteria.[18] One study of a Harvard University entering class found that the number of white students admitted under the "alumni preference" category exceeded the total number of all African American, Native American, Mexican American, and Puerto Rican students admitted.[19] Significantly, the use of certain nonmerit criteria such as genealogy has been ruled to be legal by the Office of Civil Rights of the U.S. Department of Education.[20]

Conclusion

The provision of effective recruitment, retention, and scholarship programs is one way that majority-white institutions of higher education can remedy the under-representation of African Americans and other students of color on their campuses and in graduating classes. One value of financial aid and other support programs earmarked for African Americans lies in the fact that they offset to a degree the negative image and milieu of these predominantly white places. Even modest support programs may be taken by African American parents and students as a sign that the black presence is desired on campus, at least by some whites. Given that signs of not being wanted are abundant on these campuses, effective recruitment and retention efforts provide critical symbols of personal and group recognition for African Americans.

Historically, the commitments of many white university officials to recruitment and retention programs for students of color have been reluctant or modest. Plaguing the efforts of traditionally white universities to recruit and retain African American students today is a perception among many African Americans that such efforts are not sincere but are based only on a need to exhibit a few black students to improve student statistics and to dress up a poor racial relations image. As we saw in the focus groups, black parents and students made it clear that this university's attempts at recruiting and retaining black students are very inadequate. In their view an improved outreach by mainly white institutions like State University to African American communities would require a full recognition of African American culture and of black churches and other black community organizations.

Some research shows that well-funded and conscientiously implemented recruitment and retention programs for African American students at predominantly white campuses increase retention and graduation rates. Over the decade of the 1980s, for example, programs to increase the graduation rates of black students at the University of Virginia were reportedly successful, raising the five-year

graduation rate from fifty-eight percent in 1983 to seventy-eight percent in 1989. The latter figure was much higher than the thirty-eight
percent figure for thirty-three universities in a data exchange program
with the University of Virginia. This increase was achieved in part by
making admissions more selective, but it was also facilitated by the
development of substantial university support programs that provided
academic counseling and tutoring, including a peer-advising program.[21] Federal support programs for low-income, first-generation
students, such as the Student Support Services Program, have also
been effective in dozens of colleges across the nation. One research
study found that low-income students who got support from these
federal programs in the form of comprehensive tutoring, instructional
help, and counseling "were more than twice as likely to remain in
college as students without benefit of these services."[22] Unfortunately,
the federal government has so far provided modest funding for effective retention programs, and since the early 1990s conservative state
and federal government officials have even tried to reduce or eliminate both support and financial aid programs.

A handful of retention and other support programs that focus only
on black students are not nearly enough to fully integrate and de-
racialize predominantly white campuses, a point one black parent
underscored:

> Well, you can't say, well, they [black students] get it [a scholar-
> ship], and that's just going to erase racism in the State Univer-
> sity. . . . The thing is the State University, the attitudes have to
> change, the way people interact with other people. When you go
> to the front office, and someone has to interact with you—you
> interact with that person the way you would interact with anyone
> else. You interact with a student just like you would interact with
> anyone else. I feel that it's a lot more complex than giving a
> scholarship. . . .

From an African American perspective, even the best recruitment and
retention efforts on behalf of African American students need to be
supplemented with efforts to change the ingrained character of white
thinking and acting in regard to racial matters.

The full integration of traditionally white institutions of higher
education will have to be a two-way street. It will mean more than
the one-way assimilation of African American students to a dominant
white campus culture. Two-way integration means that white administrators, faculty members, staff members, and students listen carefully
to African American students and parents, individually and collectively, and make major adjustments in their own attitudes and per-

spectives, as well as alterations in discriminatory practices in all areas of campus life.

College and university "integration," in the terms defined by white powerholders, has not worked. Perhaps it is time to try a democratic approach in which all voices, including those of African American students and parents, are seriously recognized and considered. Today, even the white commitment to one-way integration is on the wane. In one focus group, a mother noted this oscillation in white policy toward African Americans:

> At first everything was segregated. Then they wanted to give us all this stuff for the black people, and I think they called it "affirmative action" or something. And now it's like, "No we can't do this anymore. Take this away." So it's like they always want to keep us in this little space. You're never gonna get further. . . . It's like, "Hold it." . . . "Hold it. This has to stop."

RACISM IN HIGHER EDUCATION
The Need for Change

Education is seen by most Americans as a major vehicle for individual, familial, and collective progress. A high school diploma is now seen as the birthright of all Americans. In contrast to most European countries, in the United States a college education is often said to be within the reach of every child with the ability to do well. Strong egalitarian ideals are expressed in the best traditions of the U.S. system of higher education.

Yet, in practice, few colleges and universities throw their doors open to all those who meet reasonable standards of admission. In the United States higher education actually confers privileges "only to the few who can take advantage of them."[1] Higher education is widely considered to be only for those who have the abilities to master the complex matters that are studied in its learning centers, for those who are academically qualified. This type of screening for talent need not be undemocratic so long as the supportive stimuli and socio-economic environments, the financial and human investments, and the recognition required to elicit the natural talents in all people are distributed equally throughout the society. We know that this equalization of environments, resources, and opportunities is a very difficult task for any society to achieve or even to undertake. It is certainly a task that most U.S. policymakers have shied away from for centuries, the profession of venerable ideals notwithstanding.

Racial barriers of the kind documented in this book are destructive of the ideal of a university as a diverse and tolerant institution with an open door for all who make the grade and have the ability for higher learning. Racial discrimination in education, which was massively and legally enforced before the 1960s and which is still practiced in many covert or informal ways today, undergirds the special privileges and perquisites U.S. society reserves for white Americans.

Both inside and outside institutions of higher learning, there has been a widespread attack on the gains made by African Americans since the 1950s. We see this attack in federal and state governments backtracking on affirmative action and moving away from the rigorous enforcement of antidiscrimination laws. We notice it in the weakening or abandonment of college and university programs for African American students, sometimes at the behest of federal and state courts. We observe it in the recent sale of hundreds of thousands of copies of books questioning affirmative action, antidiscrimination laws, and even the intelligence of African Americans and other people of color.[2] We note it in the increase in racist rhetoric of some white politicians and talk show hosts and in the multiplying of white supremacy organizations.

In recent years the United States has moved backward from its longstanding commitment to "liberty and justice for all." In our view this is the wrong direction if this nation is to survive and thrive in the next century. Instead of reaction and retrogression, U.S. educational and other societal institutions require bold, realistic, and thorough desegregation and integration policies that recognize and represent the views and values of African Americans and other people of color. So far, both educational desegregation and societal desegregation have mostly been defined and implemented by white policymakers, many of them with weak or no commitments to racial change. For that reason, their policies are, with a few exceptions, miserable failures. In our view the only viable strategy that does not lead to the racial-ethnic balkanization and increasing polarization of the United States is one that extends and takes seriously the best of our democratic ideals—by giving all Americans full recognition and a serious and powerful voice in the shaping and governance of all U.S. institutions, including colleges and universities.

The Agony of Educational Choices

The black parents we interviewed are "all American" parents who are very concerned for the future of their children. In the focus groups black parents often reveal they are no different from white parents who seek the best in opportunities for their children. A good education in a supportive setting is an indispensable part of human dignity in today's world. Black parents dream of and work hard for their children, and many seek an advanced education as a step up for them. No racial or ethnic group has been more committed to achieving the American dream of equal opportunity and success through education and hard work than African Americans. Some white stereotypes notwithstanding, the behavior and achievements of most African American parents and their children reveal a strong commitment to the value that each person should work hard and get a good education in order to secure the rewards offered by this society. However, in spite of this firm commitment, African Americans still cannot secure the full promise of the American dream.[3] According to the accounts of the parents and the students in our focus groups, legitimate black dreams of education and social mobility are being blocked by serious racial barriers at State University and other predominantly white colleges and universities.

The accounts of stereotyping, hostility, and discrimination presented by the black parents and students in our group interviews are drawn from their experiences and those of their peers. Black students on the predominantly white campus of State University report a different world from that described by those white scholars and commentators who have played down the persistence of racial hostility on college campuses. The African American students with whom we talked live in the world of a white campus culture, and they report an environment filled with racial obstacles and hurdles created not only by other students but also by white instructors, other staff members, and security personnel.

These racial hurdles vary in their character and consequences, but all are troubling or painful. Some are obvious, such as attempts to restrict black access to certain academic programs. In Chapter 4, for example, we noted that our students, as well as those at other major universities, reported problems with academic advisers who suggested that they should not take certain courses of study because African Americans do not have the skills or talent to excel in these areas. Other racial barriers, or their consequences, are less obvious. In Chapter 4, for example, we reported that black students do not seek advice from, or make role models of, the numerous white faculty members who are racially insensitive or prejudiced. As a result, many secure less information about the academic enterprise and get less of the mentoring that makes for satisfying and rewarding academic careers. Moreover, in Chapter 3 we suggested that the years spent at a university like SU typically mark a period during which most white college students can easily make friends who are important at the time and with regard to their later careers and lives. The failure of whites to foster a campus climate where cross-racial friendships can flourish not only limits black students' academic lives but also handicaps them in their later careers.

The students we interviewed are not unusual in facing racist barriers and hurdles. We have cited studies at numerous other colleges and universities that reveal campus climates to be so seriously racist that they interfere with the academic success, social adjustments, and personal development of many African American students and other students of color. For example, a 1990s report on the racial climate at the University of California (Berkeley) noted that black students "talked most starkly about the problems of academic adjustment at Cal in terms of their high visibility in classes, the sense that they were subjects of scrutiny and silent discrimination by professors, TA's, and other students."[4]

Numerous national commentators see black problems at mainly white universities as primarily a matter of poor preparation, a lack of intelligence, weak character, or family problems among black students. However, our data demonstrate that this view misses the obvious cause of many black problems on majority-white college campuses. Most African American students, including those with top grades, have some difficulties in coping with the unwelcoming climate of these college campuses. As a result of campus racism, many students must endure anguish, pain, and repressed rage, and many face the *agonizing dilemma* of enduring this suffering or dropping out of college. Alien and hostile campus environments are a major reason for the dropout (push-out) problem of African American students.

Significantly, this agonizing dilemma is not faced by white students. White students face problems at college, such as the impersonality of university bureaucracies or the callousness of professors oriented more to research than teaching. Generally, white students not only do not face the hurdles of overt racism, but they also do not face the accentuation of the problem of bureaucratic impersonality that racism often creates. Recall, for example, the University of California report that noted that the impersonality of large educational institutions is "heightened for anyone who . . . experiences his/her situation as marginal."[5]

Like the students, most of the parents we interviewed in the focus groups do not see a friendly or consistently receptive environment for African American students at places like State University. They too perceive an array of racial barriers from many whites to student access, self-esteem, achievement, and academic success. As a result of this knowledge and experience, black parents also face agonizing decisions about sending their children to mostly white campuses and about recommending these campuses to other black youth.

As we discussed in Chapter 2, African American parents worry about whether a predominantly white college is the best place academically and socially for black children. As a solution for the racist barriers at such colleges, they sometimes suggest that a black college or university is a much more supportive place and should be carefully considered or chosen. The parent focus groups are replete with evidence of their agonizing decisions. Take, for instance, this statement from one very concerned mother:

> Then, when I finished high school, I was going to go to a black college. And I regret right now that I didn't do it. I went to a city college in New York, and I'm really sorry that I did that. Because I don't think . . . and you are talking about State University . . . I don't think that you get the same kind of supports that you get in a black school. [A black father adds] You don't. [Then, another mother adds] Life-lasting friendships, and associations from the black schools.

The discussion continues in this vein. Note that white college students seldom face the problem of giving up significant social support and normal participation in everyday campus activities just to be students in good academic programs.

The parents sometimes talk specifically about this matter as a "dilemma," as in this parent's comment about a daughter who was trying to choose a college:

> What undergrad is supposed to do is a factor. And my daughter was very set on a black university, where many members of my family have gone. And I wanted her to go there. But I also knew that she was going to make connections in college that will last for her life. And the people you spend your undergrad with very often are the CEO's of tomorrow. So it was a dilemma. Do I want her to identify with who she is ethnically, or do I want her to start the groundwork for her future career? By meeting the quote, unquote, "right people." And I tried to give her the pros and cons of both.

Another mother used similar terminology:

> And I think another thing is you want your child to sort of find themselves. I want my daughter to find herself at a black institution. But at the same time understanding and realizing what she's

> going to be faced against further down the road. So you're in a
> dilemma. You really don't know if you should send your child to
> a white institution or a black institution.

A parent's desire that a child find herself or himself as a person in college is a legitimate goal. This requires a supportive environment that
helps create a strong self-image and healthy self-esteem. The agonistic
dilemma and struggle of the black parents and their college-bound
children shows the personal and family consequences of an academically excellent but still racist reputation and climate at State University. Moreover, in an earlier chapter we underscored the point that,
unlike white parents and students, black parents and their children
often confront a poor racial climate at the public universities which
the parents help finance with their taxes. Black parents, and thus black
communities generally, do not benefit as much as they should from
these important educational institutions.

As we have seen, the poor racial climates at predominantly white
colleges and universities force many parents and students to consider
black institutions of higher learning. African American parents have
long been aware that black colleges have advantages for the personal
and academic health of black children. For many decades historically
black colleges have graduated a disproportionate share of all black college graduates, although the proportion of black students going to
black colleges has declined over the last three decades. In 1968 eight
in ten African Americans receiving college degrees got them at black
institutions. This proportion declined significantly, to less than one-
third, over the next few decades as black students moved into predominantly white colleges and universities. Today, although black
institutions make up just three percent of the nation's 3,200 colleges,
they graduate twenty-seven percent of African Americans receiving
college degrees.[6]

Sociologist John Butler has argued that black colleges have pro-
duced a disproportionate number of the nation's black professionals
and business people.[7] Other analysts of black colleges have recently
estimated that more than three quarters of black Ph.D.s, army officers,
federal judges, and doctors went to black colleges for their undergraduate work.[8] Moreover, other research explains why black colleges are
so effective in producing graduates. For example, psychologist
Jacqueline Fleming has reported on a study of 2,500 black students in
fifteen colleges and universities. She found that black students who
went to black colleges did better than those at white colleges because
they had greater social support.[9] In Chapter 2 we cited other research
that corroborates this finding. Black students at historically black colleges average greater relative academic gains than those on white cam-

puses because of the more supportive academic and social environment at the black college campuses.[10]

Nonetheless, today about eight in ten black college students go to
majority-white colleges and universities, and this proportion seems
likely to remain that large in the foreseeable future. There are only
one hundred or so predominantly black colleges and universities left
in the United States, and they only enroll a minority of African
American students. In recent years that enrollment has grown somewhat, as black students at white colleges have left and other students
who might have gone to mostly white schools changed their minds.
Unfortunately, the federal courts have created a situation that fosters
the dismantling of many black colleges. At the very time of this resur-
gence of interest, a number of the black colleges and universities are
under threat of extinction. For instance, federal court decisions to
force several Southern states to take aggressive action to dismantle
their still largely segregated university systems have threatened the
existence of a number of historically black colleges and universities.
The response of white state officials to the court decisions has frequently been to close the black schools and merge them with the predominantly white schools.[11] It seems likely that the mostly white
colleges will be places where most African American students get
their college educations for some time to come.

Bringing Major Changes to Higher Education

In recent years a number of African American analysts of the U.S.
racial situation have moved away from the solutions of desegregation
and integration, which they view as failures, to emphasize the creation and use of African American institutions. For instance, the emi-
nent African American scholar Derrick Bell, once optimistic about
racial desegregation, has argued that racism is so fundamental that
African Americans will never gain equality with white Americans.
Whites have made a few modest changes, such as passing unenforced
laws and allowing a few blacks into professional and managerial positions, but these are insufficient and fleeting.[12] In addition, the distinguished African American law professor Roy Brooks, in the past a
staunch supporter of integration strategies, has moved to a position
accenting "limited separation." While still supporting the ideal of
integration, which is not working in his view, Brooks argues that vol-
untary racial separation can create a more nurturing environment for
many African Americans and must be developed alongside attempts at
integration. Brooks has in mind community-created institutions such
as African American schools, special networks of middle-class African

Americans to provide capital for small businesses, and aggressive support for black candidates.[13]

This realism about racial desegregation is based on lucid interpretations of gloomy facts. We agree that until the ideal of racial integration can be made to work, African Americans will have to devise limited-separation and community development strategies to survive under racist conditions. We agree that tokenism and the good will of a few devoted whites cannot change the structure of modern racism, both on and off college campuses.

Yet we cannot accept the most pessimistic view of the future of racial relations. U.S. history is full of apparently impossible problems that have been redressed or overcome. Even democracy was once thought to be impossible, but much democracy has taken root in this nation. It is our belief that the scourge of white racism can and must be overcome. Nonviolent protests by thousands of black and white Americans in the 1960s and 1970s forced aggressive action against racism and brought about major changes in U.S. racial relations. Today, aggressive action can again be taken by Americans to overcome racial barriers throughout this society. As we see it, the solution is not a single magic bullet, but the inauguration of many new antiracist organizations and protests by people of color and by supportive white Americans. This organization can start with small numbers and build to a nationwide antiracist coalition encompassing people from all the nation's many racial and ethnic groups. These efforts need to generate a new way of antiracist feeling, thinking, and acting by the majority of white Americans and a new social structure of racial-ethnic integration and equality throughout all sectors of U.S. society, including the halls of academia.

In the 1960s and early 1970s people of color made significant progress when many traditionally white colleges and universities initiated programs to recruit more faculty, students, and administrators of color. Largely generated by active protests during and after the civil rights era, the federal government's prodding of colleges and universities to strive for modest affirmative action goals contributed significantly to these increased efforts. Crucial to this progress in higher education since the 1960s have been numerous programs through which the government encouraged predominantly white colleges and universities to take action to desegregate their operations. These included programs like the following: (1) The Department of Education established a number of initiatives and programs designed to increase the participation in predominantly white institutions by researchers who are women or members of underrepresented racial and ethnic groups. It has awarded fellowships to individuals from these groups to facilitate careers in higher education. (2) In making grants for new facilities the Department of Education has given priority to institutions serving a significant number of economically disadvantaged students and students of color. The department has offered grants promoting the education of students of color in the sciences to institutions with at least ten percent of their enrollments composed of traditionally underrepresented students. (3) The departments of Justice, Agriculture, Defense, and Health and Human Services, and the National Science Foundation, and numerous other federal agencies have created small set-aside programs for universities engaged in the goal of greater participation of people of color. Since the 1960s these and similar programs have offered financial support to encourage the traditionally white (and male) institutions to incorporate more women and students and faculty of color into their programs. In spite of their modest scope, these federal programs have generally been successful in getting many institutions of higher education to take a few steps to desegregate, often without their making serious reallocations of funds from university budgets.[14]

Coupled with the hard work and aggressive efforts of the black, female, and other victims of traditional discrimination, these action programs have helped to change the face of higher education. In part because of these and other antidiscrimination efforts, women today represent about half of all undergraduate students and half of the students of law, medicine, and other professional and graduate schools. In addition, the African American proportion of students in traditionally white colleges and universities increased significantly from the 1960s to the 1980s. Helped by government affirmative action programs and related aid programs, the college attendance rate for black high school graduates grew to nearly that of white high school graduates by the late 1970s.[15]

As we see the future, effective solutions for the racism that continues to plague higher education will not come from denying its reality or from parroting the abstract ideal of universities as distinctively open and tolerant places. Serious solutions will likely come in the same way that they have come in the past, from the organized protests of those who suffer racial oppression and from some national white leaders who, finally, respond and realize that substantial resources should be reallocated so as to achieve the principled goals of tolerance, equality, and justice. Without new and energetic affirmative action programs, enforceable antidiscrimination legislation, and real public accountability for civil rights goals, the traditionally white institutions of higher education will continue to be substantial bastions of white interests, power, and privilege.

Between 1964 and 1991 four major civil rights acts made much discrimination illegal, but they have not ended the millions of cases of blatant, subtle, and covert discrimination in business, jobs, housing, public accommodations, and education that African Americans and other people of color face each year. Indeed, existing governmental antidiscrimination agencies (such as the EEOC) are currently too modest and understaffed to remedy this widespread racial discrimination. As a first step toward a solution for the U.S. racial relations crisis, these federal and state antidiscrimination agencies need to be greatly expanded and strengthened to enforce equality of opportunity in all sectors of this society.

In addition, we need specific and aggressive government action in higher education that goes beyond the aforementioned affirmative action programs. There is much more that federal, local, and state governments can and should do. Legislative and executive actions to deny federal funds to colleges and universities that exclude or restrict women and people of color in regard to important campus programs have been relatively effective in bringing colleges and universities into compliance with some governmental guidelines. It is illegal to exclude women or people of color from scholarships and fellowships, work-study opportunities, and access to university facilities such as athletic facilities. The threat of denial of federal funds could be used to pressure the colleges and universities to take action against some of the serious racial discrimination, particularly that by administrators, faculty members, and other college employees, that we have documented in this book. Moreover, research funding agencies, public and private, are in a position to bring about additional changes in racial barriers on most university campuses. Not only do they define research agendas, but they also establish research standards. Consider the recent National Institutes of Health (NIH) guidelines that require the inclusion of women and people of color in research studies involving human subjects.[16] Until recently, researchers normally used all-white samples, asserting cost as the reason for excluding people of color. This common research practice resulted in increased knowledge about white health and much ignorance about the health of people of color and about how therapies might affect the latter differently. In addition, the NIH has pressed for changes at academic meetings by promulgating rules on the inclusion of women and people of color at such gatherings, regulations reflecting the idea that the "value of scientific meetings is enhanced by including participants from all segments of the scientific population ... in both the planning and conduct of such meetings."[17] More actions such as these could help in reducing the white male hold over most research efforts and programs on traditionally white college campuses.

Another area for meaningful government action and legislation is in regard to the enforcement of real merit standards for faculty hiring and promotions at traditionally white colleges and universities. Most of these universities need to be prodded into applying objective standards for faculty hiring and promotions and into meaningfully accounting for their application. White male privilege has thrived under the protection of poorly defined or highly subjective hiring, promoting, and compensating criteria for faculty members. Current legislation often exempts universities from public disclosure rules on critical personnel decisions, making accountability of decisions practically impossible.[18] A cloak of secrecy is an open invitation for the mistreatment of faculty of color. Without the first step of making these standards public, there is little chance for an open debate on the real and potential biases in the use of traditional faculty hiring, promotion, and compensation standards.

Since the 1980s conservative politicians, both at the state and the federal level, have inaugurated a massive effort to eliminate most affirmative action and set-aside programs. This has included an all-out attack on financial aid and other remedial programs targeting racial discrimination in higher education. Moreover, in recent years a more conservative Supreme Court has limited the extent and effectiveness of affirmative government action to redress discrimination, in higher education and in other institutions, against women and people of color. These steps are wrongheaded and ignore the demographic trend toward a U.S. population whose majority will not be white sometime in the next few decades. New political efforts and organizations committed to reversing these reactionary laws and decisions will be necessary if the United States is to meet the many needs of its emerging new majority.

The Need for Bold Leadership on College Campuses

A critical part of the solution for the problems the African American students and parents have identified lies within the colleges and universities themselves. We realize that significant changes will come only with bold and pathbreaking college leadership. A first indispensable step is the one taken in this book: To listen carefully to the voices of those who are being injured by the current state of racial barriers on campus. A second step is to take black students and staff seriously, to recognize them fully as legitimate members of the campus community, and to engage them in a meaningful dialogue directed at integrating campus culture and social structures.

Strong university and societal leadership that has zero tolerance for racial discrimination in any form is an important step. However, if the top academic leaders—the provosts, vice presidents, presidents, and chancellors—take such action, they may be placed in a difficult position. On the one hand, they must establish antidiscrimination guidelines for their mostly white subalterns; on the other, they depend on these subordinates for their cooperation in running the educational enterprise. The top educational leaders need deans, associate deans, and departmental chairs to make day-to-day decisions. It will require top academic leaders with great courage and vision to get lower-level administrators to act aggressively against campus discrimination in all its blatant and subtle forms.

In their turn, the deans and chairs need to exercise strong educational leadership against racial discrimination. At this level the senior administrators may have problems with white faculty members similar to those that the provosts and presidents may have with white deans and chairs. It is difficult to pressure or chastise white faculty at the same time that administrators need to encourage faculty to meet classes, attend committee meetings, and publish research. In most universities the academic departments are headed by a chair, who is usually key in everyday decisions. It is in the departments that courses are offered and staffed, and that requirements for majors are usually determined. Students and faculty, including students and faculty of color, live substantially within campus departments. There they receive many symbolic, psychological, and monetary rewards. As we have seen in our focus groups, in these places African American students and faculty encounter everyday discrimination. Flaws in departmental leadership that affect all students have a particularly injurious effect on students of color, for as a rule they are already marginalized and have fewer resources.

Real changes in racial relations on campus will require that higher-level and departmental administrators develop the vision and courage to pressure faculty and staff members to take significant action against the range of racial barriers in their spheres of influence. For example, most faculty hiring is in the hands of departments. Without substantial pressure from higher administrators, such as a freeze on departmental hiring until the number of black faculty members reaches a critical mass, most white faculty members will likely participate in, or acquiesce to, the maintenance of overwhelmingly white departments. It is also at the level of departments and divisions that much academic advising takes place. The complaints about advising that the students in the focus groups made are typical of those made by African American students at other predominantly white campuses. The solution for this national problem involves recruiting more African American advisers and securing meaningful long-term training for white advisers in relating to the needs and interests of African American students.

Expanding Multiculturalism on College Campuses

A central aspect of the racial relations problem on majority-white college campuses lies in the prejudicial attitudes and self-images of many white students, faculty, administrators, and other staff members. Some critical analysts of racial problems on college campuses make good suggestions for improving diversity but miss the need to deal directly with white hostility to students of color and with actual discrimination.[19] Indeed, some major racial climate reports that document the problems faced by blacks and other students of color miss this point as well. For example, a Michigan State University report cited in previous chapters is typical of many college reports. Its conclusions accent the point that the university's racial environment is "complex and not easily explained," substantially because that climate is created "by an uncountable collection of individual actions and interactions among students, faculty, and staff." The emphasis is entirely on individual actions, and the report closes with no specific suggestions on eradicating racial discrimination other than to note that "small, seemingly insignificant, actions can result over time in major positive changes."[20]

Clearly, the attitudes of many whites must change inside institutions of higher education. Such change will require, among other things, what educator Joyce King calls a liberatory pedagogy. In her research King found that most white students knew very little about, and made no critical ethical judgments about, racial and class hierarchies and inequalities in the existing social order. They showed an unawareness of their own subjective identities and identified strongly with the stratified social order. King notes that "most students from economically privileged, culturally homogeneous backgrounds are generally unaware of their intellectual biases and monocultural encapsulation."[21] At the same time, many of these students strongly maintained that they personally opposed racial prejudice and discrimination.

However, when African Americans actually encounter white Americans in educational settings where there have been few African Americans until recent decades, they usually encounter negative beliefs about black abilities and values and an image, overt or hidden, of white superiority. On and off college campuses, a majority of white Americans share a heritage permeated by racialized thinking. Much of this racial thought is conscious, but some is half-conscious or even subconscious.[22] Research on racial prejudice indicates that a substantial majority of whites are pervaded with a racial consciousness that is more than simple prejudice and stereotyping; it is rather a broader structure of racialized thought, a way of organizing and processing information about whiteness as well as about African Americans and other people of color.[23]

In higher education the philosophy and practice of multiculturalism target problems of white racist thought, ideology, and action. Well-implemented, multicultural policies can provide a major way to incorporate recognition of and respect for the cultures and views of many different peoples into predominantly white institutions. Multiculturalism is a diverse umbrella covering a range of viewpoints, from modest changes in the curriculum to a massive overhauling of the white-controlled apparatus of education. In spite of intense opposition from powerful white (especially white male) elites, a broad movement pressing for expanded multicultural programs and policies in higher education has developed across the United States. This movement is fueled in part by the concerns about justice for African Americans, Latinos, Asian Americans, Native Americans, and other supportive Americans.

New and extensive multicultural programs for college and university campuses are critical for the reduction of white prejudice, hegemony, and privilege. For that reason, many white Americans, particularly those in the political, economic, and educational elites, vigorously oppose strong and aggressive diversity programs. It is not surprising that they wish to retain their often unmerited privileges and ill-gotten power. As we have noted in earlier chapters, opposition to multiculturalism is frequently loud and substantial. Because they do not see racial barriers in U.S. society as major and widespread, even some liberal analysts and commentators argue that there is no need for solutions such as the "heavy artillery of multiculturalism."[24] Authors as ideologically diverse as Allan Bloom, Richard Bernstein, Arthur Schlesinger, and Dinesh D'Souza argue that today U.S. colleges and universities are facing a "radical" revolution of multiculturalism. Schlesinger, for example, views multiculturalism as already dominant at all levels of education and as entailing "an astonishing repudiation" of the idea of "a unifying American identity."[25] Among critics of multiculturalism one also finds the unsubstantiated notion that most traditionally white colleges and universities have implemented numerous required courses that replace white authors, particularly famous European writers, with contemporary authors of color. However, research on college and university courses has discovered that required reading lists are still composed overwhelmingly of authors who are white European or European American. According to the research we have examined, most college and university courses use no writings from women or people of color as required material.[26]

Indeed, one of the goals of multiculturalism is to change this dominance of white male writers in college curricula. The alternative to this white sovereignty is a meaningful pluralism of culture and perspectives, not the "minority dominance" feared by some critics of higher education. An effective multicultural curriculum can signal a definite change in respect for the culture and traditions of African Americans and other people of color. Such multiculturalism would involve a major change in the state of the white mindset now prevalent on many campuses. One or two courses added for cosmetic reasons and relegated to the margins of the curriculum will likely have an offensive effect on students of color. From a strong multiculturalism viewpoint, the cultural diversity and racial-ethnic relations courses must be substantial and at the center of the curriculum. In addition, a strong multicultural orientation in all relevant courses can bring about a dramatic shift in the peripheral position academia usually reserves for non-Anglo cultures and perspectives.

These curriculum changes are not just for the benefit of students and faculty of color. As we noted above, the changes multiculturalism can bring are especially important for whites whose age-old prejudices about people of color and fictions of the white self handicap them in dealing with other people around the globe. The sincere fictions of whites prevent them from operating productively in a racially diverse nation and world.[27] True multiculturalism means mutual learning. The recent *Diversity Project* report at the University of California (Berkeley) concluded that "pluralism in America can only be achieved if everyone does some changing. Every group will need to learn new ways of navigating into territories in which they do not have the power or control to define what is normal. . . . For whites in California, it may sometimes mean learning how to be 'a minority.'" To accomplish the goal of real pluralism each group must "be able to draw upon the integrity of their own cultural experience" and come to see the others "as resources, recognizing different and complementary competencies."[28]

Changing the historical views and memories of white Americans is important to multicultural efforts. The African American educator W.E.B. Du Bois some time ago argued that we cannot settle the question of racial equality in the United States by forgetting the "slave trade and slavery, and the struggle for emancipation" or the "whole cultural history of Africans in the world." Late in his life he strongly asserted that "What I have been fighting for and am still fighting for is the possibility of black folk and their cultural patterns existing in America without discrimination; and on terms of equality."[29] As we interpret it, multicultural programs should work to change the collective memory of white Americans so that they too remember, understand, and feel the pain of the African slave trade and other exploitative and oppressive aspects of the racist history of the United States. From this vantage point, multiculturalism could help whites to acknowledge and understand the cultural contributions of Africans and African Americans to U.S. society and culture. The ability to *recognize,* accurately and empathetically, other people and their histories as legitimate is a critical element of an effective multicultural policy. Moreover, in our view effective multicultural programs and courses should encompass a hard and critical analysis of the power and resource imbalance that underlies U.S. racial relations.

In spite of their "radical" image in much mainstream writing about academia, it appears that the majority of white college faculty are not supportive of substantial and expanded multicultural policies and programs. For example, in the early 1990s the faculty at the University of Washington overwhelmingly voted down a proposal to add *one* cultural diversity course to the university's degree requirements. The required course would have been selected from a list of courses on some aspect of racial relations, ethnicity, gender, religion, or disability. According to an analysis by Ruth Sidel, many faculty members there felt that the course suggestion was part of the hysteria over "political correctness," a threat to the Eurocentric curriculum, or just academically illegitimate. One black student active in lobbying for the requirement suggested that it did not pass because "there are too many white men on the faculty." In his view "a system of white supremacy exists" at the University of Washington.[30] The overwhelming preponderance of whites in university faculties means that the views of people of color often are not recognized or taken seriously. A report at the University of California (Berkeley) noted that while the campus is composed of a majority of students of color, the faculty is still eighty-nine percent white. The report also criticized the "circling of the wagons" of white faculty who are making a "last ditch effort to fend off multiculturalism and diversity."[31]

For this reason many multicultural advocates are pressing for substantial increases in college instructors who are people of color. Major structural changes must be made on college campuses, including the composition and character of college faculties. An indispensable first step in eradicating certain types of discrimination on mainly white college campuses is to increase the proportion of faculty of color. Their currently low numbers are testimony to the lack of commitment to educational equality at most traditionally white colleges and universities. In the social space of the university, the position of faculty member is one of the most visible and respected. The composition of the faculty indicates whose knowledge is valued highly. African American faculty and other faculty of color are important to the education of all students. Indeed, large numbers of white students have lived in a white bubble in which they have not had to interact with or get to know people of color. If a critical mass of faculty of color is added to a typical majority-white campus, most white students will have their first opportunities to interact in a substantial way with people of color who occupy positions of high status.

For African American students, faculty members who share their culture are often a source of pride and admiration, living symbols of what they can achieve. Black faculty provide essential mentorship, advising, and role modeling for black students. Black faculty and other faculty of color can represent a major source of advice and assistance for white administrators and faculty. A substantial increase in these faculty of color will also aid in the governance of a university committed to increased equality and the elimination of discrimination. An overwhelmingly white faculty may not make pedagogical decisions to provide the best educational climate for a student body with large numbers of students of color. In our focus groups, both students and parents underscore the scarcity of black faculty and staff on the SU campus, a condition that deprives the students of role models and of a key aspect of human recognition. On predominantly white campuses black faculty and administrators are largely absent in the important control positions that affect transmissions along the educational pipeline. Their numbers must be increased. The students and parents in our focus groups hold this view, and it is common among students of color on other university campuses. Some self-studies on college campuses have also made this point. For example, a recent report at the University of Nevada (Las Vegas) noted the "chilly climate" for students of color on that campus and called on the campus administration to recruit more faculty of color.[32] It is probable that there will be no significant improvement in the racial climates of majority-white colleges and universities until faculty and staff of color are a critical mass among the faculty members and administrators who make the important decisions shaping campus rules, cultures, and climates.

Repeatedly, the black students and parents we interviewed call attention to African American students not being recognized as full members of the campus community. From university publications to the daily rhythm of life on campus, many symbols, comments, and actions suggest to black students that they really do not belong. The strength of their perceptions and feelings on these matters underscores the need for making majority-white educational institutions more welcoming to students whose cultures are not those of the dominant group. If we are to make predominantly white campuses truly welcoming to students of color, we must move away from the self-segregating and excluding ways of the dominant culture in the direction of a more universalistic conception of a university. Expecting harmony among different racial and ethnic groups on campus, while at the same time preserving the superiority of the white group, is clearly naive and unrealistic.

As we understand it, multiculturalism can be an important tool for moving in the direction of full recognition for all racial and ethnic groups. From the perspective of human recognition, multiculturalism is a way of telling black students and other students of color that their presence and their cultures are important to the comprehensive development of a university. Multiculturalism gives students the message that all people have a right to grow morally and intellectually and that the university is a repository of the best in the heritages of all groups in this nation. As we see it, the goal of universities should be to become what Dr. Martin Luther King, Jr., called the "beloved community." The scholar bell hooks has developed King's concept and suggested that many people in the United States still long to live in a community "where loving ties of care and knowing bind us together in our differencs."[33] In this type of respectful community the scourge of racism will come to an end. This kind of beloved community will come about "not by the eradication of difference but by its affirmation, by each of us claiming the identities and cultural legacies that shape who we are and how we live in the world."[34] This ideal of community is close to the old ideal of what a university should be. When university communities find the courage to live up to this ideal of active respect for diversity of people and cultures, we will see an end of racism on college campuses and perhaps in the larger society.

Conclusion

Multicultural changes are coming to predominantly white colleges and universities whether their leading faculty and top administrators take action or not. Over the next few decades major changes in the demographic composition of the United States will force actions to be taken against racism in higher education, as more students of color refuse to accept an inferior position on these campuses. By the middle of the twenty-first century, if current demographic trends continue, the United States will be a nation in which European Americans are the statistical minority. Although the majority of the U.S. population currently has its ancestral roots in Europe, around the year 2055 the majority of Americans will be of African, Asian, Latin American, Middle Eastern, or Native American ancestry. Significantly, well before the middle of the twenty-first century, more than half of all college-age Americans will be people of color.[35]

Major demographic changes are already observable in the composition of major colleges and universities. A study at the University of California (Berkeley) noted large demographic shifts in the makeup of the student population since 1968. In 1968 only four percent of the students were black or Latino; by 1991 the entering class at Berkeley was twenty-eight percent black or Latino. Also in 1991 another one-third of the students were Asian American.[36] By the early 1990s whites were less than half of the students at what is one of the nation's largest and most prestigious universities. While recent changes in the affirmative action admissions policies at Berkeley may to some degree reduce this trend, in the long run Berkeley and most other tradition-ally white colleges and universities will face growing pressures to meet the educational needs of communities of color.

Because of the increasing weight of their numbers and votes, people of color are already, if gradually, achieving greater social, cultural, and political influence in the United States. Changes in the cultural and political power of people of color in cities like Los Angeles can already be seen.[37] These relatively new sociopolitical forces are slowly forcing a public examination of the nation's failure to achieve the equality-and-justice ideals proclaimed for more than two hundred years. These forces are pressing for a reexamination of one-way assimilation assumptions and the notion of white social and cultural superiority in higher education and other sectors of U.S. society. Sociopolitical changes will play an even greater role in the future shaping of schools, colleges, workplaces, and neighborhoods. Most people of color do not want to forget their history and culture in order to adopt a history and culture that so far has defined them as inferior and unwelcome. Most do not accept the idea that they are flawed by inferior intelligence. Most will not gracefully accept for themselves and their children the often menial positions that white powers that be would have them accept. And most will not tolerate restrictions on their full participa-tion in U.S. institutions of higher education.

Early cultural pluralists like Horace Kallen, a brilliant Jewish Amer-ican analyst who first wrote on these matters in the 1910s, argued that without pluralistic interaction and cross-fertilization countries would stagnate and die.[38] Fortunately, people of color inside and outside academia now regularly articulate this perspective. Even a few promi-nent white leaders are beginning to see that U.S. society can no longer afford the continuation of racially restrictive and exclusionary practices. Over the last decade the idea that U.S. economic and edu-cational systems should respond to the twin challenges of a multicul-tural society and of a global economy has been gaining ground among a modest number of economic and political leaders. The interest in multicultural programs and policies among business leaders is in part because U.S. workforces are becoming more diverse in racial and eth-nic terms. Another reason for this response is the fact that the corporate economy is now global and multicultural. Today, the U.S. economy produces not only for its own population and but also for other countries around the world, and much of what the people of the United States consume comes from around the globe. Because U.S. companies trade with partners in many countries with an array of racial and ethnic groups not of European origin, the economic future of the United States and the general welfare of its citizens depends on an ability to understand, get along with, and trade with peoples who are neither white nor European. For the most part, these abilities are learned, or not learned, in U.S. schools, colleges, and universities.[39]

As we see the future, a return to an age of unchallenged white-European cultural, economic, and political hegemony in the United States or across the globe will not be possible. In recent years protests in central cities by some young people of color and protests on college campuses by other young people of color, in both cases against white dominance, are clear signals that racial change is coming. We have previously noted the protests of African American students at places such as Grinnell College and Rutgers University. We are likely to see many more such protests in the years ahead. Most African American youth—and their parents—are enraged over persisting racism on and off college campuses. They hold strongly to the highest ideals of freedom, justice, and equality, and many are pressing the nation's white leaders to live up to these long-standing promises.

All over the world, racial, ethnic, gender, and other subordinated groups are aggressively pressing for greater power and resources, for increased political and social recognition. Struggles over racial and ethnic recognition are commonplace around the globe, from Brazil, to the former Yugoslavia, to the former Soviet Union, to South Africa and India. Today, much of Europe is moving toward the creation of a supranational country with the ultimate idea of doing away with many cultural, language, and national frontiers. The nation of South Africa is in the process of setting up majority rule and dismantling its apartheid system of disenfranchisement and exploitation of black Africans by the descendants of white European settlers. Once South Africa's racist system was the target of much criticism, and even economic boycotts, by many people, including many whites, in the United States. Can the U.S. system of white racism survive in the midst of such global changes?

NOTES

Notes to Preface

1. Doreen Carvajal, "A Career in the Balance; Rutgers President Starts a Firestorm With Three Words," *New York Times* (February 6, 1995): B1.
2. John Leo, "The Rutgers Star Chamber," *U.S. News & World Report* (February 20, 1995): 22.
3. Angela Ards, "Dear Students, From a Friend," *The Village Voice* (February 28, 1995):17.
4. Miles Seligman, Michael Carlson, Jeff Klein, Paul Park, and Karl Eric Reif, "Jock-beat," *The Village Voice* (February 21, 1995): 121.
5. Christopher Shea, "Protests Centering on Racial Issues Erupt on Many Campuses This Fall," *Chronicle of Higher Education* (November 25, 1992): A23.
6. Shelby Steele, "The Recoloring of Campus Life," *Harper's* (February, 1989): 49.
7. Richard Bernstein, *Dictatorship of Virtue: Multiculturalism and the Battle for America's Future* (New York: Alfred A. Knopf, 1994), 3–4.
8. "Black Students and Educational Aspirations," *Race Relations Reporter* (August 15, 1994): 1.
9. W.E.B. Du Bois, *The Education of Black People* (Amherst: University of Massachusetts Press, 1978), 100–101.

Chapter 1

1. As quoted in Jo Ann Gerdeman Thompson, *The Modern Idea of the University* (New York: Peter Lang, 1984), 266–67.

2. John Henry Newman, "The Idea of a University," in *The Idea of a University*, ed. M. J. Svalic (San Francisco: Rinehart Press, 1960 [1852]), 15–16.

3. See Allan Bloom, *The Closing of the American Mind* (New York: Simon and Schuster, 1987), 91; Dinesh D'Souza, *Illiberal Education: The Politics of Race and Sex on Campus* (New York: Vintage, 1991), 13–15, 229–44; Richard Bernstein, *Dictatorship of Virtue: Multiculturalism and the Battle for America's Future* (New York: Alfred A. Knopf, 1994); Arthur Schlesinger, Jr., *The Disuniting of America: Reflections on a Multicultural Society* (New York: Norton, 1991).

4. Bloom, *The Closing of the American Mind*, 89.

5. Bloom, *The Closing of the American Mind*, 90.

6. Bloom, *The Closing of the American Mind*, 91.

7. D'Souza, *Illiberal Education*, 236.

8. Shelby Steele, " The Recoloring of Campus Life," *Harper's* (February, 1989): 49.

9. Bloom, *The Closing of the American Mind*, 93. His italics.

10. Steele, " The Recoloring of Campus Life," 51.

11. D'Souza, *Illiberal Education*, 244.

12. D'Souza, *Illiberal Education*, 257.

13. Bernstein, *Dictatorship of Virtue*, 4.

14. Bernstein, *Dictatorship of Virtue*, 206.

15. Bernstein, *Dictatorship of Virtue*, 62.

16. Bernstein, *Dictatorship of Virtue*, 80.

17. Schlesinger, *The Disuniting of America*, 13, 16–17.

18. Schlesinger, *The Disuniting of America*, 124–25.

19. George Keller, "Black Students in Higher Education: Why So Few?" *Planning for Higher Education* 17 (1988–1989): 50–56.

20. Martin E.P. Seligman, "When Black Americans Play the Blame Game, They're Bound to Lose," *Chicago Tribune* (February 10, 1993): Zone N, 19.

21. Seligman, ""When Black Americans Play the Blame Game, They're Bound to Lose," 19.

22. Joe R. Feagin and Melvin P. Sikes, *Living with Racism: The Black Middle Class Experience* (Boston: Beacon Press, 1994), 94.

23. Lynne Duke, "Ugly Racial Melee Shakes Students, Officials at Small Michigan College," *Washington Post* (April 12, 1992): A3; Jerry Thomas, "Brawl May Empty College of All Blacks," *Chicago Tribune* (April 26, 1992): C23. This section draws on Joe R. Feagin and Hernán Vera, *White Racism: The Basics* (New York: Routledge, 1995), chapter 2.

24. Don Gonyea, "Olivet College Copes with Racial Tension," All Things Considered, National Public Radio, April 29, 1992.

25. Isabel Wilkerson, "Racial Tension Erupts, Tearing a College Apart," *New York Times* (April 13, 1992): A14.

26. "Olivet Disciplinary Panel to Begin Investigation of Racial Brawl," United Press International (April 15, 1992): BC cycle, n.p.; Charles Grose, "Racial Relations as a Catalyst for Institutional Change," unpublished research paper, Mankato State University, 1995.

27. Gonyea, "Olivet College Copes with Racial Tension."

28. Gonyea, "Olivet College Copes with Racial Tension."

29. Duke, "Ugly Racial Melee Shakes Students," A3.

30. Wilkerson, "Racial Tension Erupts, Tearing a College Apart," A14.

31. Thomas, "Brawl May Empty College of All Blacks," C23.

32. Reported from the *Des Moines Register* (January 3, 1995) in "Racism in Education," *The Race Relations Reporter* (May 15, 1995): 3.

33. Jacqueline Fleming, *Blacks in College: A Comparative Study of Students' Success in Black and in White Institutions* (San Francisco: Jossey-Bass, 1984), 47–63; Walter R. Allen, Edgar G. Epps, and Nesha Z. Haniff (Eds.), *College in Black and White* (Albany: SUNY Press, 1991); Walter R. Allen, "The Color of Success," *Harvard Educational Review* 62 (Spring 1992): 27.

34. Walter R. Allen, "Introduction," in *College in Black and White*, eds. Walter R. Allen, Edgar G. Epps, and Nesha Z. Haniff (Albany: SUNY Press, 1991), 12.

35. Anti-Defamation League, *Highlights from an Anti-Defamation League Survey on Racial Attitudes in America* (New York: Anti-Defamation League, 1993), 10.

36. See National Opinion Research Center, University of Chicago, "1994 General Social Survey."

37. National Opinion Research Center, University of Chicago, "1994 General Social Survey."

38. Reported in "Survey Finds Minorities Resent Whites And Each Other," *Jet*, March 28, 1994, 14.

39. Richard Herrnstein and Charles Murray, *The Bell Curve: Intelligence and Class Structure in American Life* (New York: Free Press, 1994).

40. Richard Kluger, *Simple Justice: The History of Brown v. Board of Education and Black America's Struggle for Equality* (New York: Knopf, 1975), Vol. II, 801.

41. Gunnar Myrdal, *An American Dilemma* (New York: McGraw-Hill, 1964 [1944]), Vol. II, 633.

42. Jim Crow railroad cars originated in Massachusetts. On segregation in the North, see Lerone Bennett, Jr., *Before the Mayflower: A History of the Negro In America, 1619–1964*, rev. ed. (New York: Penguin Books, 1964), 152, 212.

43. Allen B. Ballard, "Academia's Record of Benign Neglect," *Change* 5 (March 1973): 27–33; see also Allen B. Ballard, *The Education of Black Folk: The Afro-American Struggle for Knowledge in White America* (New York: Harper and Row, 1973).

44. Myrdal, *An American Dilemma*, Vol. II, 633; Letter from Francis J. Dallett, Univesity Archivist, to editor, *Princeton Alumni Weekly*, June 2, 1970, in Firestone Library, Princeton University. One black student was admitted in the 1700s but did not graduate from Princeton.

45. Ballard, "Academia's Record of Benign Neglect," 27–33; Ballard, *The Education of Black Folk*.

46. "Study Reveals That Most Southern Colleges Remain Segregated," *Jet* (June 12, 1995): 12.

47. Carolyn A. Dorsey, "Black Faculty at White Institutions Before 1900." *Western Journal of Black Studies* 14 (Spring 1990): 1–8.

48. Ballard, "Academia's Record of Benign Neglect," 27–33.

49. See "Study Reveals That Most Southern Colleges Remain Segregated," 12.

50. Carter Woodson, *The Mis-education of the Negro* (Washington, D.C.: Africa World Press, [1933] 1990).

51. *Brown v. Board of Education of Topeka* 347 U.S. 483, 493 (1954).

52. A number of recent reports have cited the growing racial unrest on college campuses. See Gail E. Thomas, "Race Relations and Campus Climate for Minority Students at Majority and Minority Institutions: Implications for Higher Education Desegregation," report prepared for the Southern Education Foundation, Texas A&M University, 1995.

53. Ralph Ellison, *Invisible Man* (New York: Vintage Books, 1989), 3.

54. See Erving Goffman, *Interaction Ritual: Essays on Face-to-Face Behavior*, Garden City, N.Y.: Anchor Books, 1967, 7–15.

55. Jurgen Habermas, "Struggles for Recognition in the Democratic Constitutional State,"

in *Multiculturalism*, ed. Amy Gutman (Princeton, N.J.: Princeton University Press, 1994), 107–48. The Habermas article is a commentary on an article by Charles Taylor.

56. Jessica Benjamin, *The Bonds of Love: Psychoanalysis, Feminism, and the Problem of Domination* (New York: Pantheon, 1988), 12, 15.

57. See, for example, Charles H. Cooley, *Human Nature and the Social Order* (Glencoe, Illinois: Free Press, 1956), 187–88.

58. See Dorothy Lee, *Freedom and Culture* (Englewood Cliffs, N.J.: Prentice Hall, 1959), 5, 20–133; Marimba Ani, *Yurugu: An African-Centered Critique of European Cultural Thought and Behavior* (Trenton, N.J.: Africa World Press, 1994).

59. On the use of focus groups, see Charles E. Basch, "Focus Group Interview: An Underutilized Technique for Improving Theory and Practice in Health Education," *Health Education Quarterly* 14 (Winter 1987): 411–48.

60. Those who agreed to participate in the group interviews were told that their names would not be used in the research write-ups of focus group discussions and questionnaires. Most personal, place, and college or university names, as well as certain other information, have been disguised in the focus group comments to protect the anonymity of the participants or of the university. For example, the names of certain colleges or universities have been replaced with "a predominantly black institution" or a "predominantly white university" where this seemed necessary. We have edited the comments for punctuation and to reduce repetitious phrases like "um" and "you know." We have also edited numerous comments lightly for grammar and have sometimes inserted a bracketed word for clarity. Ellipses have been omitted at the beginning of most comments—and at the end of comments where the thought being communicated seemed complete. The focus groups were conducted in the early 1990s, and the recruitment and taping of the seven groups were done by experienced market research firms.

61. The student focus groups were drawn randomly from a list of all black juniors and seniors at State University (excluding a few special students). All were full-time students. About half were seniors. There was a diversity of majors. On class and age variables the screened-in group and the actual participants were similar. The screening and recruiting process brought in more males than females into the final focus groups. This sixty-one percent of males was fairly close to the male percentage (fifty-five percent) in the screened-in group. The final male proportion is higher than for the campus as a whole, so males were overrepresented. This may be because of the greater willingness of college men to go to an off-campus facility at night.

62. The parents were randomly drawn from phone books in these areas. Each was screened for the following qualifications: African American; has lived in this state or nearby for at least ten years; has at least one child aged ten to twenty-seven years; and has plans for their child to attend college, or has a child who has attended college during the past decade. These characteristics were chosen so we would ensure interviewing adults who have been in the state long enough to be knowledgeable about state educational institutions, and who have at least one child whose age is close enough to the usual college student's age for them to have considered the possibility of a college education.

63. Seventy-six percent of the parents were aged thirty-one to fifty. Thirty-six percent had a high school education or less, with just under half having one to four years of college and about fifteen percent with some postgraduate work. A fifth were homemakers, retired, or students, while just over half were white-collar employees and just over a fifth were employed in blue collar or trade jobs. These demographic distributions are close to the demographic distributions on the larger, screened-in group of black parents drawn in the random sampling process.

Chapter 2

1. See Hernan Vera and Andrew Gordon, "The Beautiful American: Fictions of the White Messiah in the American Cinema," unpublished research paper, University of Florida, 1995.

2. James W. Loewen, *Lies My Teacher Told Me: Everything Your American History Textbook Got Wrong* (New York: The New Press, 1995), 161.

3. Comments from the focus groups have been edited to protect the respondents' anonymity.

4. See Joe R. Feagin and Melvin P. Sikes, *Living with Racism: The Black Middle Class Experience* (Boston: Beacon Press, 1994), 16–23; and Sarah and A. Elizabeth Delany, *Having Our Say: The Delany Sisters' First 100 years* (New York: Kodansha International, 1993), chapter 6 and passim.

5. See John S. Mbiti, *African Religions and Philosophies* (New York: Anchor Press, 1970); Mircea Eliade, *The Sacred and the Profane* (New York: Harcourt Brace. 1959), 21; Dona Marimba Richards, "European mythology: the Ideology of Progress," in *Black Contemporary Thought,* Molefi Asante and Abdulai Vandi, eds., (Los Angeles: Sage Publications, 1985), 218.

6. See Allan Bloom, *The Closing of the American Mind* (New York: Simon and Schuster, 1987), 91; Dinesh D'Souza, *Illiberal Education: The Politics of Race and Sex on Campus* (New York: Vintage, 1991), 13–15, 229–44; Richard Bernstein, *Dictatorship of Virtue: Multiculturalism and the Battle for America's Future* (New York: Alfred A. Knopf, 1994); Arthur Schlesinger, Jr., *The Disuniting of America: Reflections on a Multicultural Society* (New York: Norton, 1991).

7. Todd Ackerman, "UT Minority Survey Critical," *Houston Chronicle* (January 29, 1994): A31.

8. See Walter R. Allen and Nesha Z. Haniff, "Race, Gender, and Academic Performance in U.S. Higher Education," *College in Black and White,* eds. Walter R. Allen, Edgar G. Epps, and Nesha Z. Haniff (Albany: SUNY Press, 1991), 96; Jacqueline Fleming, *Blacks in College: A Comparative Study of Students' Success in Black and in White Institutions* (San Francisco: Jossey-Bass, 1984), 47–63.

9. There was one "no answer."

10. See Feagin and Sikes, *Living with Racism*, 307–11.

11. See Marimba Ani, *Yurugu: An African-Centered Critique of European Cultural Thought and Behavior* (Trenton, N.J.: Africa World Press, 1994).

12. *Studies of Intercollegiate Athletics: The Experiences of Black Intercollegiate Athletes at NCAA Division I Institutions* (Palo Alto: American Institutes for Research Center for the Study of Athletics, 1989).

13. *Studies of Intercollegiate Athletics.*

14. Natasha Tarpley, "Voices from the College Front," *Essence* (October, 1993): 65.

15. Ralph Ellison, *Invisible Man* (New York: Vintage Books, 1989), 3.

Chapter 3

1. See Dorothy Lee, *Freedom and Culture* (Englewood Cliffs, N.J.: Prentice Hall, 1959), 5, 20–133; Marimba Ani, *Yurugu: An African-Centered Critique of European Cultural Thought and Behavior* (Trenton, N.J.: Africa World Press, 1994).

2. See Claude Levi-Strauss, *Structural Anthropology* (New York: Doubleday Anchor, 1967), 282.

3. See Thorstein Veblen, *The Theory of the Leisure Class* (New York: Penguin, 1979), 46.

4. See Stanford M. Lyman and Marvin B. Scott, "Territoriality: A Neglected Sociological Dimension," *Social Problems* 15 (1967): 236–49.

5. See Ani, *Yurugu: An African-Centered Critique of European Cultural Thought and Behavior*; Frances Cress Welsing, *The Isis Papers: Keys to the Colors* (Third World Press: Chicago, 1991).

6. Allan Bloom, *The Closing of the American Mind* (New York: Simon and Schuster, 1987), 91.

7. Bloom, *The Closing of the American Mind*, 92.

8. Bloom, *The Closing of the American Mind*, 92.

9. Institute for the Study of Social Change, *The Diversity Project: Final Report* (Berkeley: University of California, 1991), 44.

10. George Keller, "Black Students in Higher Education: Why So Few?" *Planning for Higher Education* 17 (1988–1989): 50–54.

11. Keller, "Black Students," 55.

12. Dinesh D'Souza, *Illiberal Education: The Politics of Race and Sex on Campus* (New York: Vintage, 1991), 236.

13. Anthony R. D'Augelli and Scott L. Hershberger, "African American Undergraduates on a Predominantly White Campus: Academic Factors, Social Networks, and Campus Climate," *Journal of Negro Education*, 62 (1993): 67–81.

14. Walter Allen, *Gender and Campus Race Differences in Black Student Academic Performance, Racial Attitudes and College Satisfaction* (Atlanta: Southern Education Foundation, 1986).

15. The data were presented at a New Orleans conference. We draw on the account in Alice Dembner, "Campus Racial Lines May Be Blurring; Study Counters Notion That Minorities Segregate Selves," *Boston Globe* (April 5, 1994): 1.

16. Reported from the *New York Times* (October 10, 1994) in "Racism in Education," *The Race Relations Reporter* (November 15, 1994): 4.

17. Lyman and Scott, "Territoriality: A Neglected Sociological Dimension," 236–49.

18. For example, black students at the University of Florida have periodically made this complaint.

19. See Feagin and Sikes, *Living with Racism*.

20. See Bloom, *The Closing of the American Mind*, 35.

21. See Bloom, *The Closing of the American Mind*; and Arthur Schlesinger, Jr., *The Disuniting of America: Reflections on a Multicultural Society* (New York: Norton, 1991).

22. Walter R. Allen, "Black and Blue: Black Students at the University of Michigan," *LSA Magazine* 6 (Fall, 1982): n.p.

23. Southern Regional Education Board, *Racial Issues on Campus: How Students View Them* (Atlanta: Southern Regional Education Board, 1990), 11.

24. D'Augelli and Hershberger, "African American Undergraduates on a Predominantly White Campus," 76.

25. Cynthia A. Villis, Stephen Parker, Robert P. Gordon, *Institutionalizing Cultural Diversity: Assessment, Year One* (San Diego: University of San Diego, 1993), 27.

26. Joe R. Feagin, *Final Report: Survey of Minority Undergraduate Students*, unpublished, 1993.

27. Urban Affairs Programs, *The Graduate School Climate at MSU: Perceptions of Three Diverse Racial/Ethnic Groups* (East Lansing: Office of the Provost, 1995), Table 20.

28. Howard J. Ehrlich, *Campus Ethnoviolence and the Policy Options* (Baltimore: National Institute Against Prejudice and Violence, 1990), iii.

29. Here we draw in part on 1993–95 issues of *The Race Relations Reporter*.

30. Richard Bernstein, *Dictatorship of Virtue: Multiculturalism and the Battle for America's Future* (New York: Alfred A. Knopf, 1994), 205–206.

31. Bernstein, *Dictatorship of Virtue*, 206.

32. Ralph Ellison, *Invisible Man* (New York: Vintage Books, [1947] 1989), 3.

33. D' Augelli and Hershberger, "African American Undergraduates on a Predominantly White Campus," 67–81.

34. Marvalene Styles Hughes, "Black Students' Participation in Higher Education," *Journal of College Student Personnel*, 28 (1987): 532–45.

35. Thomas B. Edsall and Mary D. Edsall, "When the Official Subject is Presidential Politics, Taxes, Welfare, Crime, Rights, or Values—the Real Subject Is Race," *Atlantic*, Vol. 267 (May, 1991): 53–55; Thomas B. Edsall, with Mary D. Edsall, *Chain Reaction* (New York: Norton, 1991–92), 15.

36. Quoted in Denise K. Magner, "Blacks and Whites on the Campuses: Behind Ugly Racist Incidents, Student Isolation and Insensitivity," *Chronicle of Higher Education*, April 26, 1989, pp. A27–A29.

37. For discussions of disparities in media treatment of black and white anti-Semitism, see Feagin and Vera, *White Racism,* 79–80.

38. Mary Jordan, "College Dorms Reflect Trend of Self-Segregation," *Washington Post*, March 6, 1994, p. A1.

39. Bloom, *The Closing of the American Mind,* 91.

40. Cited in Dembner, "Campus Racial lines May Be Blurring," 1.

41. Institute for the Study of Social Change, *The Diversity Project*, 16.

42. Institute for the Study of Social Change, *The Diversity Project*, 29.

43. Institute for the Study of Social Change, *The Diversity Project,* 29.

44. Ruth J. Simmons, "Report on Campus Race Relations," Princeton University, March 1, 1993, 3.

45. Marvalene Styles Hughes, "Black Students' Participation in Higher Education," *Journal of College Student Personnel* 28 (1987): 532–45.

46. A summary of William Sedlacek's pioneering research, with extensive citations, can be found in William E. Sedlacek, "Using Research to Reduce Racism at a University," Research Report 2–94, Counseling Center, University of Maryland, College Park, Maryland.

47. Walter R. Allen, "Black Student, White Campus: Structural, Interpersonal, and Psychological Correlates of Success," *Journal of Negro Education* 54 (1985): 134–47.

48. Reported from the *Lafayette Journal & Courier* (April 19, 1994) in "Racism in Education," *The Race Relations Reporter* (June 15, 1994): 3.

49. See for example, Keller, "Black Students," 50–56.

50. Shelby Steele, " The Recoloring of Campus Life," *Harper's* (February, 1989): 53.

51. Office of the President, "Report of the Diversity Committee," unpublished report, Colgate University, August 21, 1990, 9.

52. Jacqueline Fleming, *Blacks in College: A Comparative Study of Students' Success in Black and in White Institutions* (San Francisco: Jossey-Bass, 1984), 155.

53. Southern Regional Education Board, *Racial Issues on Campus: How Students View Them* (Atlanta: Southern Regional Education Board, 1990), 11.

54. Urban Affairs Programs, *The Graduate School Climate at MSU: Perceptions of Three Diverse Racial/Ethnic Groups* (East Lansing: Office of the Provost, 1995), Tables 18–19.

Chapter 4

1. Cited in Denice Ward Hood, "Academic and Noncognitive Factors Affecting the Retention of Black Men at a Predominantly White University," *Journal of Negro Education* 61 (1992): 518.

2. John Henry Newman, "The Idea of a University," in *The Idea of a University*, ed. M. J. Svalic (San Francisco: Rinehart Press, 1960 [1852]), 15–16.

3. Center for Applied Research, "Survey of Ethnic Minority Students," University of Nevada at Reno, August 1993, 52.

4. Joe R. Feagin, *Final Report: Survey of Minority Undergraduate Students*, unpublished, 1993.

5. Urban Affairs Programs, *The Graduate School Climate at MSU: Perceptions of Three Diverse Racial/Ethnic Groups* (East Lansing: Office of the Provost, 1995), Table 20.

6. Gloria J. Edmunds, "Needs Assessment Strategy for Black Students: An Examination of Stressors and Program Implications," *Journal of Non-White Concerns in Personnel and Guidance* 12 (1984): 48–56.

7. Institute for the Study of Social Change, *The Diversity Project: Final Report* (Berkeley: University of California, 1991), 29.

8. For a discussion of the importance of white conceptions of the white self, see Joe R. Feagin and Hernán Vera, *White Racism: The Basics* (New York: Routledge, 1995), 135–62.

9. Joe R. Feagin, "Barriers to Black Students in Higher Education: Learning from Qualitative Research," published position paper, Center for Research on Minority Education, University of Oklahoma, 1989.

10. Office of the President, "Report of the Diversity Committee," unpublished report, Colgate University, August 21, 1990, 9.

11. Urban Affairs Programs, *The Graduate School Climate at MSU*, Tables 20 and 22.

12. Roberta M. Hall and Bernice R. Sandler, *The Classroom Climate: A Chilly One for Women?* (Washington, D.C.: Association of American Colleges, 1982); see also Joe R. Feagin and Nijole Benokraitis, *Modern Sexism: Blatant, Subtle and Covert Discrimination*, 2nd ed. (Englewood Cliffs, N.J.: Prentice Hall, 1995).

13. Institute for the Study of Social Change, *The Diversity Project*, 17.

14. Institute for the Study of Social Change, *The Diversity Project*, 17, note.

15. Ruth J. Simmons, "Report on Campus Race Relations," Princeton University, March 1, 1993, p. 11.

16. Dinesh D'Souza, *The End of Racism: Principles for a Multiracial Society* (New York: Free Press, 1995), 491–93.

17. bell hooks, *Killing Rage: Enduring Racism* (New York: Henry Holt and Co., 1995), 20, 29.

18. Urban Affairs Programs, *The Graduate School Climate at MSU*, Tables 20 and 22.

19. We draw on a summary of the *Chronicle* article in "Racism in Education," *The Race Relations Reporter* (January 15, 1994): 3.

20. Valora Washington and William Harvey, *Affirmative Rhetoric, Negative Action* (Washington: George Washington University, 1989), 6.

21. Washington and Harvey, *Affirmative Rhetoric, Negative Action*, 7, 20.

22. Affirmative Action Office, "Faculty Survey," University of Nevada at Las Vegas, September, 1993, 3.

23. Kenneth W. Jackson, "Black Faculty in Academia," in *The Racial Crisis in American Higher Education*, eds. Philip G. Altbach and Kofi Lomotey (Albany: SUNY Press, 1991), 143.

24. Washington and Harvey, *Affirmative Rhetoric, Negative Action*, 26.

25. See Pierre Bourdieu and Jean-Claude Passeron, *Les Héritiers: Les Étudiants et La Culture* (Paris: Les Edition de Minuit, 1964), 25.

26. Ruth J. Simmons, "Report on Campus Race Relations," Princeton University, March 1, 1993, 2.

Chapter 5

1. The rest were uncertain.

2. Joe R. Feagin, *Final Report: Survey of Minority Undergraduate Students*, unpublished, 1993.

3. Erving Goffman, *Encounters: Two Studies in the Sociology of Interaction* (Indianapolis: Bobbs-Merril Company, Inc., 1961), 7.

4. The hate stare was vividly described by white journalist John Howard Griffin in an account of travels in the 1950s as a white man temporarily dyed black. See John Howard Griffin, *Black Like Me* (Boston: Houghton Mifflin, 1961).

5. See Joe R. Feagin and Melvin P. Sikes, *Living With Racism: The Black Middle Class Experience* (Boston: Beacon Press, 1994), 63–64.

6. Feagin and Sikes, *Living with Racism*, 47–56.

7. Institute for the Study of Social Change, *The Diversity Project: Final Report* (Berkeley: University of California, 1991), 29.

8. Reported from the *Hackensack Record* (September 20, 1994) in "Racism in Education," *The Race Relations Reporter* (October 15, 1994): 4.

9. See Feagin and Sikes, *Living with Racism*, chapter 3.

10. See Joe R. Feagin and Hernan Vera, *White Racism: The Basics* (New York: Routledge, 1995), 109–23.

11. See, for example, Edward T. Hall, *The Silent Language* (Garden City, New York: Anchor Books, 1973).

12. See Joe R. Feagin and Clairece Y. Feagin, *Racial and Ethnic Relations*, 5th ed. (Englewood Cliffs, N.J.: Prentice-Hall, 1996), 247–48; and Kim Lersch, "Current Trends in Police Brutality: An Analysis of Recent Newspaper Accounts," Gainesville, University of Florida, unpublished master's thesis, 1993.

13. Ruth Sidel, *Battling Bias: The Struggle for Identity and Community on College Campuses* (New York: Viking, 1994), 125.

14. Bonnie J. Morris, "The Pervasiveness of Campus Racism," letter to editors, *The Chronicle of Higher Education* (May 12, 1993): B5; Michelle N-K Collison, "Black Students Complain of Abuse by Campus Police," *Chronicle of Higher Education* (April 14, 1993): A35–A36.

15. Sidel, *Battling Bias*, 84.

16. See Feagin, *Final Report*.

17. Reported from the *Pocono Record* (February 28, 1995) in "Racism in Commerce," *The Race Relations Reporter* (April 15, 1995): 3.

18. Feagin, *Final Report*.

19. Center for Applied Research, "Survey of Ethnic Minority Students," University of Nevada at Reno, August 1993, 53.

20. Ruth J. Simmons, "Report on Campus Race Relations," Princeton University, March 1, 1993, 11.

21. Karen Houppert, "More Than Words: Inside the Rutgers Student Movement," *The Village Voice* (February 28, 1995): 133.

Chapter 6

1. Walter R. Allen and Joseph O. Jewell, "African American Education since *An American Dilemma*," paper presented at a Morehouse Research Institute conference, April 20–23, 1994, 9; Anonymous, "Vital Signs: Statistics That Measure the State of Racial Equality," *Journal of Blacks in Higher Education* 1 (Spring 1995): 53.

2. Arnold L. Mitchem, "Testimony," Senate Labor and Education Committee, Federal Document Clearing House, May 17, 1994.

3. See George Keller, "Black Students in Higher Education: Why So Few?" *Planning for Higher Education* 17 (1988–89): 50–54.

4. Southern Regional Education Board, *Racial Issues on Campus: How Students View Them* (Atlanta: Southern Regional Education Board, 1990), 11.

5. Institute for the Study of Social Change, *The Diversity Project: Final Report* (Berkeley: University of California, 1991), 29.

6. Stephen L. Carter, "Color-blind and Color-Active," *The Recorder* (January 3, 1992): 6.

7. *Kirwan v. Podberesky*, 115 Sup. Ct. 2001 (1995).

8. David Folkenflik, "Democrats Snipe at Cuts in Student Loans; Republicans Hope Votes Will Feel Balancing Budget Is More Important," *Baltimore Sun* (October 26, 1995): 3A.

9. Rebecca Huntington, "Lewis-Clark State: Students' Protest Recalls Hooverville; GOP-Backed Cuts Would Hurt LSCS, Students Warn," *Lewiston Morning Tribune* (October 11, 1995): 5A.

10. Robbie J. Seward, Marshall R. Jackson, Sr., James Jackson, "Alienation and Inter-actional Styles in a Predominantly White Environment: A Study of Successful Black Students," *Journal of College Student Development* 31 (1990): 509–15.

11. Bebe Moore Campbell, "To Be Black, Gifted, and Alone," *Savvy* 5 (December 1984): 69.

12. Institute for the Study of Social Change, *The Diversity Project*, 40.

13. Ruth J. Simmons, "Report on Campus Race Relations," Princeton University, March 1, 1993, 3, 11.

14. See Joe R. Feagin and Melvin P. Sikes, *Living with Racism: The Black Middle Class Experience* (Boston: Beacon Press, 1994), chapter 3.

15. Institute for the Study of Social Change, *The Diversity Project,* 30.

16. Institute for the Study of Social Change, *The Diversity Project,* 30.

17. Allan Nairn, *The Reign of ETS: The Corporation that Makes Up Minds* (Washington, D.C.: Allan Nairn and Associates, 1980).

18. Sources are cited in Institute for the Study of Social Change, *The Diversity Project,* 5.

19. Jerome Karabel and David Karen, "Go to Harvard, Give Your Kid a Break," *New York Times* (December 8, 1990): Section 1, 25.

20. Institute for the Study of Social Change, *The Diversity Project,* 5.

21. [No author] "Black Student Graduation Rates on Increase," United Press International (December 28, 1989): BC cycle.

22. Mitchem, "Testimony," Senate Labor/Education Committee. The study was done by the Systems Development Corporation.

Chapter 7

1. Brand Blanshard, "Democracy and Distinction in American Education," *On the Meaning of the University*, ed. S. M. McMurrin (Salt Lake City: University of Utah Press, 1976), 33.

2. See, for example, Richard Herrnstein and Charles Murray, *The Bell Curve* (New York: Free Press, 1994), which reportedly has sold 400,000 copies.

3. See Joe R. Feagin and Melvin P. Sikes, *Living with Racism: The Black Middle Class Experience* (Boston: Beacon Press, 1994), 33–35.

4. Institute for the Study of Social Change, *The Diversity Project: Final Report* (Berkeley: University of California, 1991), 29.

5. Institute for the Study of Social Change, *The Diversity Project,* 29.

6. Walter R. Allen and Joseph O. Jewell, "African American Education since *An Ameri-can Dilemma*, unpublished paper given at Morehouse Research Institute conference, April 20–23, 1994, 10–11.

7. John S. Butler, *Entrepreneurship and Self-help among Black Americans* (New York: SUNY Press, 1991), 259.

8. Erika N. Duckworth, "Shared Heritage," *St. Petersburg Times* (February 20, 1994): 1D.

9. Jacqueline Fleming, *Blacks in College: A Comparative Study of Students' Success in Black and in White Institutions* (San Francisco: Jossey-Bass, 1984), 47–63.

10. See Walter R. Allen and Nesha Z. Haniff, "Race, Gender, and Academic Performance in U.S. Higher Education," *College in Black and White*, ed. Walter R. Allen, Edgar G. Epps, and Nesha Z. Haniff (Albany: SUNY Press, 1991), 96.

11. Nathaniel Sheppard Jr., "Ruling May Hit at Black Colleges' Roots," *Chicago Tribune* (July 10, 1994): C1.

12. Derrick Bell, *Faces at the Bottom of the Well* (New York: Basic Books, 1992), 21.

13. Roy L. Brooks, *The Civil Rights Trilogy: Racial Integration, Total Separation, and Limited Separation*, unpublished manuscript, University of San Diego School of Law, 1995.

14. Scott Jaschick, "Affirmative Action Under Fire: Outcome of Congressional Review Could Radically Change the Way Colleges Operate," *The Chronicle of Higher Education* (March 10, 1995): A22–A29.

15. See Mary Frances Berry, "Affirmative Action: Political Opportunists Exploit Racial Fears," *Ethnic NewsWatch* (May 31, 1995): 29.

16. See Department of Health and Human Services, National Institutes of Health, "NIH Guidelines on the Inclusion of Women and Minorities as Subjects in Clinical Research, *Federal Register* 59, No. 59 (March 28, 1994).

17. See "Guidelines on Inclusion of Women, Minorities, and Persons with Disabilities in NIH Sponsored And/or Supported Intramural and Extramural Scientific Meetings and Conferences," *NIH Guide* 24 (April 28, 1995).

18. See, for example, *State ex rel. James v. Ohio State Univ.* Supreme Court of Ohio, 70 Ohio St. 3d 168; 637 N.E.2d 911; 1994 Ohio Lexis 1833.

19. See, for instance, Ruth Sidel, *Battling Bias: The Struggle for Identity and Community on College Campuses* (New York: Viking, 1994), 251–60.

20. Urban Affairs Programs, *The Graduate School Climate at MSU: Perceptions of Three Diverse Racial/Ethnic Groups* (East Lansing: Office of the Provost, 1995), 45.

21. Joyce E. King, "Dysconscious Racism: Ideology, Identity, and the Miseducation of Teachers," *Journal of Negro Education* 60 (1991): 142.

22. See Charles R. Lawrence, "The Id, the Ego, and Equal Protection," *Stanford Law Review* 39 (January, 1987): 317–23.

23. See Anti-Defamation League, *Highlights from an Anti-Defamation League Survey on Racial Attitudes in America* (New York: ADL, 1993), 18–25; and National Opinion Research Center, General Social Surveys, 1990, 1994.

24. Richard Bernstein, *Dictatorship of Virtue: Multiculturalism and the Battle for America's Future* (New York: Alfred A. Knopf, 1994), 199.

25. Arthur M. Schlesinger, Jr., *The Disuniting of America: Reflections on a Multicultural Society* (New York: Norton, 1991), 13, 16–17.

26. Gerald Graff, *Beyond the Culture Wars: How Teaching the Conflicts Can Revitalize American Education* (New York: Norton, 1992); James A. Banks, "Multicultural Education: Development, Dimensions, and Challenges; Multicultural Education," *Phi Delta Kappan* 75 (September, 1993): 22–24.

27. See, for example, Banks, "Multicultural Education," 22.

28. Institute for the Study of Social Change, *The Diversity Project: Final Report* (Berkeley: University of California, 1991), 53–54.

29. W.E.B. Du Bois, "Whither Now and Why," *The Education of Black Folk: Ten Critiques 1906–1960*, edited by Herbert Aptheker (Amherst: University of Massachusetts Press, 1973), 79.

30. As quoted in Ruth Sidel, *Battling Bias*, 147. See also 145–146.

31. Institute for the Study of Social Change, *The Diversity Project*, 57.

32. See Campus Committee on Ethnic Minority Affairs, "Final Report," University of Nevada, Las Vegas, November, 1993, 11.

33. bell hooks, *Killing Rage: Ending Racism* (New York: Henry Holt, 1995), 263–64.

34. hooks, *Killing Rage,* 265.

35. See Joe R. Feagin, Hernan Vera, and Barbara A. Zsembik, "Multiculturalism: A Democratic Basis for American Society," in *Primis,* eds. George Ritzer and Craig Calhoun (New York: McGraw-Hill, 1995).

36. Institute for the Study of Social Change, *The Diversity Project,* iii.

37. See Harold Brackman and Steven P. Erie, "Beyond 'Politics by Other Means'? Empowerment Strategies for Los Angeles's Asian Pacific Community," in *The Bubbling Cauldron: Race, Ethnicity, and the Urban Crisis,* eds. Michael P. Smith and Joe R. Feagin (Minneapolis: University of Minnesota Press, 1995), 282–304.

38. See Horace Kallen, *Cultural Pluralism and the American Idea: An Essay in Social Philosophy* (Philadelphia: University of Pennsylvania Press, 1956).

39. See Feagin and Vera, *White Racism,* 165–91.

INDEX